Ready Seapower

A History of the U.S. Seventh Fleet

Edward J. Marolda

DEPARTMENT OF THE NAVY
WASHINGTON, DC
2012

"The Navy is more than the 'first line of defense.' It frequently is and must be the spearhead of our military actions overseas. It is a 'first line of impact' on many occasions."

—ADMIRAL ARLEIGH BURKE,
CHIEF OF NAVAL OPERATIONS,
1955–1961

CONTENTS

Foreword		v
Chronology		vii
Introduction		xv
Chapter 1	**MacArthur's Navy**	1
Chapter 2	**Weathering Postwar Turmoil in Asia**	11
Chapter 3	**Fighting the Korean War**	23
Chapter 4	**Deterring Conflict in the Far East**	37
Chapter 5	**Combat and Confrontation**	53
Chapter 6	**Old Enemies and New Friends**	79
Chapter 7	**From the Arabian Gulf to Mount Pinatubo**	101
Chapter 8	**Safeguarding the Peace**	113
Chapter 9	**Terrorists, Pirates, and Weapons Proliferators**	127
Chapter 10	**Partners and Adversaries**	143
Appendix	**Commanders, U.S. Seventh Fleet**	171
Abbreviations		173
Acknowledgments		177
Suggested Reading		179
Index		183

Commander Seventh Fleet Vice Admiral John M. Bird discusses operations with Vice Admiral Tohru Izumi, Commander in Chief, Japan Maritime Self-Defense Force, aboard the command ship Blue Ridge (LCC 19) *in February 2009.*

FOREWORD

THE NAVAL HISTORY AND HERITAGE COMMAND published this history to enhance our understanding of the pivotal role played by the U.S. Seventh Fleet in the Western Pacific from World War II through 2010. This project is in keeping with the Command's ongoing efforts to provide naval personnel with historical information and analysis that directly support their global mission. No naval command has done more than the Seventh Fleet to defend and promote American interests in Asia. This "fighting fleet" was in the forefront of U.S. forces involved in the Pacific campaigns of World War II and the conflicts in Korea, Vietnam, and the Arabian Gulf. In the last half of the 20th century and the first decade of the 21st century, the Seventh Fleet has stood as a bulwark against aggression and partnered with America's Asian allies to maintain peace and stability in this vital region. Whether combating conventional forces, guerrillas, insurgents, pirates, or terrorists, Seventh Fleet Sailors have routinely displayed exceptional courage and dedication, serving also as ambassadors for America's core values of freedom, democracy, free market enterprise, and respect for human rights.

The author of this illustrated history, Dr. Edward J. Marolda, former Senior Historian of the Navy, brings to the topic forty-plus years of relevant scholarship and experience. He has authored, coauthored, or edited 12 highly regarded works on the Navy's history, with a special focus on its involvement in modern Asian conflicts and developments.

Rear Admiral Jay DeLoach, U.S. Navy (Ret.)
Director of Naval History

Vice Admiral Thomas C. Kinkaid and his commanders off the Philippines. Left to right, Rear Admiral Jesse B. Oldendorf, Kinkaid, Rear Admiral Theodore E. Chandler (later killed in a kamikaze attack), and Rear Admiral Russell S. Berkey (future Commander Seventh Fleet).

A flight deck officer signals the pilot of an A-4 Skyhawk to launch from carrier Coral Sea *(CVA 43) in March 1965.*

Changing of the guard. Midway *(CV 41), top, en route in August 1991 to San Diego and decommissioning, shares a pier at the Pearl Harbor naval base with* Independence *(CV 62), preparing to begin her forward deployment to Japan.*

SEVENTH FLEET CHRONOLOGY

1941, 7 December	Imperial Japanese Navy attacks U.S. Pacific Fleet at Pearl Harbor, Hawaii, igniting World War II in the Pacific.
1942, 4-6 June	U.S. naval forces defeat Japanese fleet in Battle of Midway.
1943, 19 February	U.S. Navy establishes U.S. Seventh Fleet.
1943, 26 November	Vice Admiral Thomas C. Kinkaid takes the helm as Commander U.S. Seventh Fleet.
1944, 29 February	Seventh Fleet forces land troops in the Admiralty Islands.
1944, 22 April	Seventh Fleet deploys ground forces ashore at Hollandia, New Guinea.
1944, 20 October	Allied forces land at Leyte in the Philippines.
1944, 25 October	Seventh Fleet and Third Fleet forces defeat the Imperial Japanese Navy in the Battle of Leyte Gulf.
1944, 25 October	First major kamikaze attack on U.S. naval forces results in the sinking of escort carrier *St. Lo* (CVE 63).
1944, 15 December	Seventh Fleet lands troops on Mindoro Island, Philippines.
1945, 9 January	Seventh Fleet amphibious forces deploy Army divisions ashore at Lingayen on the main Philippine island of Luzon.
1945, 15 August	General Douglas MacArthur issues General Order No. 1 directing the disarmament of Japanese forces in China and Korea.
1945, 2 September	World War II ends as Japanese officials sign surrender documents on board battleship *Missouri* (BB 63).
1945, 9 September	Admiral Thomas C. Kinkaid and Army General John R. Hodge accept the surrender of Japanese forces in southern Korea at a ceremony in Seoul.
1946, 4 July	Seventh Fleet forces are on hand off Manila for Philippine Independence Day.
1947, 1 January	Seventh Fleet renamed U.S. Naval Forces Western Pacific.
1948, 17 January	Attack transport *Renville* (APA 227) serves as the venue for a cease-fire agreement between the Netherlands and Indonesian independence groups.
1949, 25 May	Seventh Fleet departs Qingdao, China, its homeport from 1946 to 1949, for the last time.

1949, 19 August	U.S. Naval Forces Western Pacific designated U.S. Seventh Task Fleet.
1949, 1 October	Communist leader Mao Zedong (Mao Tse-tung) establishes the People's Republic of China.
1950, 12 January	Secretary of State Dean Acheson announces a U.S. defensive perimeter in the Western Pacific that excludes South Korea and Taiwan from American protection.
1950, 11 February	U.S. Seventh Task Fleet redesignated U.S. Seventh Fleet.
1950, 14 February	People's Republic of China and Soviet Union sign a 30-year Treaty of Friendship, Alliance, and Mutual Assistance.
1950, 25 June	Communist North Korea, with the support of the People's Republic of China and the USSR, invades South Korea.
1950, 27 June	At the direction of President Harry S. Truman, Seventh Fleet steams near Taiwan to discourage a Chinese Communist invasion of the Chinese Nationalist-held island.
1950, 3 July	Seventh Fleet carrier *Valley Force* (CV 45) and Royal Navy carrier *Triumph* carry out the first naval attacks on North Korea with strikes against targets near Pyongyang.
1950, 4 August	Commander Seventh Fleet establishes the Formosa Patrol Force (Task Force 72), which operates for almost three decades as the Taiwan Patrol Force.
1950, 15 September	Seventh Fleet and UN warships and ground troops execute an amphibious assault at Incheon (Inchon), South Korea, that routs the invading North Korean army and liberates the country.
1950, 25 November	Chinese People's Liberation Army launches a major offensive that forces the withdrawal of U.S. and UN forces from North Korea.
1950, 24 December	Seventh Fleet and other UN naval forces evacuate close to 200,000 troops and refugees from Hungnam, North Korea.
1951, 30 August	United States and Republic of the Philippines sign a Mutual Defense Treaty.
1951, 1 September	Australia, New Zealand, and the United States sign the ANZUS Security Treaty.
1953, 5 March	Soviet dictator Joseph Stalin dies.
1953, 27 July	Belligerents sign a cease-fire agreement that ends the fighting in Korea.
1953, 1 October	United States and Republic of Korea sign a Mutual Defense Treaty.
1954, 7 May	Ho Chi Minh's Viet Minh forces overwhelm the last French defenders of the combat base at Dien Bien Phu in Indochina.

1954, 21 July	At a conference in Geneva, Switzerland, representatives of the belligerents in the First Indochina War agree to cease-fire terms ending the conflict.
1954, 16 August	Seventh Fleet begins loading the first of 293,000 refugees from northern Vietnam who are transported to southern Vietnam in Operation Passage to Freedom.
1954, 3 September	Mao Zedong's army begins shelling Jinmen and Mazu, islands held by the forces of Chiang Kai-shek's Nationalist government on Taiwan.
1954, 8 September	At a meeting in Manila, the United States, Australia, Great Britain, France, Pakistan, the Philippines, New Zealand, and Thailand agree to establish the Southeast Asia Treaty Organization (SEATO) to counter Communist inroads.
1954, 2 December	United States and Republic of China sign a Mutual Defense Treaty.
1955, 20 January	Chinese Communist forces seize Yijiangshan Island in the Dachens chain.
1955, 28 January	Congress passes the Formosa Resolution to support the Republic of China in its confrontation with the People's Republic of China.
1955, 6 February	Seventh Fleet ships begin the evacuation of Chinese Nationalist troops and civilians from the Dachen Islands.
1958, 23 August	Chinese Communist forces begin shelling Chinese Nationalist positions on Jinmen Island in the Taiwan Strait, sparking a confrontation with the United States.
1958, 6 October	Mao Zedong ends the Taiwan Strait crisis with the announcement that his forces will shell Jinmen only on odd days.
1960, 19 January	United States and Japan sign a Treaty of Mutual Cooperation and Security.
1962, 17 May	At the direction of President John F. Kennedy, Seventh Fleet deploys Marine and other U.S. forces to Thailand as a deterrent to Communist advances in neighboring Laos.
1962, 23 July	At a conference in Geneva, Switzerland, the United States and other nations agree to the neutralization of Laos in the ongoing conflict in Southeast Asia.
1963, 1 November	Military coup in South Vietnam results in the assassination of President Ngo Dinh Diem.
1963, 22 November	President John F. Kennedy is assassinated in Dallas, Texas.
1964, 2 August	North Vietnamese torpedo boats attack Seventh Fleet destroyer *Maddox* (DD 731) in the Gulf of Tonkin.
1964, 7 August	Congress passes the Tonkin Gulf Resolution, enabling President Lyndon B. Johnson to employ military means against Communist forces in Southeast Asia.

1965, 8 March	Seventh Fleet amphibious units land the 9th Marine Expeditionary Brigade at Danang, South Vietnam.
1965, 11 March	The Market Time anti-infiltration operation that will involve Seventh Fleet, U.S. Coast Guard, and Vietnam Navy forces, gets underway off the coast of South Vietnam.
1965, 15 March	Task Force 77 carriers launch the Navy's first strikes of the Air Force–Navy Rolling Thunder bombing campaign against North Vietnam.
1966, 26 October	Fire on board carrier *Oriskany* (CVA 34) in the Gulf of Tonkin kills 44 naval aviators and crewmen.
1967, 29 July	Catastrophic fire on the flight deck of carrier *Forrestal* (CVA 59) leads to the death of 134 Sailors.
1968, 23 January	North Korean naval forces seize intelligence ship *Pueblo* (AGER 2) in international waters.
1968, 31 January	Communist forces launch the Tet Offensive in South Vietnam.
1968, 31 March	President Lyndon B. Johnson announces the end of bombing in North Vietnam above of the 19th parallel.
1969, 15 April	North Korean MiGs shoot down a Navy EC-121 reconnaissance plane, killing the entire crew of 31.
1971, 9 December	Washington orders the *Enterprise* (CVAN 165) battle group to deploy to the Indian Ocean in connection with the Indo-Pakistan War.
1972, 21 February	President Richard M. Nixon meets with Chinese Communist leader Mao Zedong in China.
1972, 30 March	North Vietnam launches the multipronged Easter Offensive into South Vietnam.
1972, 9 May	Navy and Marine aircraft flying from carrier *Coral Sea* (CVA 43) mine the approaches to North Vietnam's Haiphong harbor.
1972, 10 May	Seventh Fleet and U.S. Air Force aircraft launch the Linebacker I bombing campaign against North Vietnam.
1972, 18 December	As directed by President Richard M. Nixon, Task Force 77 and Air Force planes inaugurate the Linebacker II strikes on Hanoi and Haiphong.
1973, 27 January	Vietnam War is over for the United States with the signing of the Paris Agreement on Ending the War and Restoring Peace in Vietnam.

1973, 6 February	Seventh Fleet's Mine Countermeasures Force (Task Force 78) begins operations to ensure the waters of North Vietnam are free of U.S.-laid mines, a requirement of the Paris peace agreement.
1975, 12 April	Seventh Fleet and Marine forces evacuate Americans, Cambodians, and others from Phnom Penh, Cambodia, in Operation Eagle Pull.
1975, 30 April	Seventh Fleet directs the Operation Frequent Wind evacuation that ends the U.S. presence in South Vietnam.
1975, 15 May	Navy and Marine units recover merchant ship SS *Mayaguez*, seized two days before by Cambodia's Khmer Rouge.
1976, 21 August	In response to the brutal axe murder of two U.S. Army officers by North Korean soldiers, Seventh Fleet and other U.S. and South Korean units mount a massive show of force in and around the peninsula's Demilitarized Zone.
1979, 1 January	United States and People's Republic of China establish diplomatic relations.
1979, 17 February	People's Republic of China attacks Socialist Republic of Vietnam to "teach the Vietnamese a lesson."
1979, 27 December	Soviet army invades Afghanistan.
1983, 1 September	Soviet MiG shoots down a KAL airliner off Sakhalin Island, killing all on board.
1986, 5 November	For the first time since 1949, warships of the Seventh Fleet visit the Chinese port of Qingdao.
1989, 4 June	China's People's Liberation Army crushes a pro-democracy movement in Beijing's Tiananmen Square.
1989, 1 December	Seventh Fleet units support the government of the Philippines when military elements stage a coup in Manila.
1990, 2 August	Saddam Hussein's Iraqi forces invade Kuwait.
1990, 7 August	As directed by President George H.W. Bush, Seventh Fleet and other U.S. forces launch Operation Desert Shield.
1991, 17 January	Seventh Fleet and other UN coalition forces initiate Desert Storm air and naval operations against Iraqi armed forces.
1991, 24 February	Coalition ground forces begin the ground assault into Kuwait.
1991, 28 February	UN coalition concludes combat operations against Iraq.

1991, 9 May	In Operation Sea Angel, Seventh Fleet and other forces begin humanitarian assistance to the victims of typhoon-devastated Bangladesh.
1991, 16 June	Seventh Fleet forces begin transporting evacuees to Cebu Island in the Philippines from U.S. Naval Base Subic Bay, hit hard by the eruption of volcanic Mount Pinatubo.
1992, 24 November	Seventh Fleet ends the almost 100-year U.S. military presence at U.S. Naval Base Subic Bay.
1993, 12 March	North Korea declares "state of readiness for war" and announces intention to withdraw from the Nuclear Non-Proliferation Treaty.
1996, 11 March	Washington directs the *Nimitz* (CVN 68) and *Independence* (CV 62) carrier battle groups to concentrate near Taiwan as a deterrent to aggressive behavior by the People's Republic of China.
1994, 21 October	United States and North Korea concur on an agreed framework to limit the latter's development of nuclear weapons.
1997, 1 July	United Kingdom transfers sovereignty of its Hong Kong crown colony to the People's Republic of China.
1998, 19 January	United States and People's Republic of China sign a Military Maritime Consultative Agreement for military-to-military contacts.
1998, 31 August	North Korea fires a Taepo Dong I missile over Japan.
1999, 7 May	U.S. aircraft mistakenly bomb the embassy of the People's Republic of China in Belgrade, Serbia.
1999, 15 Jun	Republic of Korea Navy combatants sink a North Korean patrol boat in the Battle of Yeonpyeong.
1999, 1 October	Seventh Fleet forces arrive off Dilli, East Timor, in support of UN Operation Stabilize.
2000, 12 October	Al-Qaeda terrorists in Aden, Yemen, detonate an explosive next to the hull of guided missile destroyer *Cole* (DDG 67), killing 17 American Sailors.
2001, 1 April	PRC fighter crashes into a U.S. EP-3E patrol plane, forcing the latter to make an emergency landing on China's Hainan Island.
2001, 11 September	Al-Qaeda terrorists crash civilian airliners into the Twin Towers of New York's World Trade Center, the Pentagon, and a field in central Pennsylvania, killing close to 3,000 people.
2001, 7 October	U.S. forces begin the fight against al-Qaeda and Taliban terrorists in Afghanistan in Operation Enduring Freedom.

2003, 19 March	Coalition forces begin combat actions against Iraq in Operation Iraqi Freedom.
2003, 31 May	President George W. Bush announces the Proliferation Security Initiative to counter proliferation of weapons of mass destruction.
2004, 28 December	In Operation Unified Assistance, Seventh Fleet units deploy to waters off Indonesia in connection with the Indian Ocean tsunami humanitarian relief.
2005, 28 June	Washington and New Delhi sign the New Framework for the U.S.-India Defense Relationship, a ten-year agreement for joint protection of sea lanes.
2005, Fall	Chief of Naval Operations calls for an international "thousand-ship navy" to defend the maritime commons.
2006, 5 July	North Korea fires Scud, No Dong, and Taepo Dong II missiles into the Sea of Japan/East Sea.
2007, 21 November	Uniformed heads of the U.S. Navy, U.S. Marine Corps, and U.S. Coast Guard sign the "Cooperative Strategy for 21st Century Seapower."
2008, 26 November	Islamist terrorists attack targets in Mumbai, India, killing 165 people.
2009, 20 March	Seventh Fleet and Republic of Korea Navy leaders sign an agreement regarding eventual ROKN assumption of operational control over contingency operations in Korea.
2009, 9 March	Ships of the People's Republic of China harass U.S. Navy research vessel *Impeccable* (T-AGOS 23) in the South China Sea.
2010, 26 March	A North Korean submarine sinks the ROKN corvette *Cheonan*, killing 46 South Korean sailors.
2010, 23 November	North Korean artillery shells South Korea's Yeonpyeong Island, killing two Republic of Korea marines and two civilians.

INTRODUCTION

U.S. INTEREST IN THE FAR EAST dates from the earliest years of the republic, when American merchant ships sailed across the vast Pacific to ply their trade in the ports of China, the Philippines, Indochina, and the East Indies. Warships of the U.S. Navy followed soon afterward to protect those commercial carriers and to promote American diplomatic interests in Asia.

The U.S. Seventh Fleet, successor to the Asiatic Squadron and Asiatic Fleet of the 19th and early 20th centuries, began making its own naval history in the early days of World War II. Unique among the nation's naval forces, the fleet has taken part in all the major conflicts and most of the crises and confrontations of the last six decades. It has defended U.S. interests and worked with America's Asian alliances to deter aggressors and maintain peace and stability in the region. The fleet's Sailors have provided humanitarian assistance and disaster relief to numerous countries devastated by natural and manmade disasters.

The fleet's area of responsibility in the 21st century encompasses 48 million square miles of the Pacific and Indian oceans, an area holding half of the world's population, 35 nations, and many of its most prosperous economies. Much of the world's energy resources and oceangoing trade passes through waters guarded by the warships, aircraft, and men and women of the U.S. Seventh Fleet, whose motto is appropriately—Ready Power for Peace.

Commander Seventh Fleet Vice Admiral Thomas C. Kinkaid, left, and his boss, Supreme Commander, Allied Forces Southwest Pacific Area General Douglas MacArthur, on board light cruiser Phoenix (CL 46) *in early 1944.*

CHAPTER 1

MACARTHUR'S NAVY

THE JAPANESE ATTACK ON PEARL HARBOR on 7 December 1941, characterized by President Franklin D. Roosevelt as a "date which will live in infamy," propelled the United States and the American people into World War II. In following months Japanese forces seized the Philippines, Malaya, and the Netherlands East Indies, in the process defeating badly outnumbered and ill-prepared U.S., British, and Dutch naval forces. In spring 1942 U.S. Pacific Fleet forces and Australian ground troops stalled the Japanese offensive in New Guinea. American ground, air, and naval units then won a hard-fought victory on Guadalcanal and in the waters of the Solomon island chain. By early 1943 Allied forces under Admiral William F. Halsey, Commander, South Pacific Forces and South Pacific Area, were poised to continue the advance northward through the Solomons, with the strong Japanese base at Rabaul on the island of New Britain as the final objective. At the same time, General Douglas MacArthur, Supreme Commander, Allied Forces Southwest Pacific Area, prepared to lead his American and Australian combat units on a divergent course west along the virtually trackless coast of northern New Guinea.

Military leaders in Washington recognized that naval power would be key to MacArthur's New Guinea offensive, so on 19 February 1943 the Navy established the U.S. Seventh Fleet under Vice Admiral Arthur S. Carpender. The fleet made its combat debut at the end of June when Rear Admiral Daniel E. Barbey, in charge of amphibious forces (Task Force 76), deployed troops ashore south of Salamaua in New Guinea and on the Trobriand and Woodlark islands. In September the flag officer, soon called by the press "Uncle Dan the Amphibious Man," ordered Australian combat troops to land east of Lae while U.S. Army paratroopers seized an airfield to the west. This combined assault from the sea and from the air, bypassing strong enemy defenses, would come to characterize the Seventh Fleet's way of war.

Vice Admiral Thomas C. Kinkaid, later recognized as one of the Navy's most successful World War II commanders, took the helm of the battle-hardened Seventh Fleet on 26 November 1943. Kinkaid served MacArthur not only as Commander Seventh Fleet but Commander Allied Naval Forces, Southwest Pacific Area, directing operations of the Australian, New Zealand, and Dutch cruisers and destroyers working for MacArthur.

Admiral Ernest J. King, Commander in Chief, U.S. Fleet and Chief of Naval Operations, selected Kinkaid for the billet because of his success cooperating with Army leaders in Alaska earlier in the war. This skill was a prized attribute because Kinkaid had to work closely with the generals commanding MacArthur's sizable formations of U.S. and Australian ground troops. He recognized that naval forces were in a supporting role in MacArthur's theater and acted accordingly. Moreover, the Navy assigned its large aircraft carriers only to the Central Pacific offensive led by Admiral Chester W. Nimitz, Commander in Chief, U.S. Pacific Fleet and Commander Central Pacific Area, so the Seventh Fleet needed protection by

Battleship Arizona *(BB 39) explodes during the Japanese 7 December 1941 attack on Pearl Harbor.*

the land-based bombers of the U.S. Fifth Air Force under Army Air Forces Lieutenant General George C. Kenney. Kinkaid once observed that "General Kenney . . . was a little difficult to deal with . . . and he thought 'Damn-Navy' was one word," but the two got on with the job at hand of beating the Japanese. For example, Kinkaid persuaded Kenney to assign an Army Air Forces officer to shipboard duty directing fighter cover for the fleet.

MacArthur often disagreed with the Navy's positions on various command, strategic, logistical, and other issues, and Kinkaid helped smooth relations between MacArthur and King, Nimitz, Halsey, and other top Navy leaders. He tried hard to foster interservice cooperation. During planning and preparation for Philippine operations, to be directed by MacArthur's command, Kinkaid ensured that the amphibious commanders from the Seventh Fleet and from Nimitz's Pacific Fleet worked in harmony.

But when Kinkaid disagreed with the general over operations involving naval forces, he did not hesitate to press his case with passion. In one instance, involving landing operations in the Philippines, Kinkaid was prepared to go over MacArthur's head to Admiral King, despite the probability that such an action would result in his firing. Before sending his fleet into the restricted maneuvering room of the Philippine islands and close-by enemy land-based aircraft, Kinkaid wanted landing operations delayed so Allied airpower could neutralize the threat. Persuaded by the analysis of Kinkaid and other naval leaders, MacArthur finally agreed to delays in the operations.

By early 1944 MacArthur's amphibious forces deployed the veteran 1st Marine Division on New Britain and bypassed Japanese forces on New Guinea to land Army troops to their rear. When the general concluded that enemy forces were weak in the Admiralties north of New Guinea, he exploited the mobility and flexibility of the Seventh Fleet to seize the strategic islands. On 29 February 1944 amphibious forces under Rear Admiral William M. Fechteler, a future Chief of Naval Operations, landed elements of the Army's 1st Cavalry Division on Los Negros. Not content to view the operation from the relative safety of light cruiser *Phoenix* (CL 46), MacArthur went ashore where troops were under fire. The general believed that personal bravery was a true mark of combat leadership. In short order U.S. forces secured the Admiralty Islands.

In an even more daring action, MacArthur used the Seventh Fleet to put two Army divisions 300 miles behind Japanese lines at Hollandia on New Guinea. This operation was a joint success story. General Kenny's Fifth Air Force, Admiral Marc Mitcher's fast carriers, and a task force of escort carriers from Halsey's Third Fleet eliminated shore-based Japanese aircraft in range of Hollandia and compelled enemy surface combatants and supply

MacArthur's Flagship

Commissioned in 1938, the *Brooklyn*-class light cruiser *Nashville* (CL 43) was a mainstay of Seventh Fleet operations in World War II. Even before deploying with Vice Admiral Thomas C. Kinkaid's fleet in early in 1943, *Nashville* joined *Hornet* (CV 8) in the famous Halsey-Doolittle bomber raid on Tokyo and later shelled Japanese forces on Kiska Island in the Aleutians. The warship, with General Douglas MacArthur frequently embarked, took part in the Seventh Fleet's major amphibious operations in the Solomons, New Guinea, the Admiralties, and the Philippines. Several months after the pivotal Battle of Leyte Gulf, a Japanese kamikaze plane hit the cruiser, killing 133 Sailors, wounding another 190, and severely damaging the ship. After stateside repairs, she was back in the fight in 1945 for operations in the Netherlands East Indies and the South China Sea.

After the Japanese surrender, *Nashville* supported operations on China's Yangtze River as part of Task Force 73 under Rear Admiral C. Turner Joy and protected amphibious ships transporting U.S. Marines to northern China. The light cruiser then took part in Operation Magic Carpet that returned millions of U.S. servicemen and women home. The Navy decommissioned *Nashville* in June 1946, placed her in "mothballs" until 1951, and then sold the cruiser to Chile. The proud Seventh Fleet veteran served in the Chilean Navy until the early 1980s.

General Douglas MacArthur, third from right, and other officers observe the landing at Leyte in the Philippines from the bridge of light cruiser Nashville *(CL 43), October 1944.*

ships to flee the area. Cut off by air and sea, the Japanese forces ashore were doomed to defeat.

MacArthur next targeted the heavily fortified island of Biak, about 325 miles northwest of Hollandia. The Imperial Japanese Navy sent battleship *Fuso*, two cruisers, and five destroyers loaded with troop reinforcements to support the island's defense. More than 200 enemy planes covered the naval flotilla. Thanks to discovery by Seventh Fleet submarines and patrol aircraft, however, the enemy force reversed course and withdrew. Conversely, covering the Allied landing at Biak were Australian heavy cruisers *Australia* and *Shropshire* and U.S. light cruisers *Phoenix*, *Nashville* (CL 43), and *Boise* (CL 47), plus several Australian and American destroyer divisions. This combined group frustrated a second Japanese attempt to reinforce the defenders of Biak. This naval support proved vital, for once U.S. Army troops landed, they needed a month to overcome the dug-in enemy garrison.

As other U.S. Navy forces deployed Allied divisions ashore at Normandy in France and the Mariana Islands in the Central Pacific during the summer of 1944, MacArthur's U.S.-Australian command, including the Seventh Fleet, finished wresting control from the Japanese of the 1,000-mile northern coast of New Guinea.

These operations were immeasurably assisted by the work of the Seventh Fleet's submarine force under Rear Admiral Ralph W. Christie. His boats, benefiting from a steady flow of "Ultra" radio intelligence gathered by MacArthur's code-breakers in Australia, sent many fully loaded enemy merchant ships to the bottom, protected the amphibious task forces from surface attack, and supplied guerrilla bands in the Netherlands East Indies and southern Philippines.

To the north, the Philippines now beckoned MacArthur. The commander of American and Filipino forces defeated there early in the war, the general had long expressed his determination to erase the memory of that catastrophic loss. When he pledged, "I shall return," in speaking of the Philippines, Allied leaders had little doubt about MacArthur's strategic preferences. Convinced by the general's argument that freeing the Philippines from the brutal Japanese occupation was a moral and military imperative, President Roosevelt gave the go-ahead for the invasion. Commanders prepared their forces for a 20 October 1944 amphibious assault on the Philippine island of Leyte.

The Battle of Leyte Gulf would test the Seventh Fleet as no other World War II fight, for the Japanese were determined to spare neither ships nor planes nor men in their desperate effort to stop the Allied Pacific offensive. As the fleet approached the Philippines, Imperial Japanese Navy commanders launched a long-prepared operation to destroy the American invasion fleet's troop transports, amphibious ships, landing craft, and any warships that got in the way. Vice Admiral Takeo Kurita's Central Force of *Yamato* and *Musashi* and 3 other battleships, 12 cruisers, and 15 destroyers headed through San Bernardino Strait on an easterly heading, intent on attacking the Leyte invasion site. After carrier planes sank *Musashi*, U.S. naval leaders thought this and other losses would compel the Central Force to reverse course and retire, but the Americans were mistaken.

Meanwhile the Southern Force of two battleships and 15 other warships, led by Vice Admirals Shoji Nishimura and Kiyohide Shima, approached Leyte Gulf through Surigao Strait. Deployed there to meet them across the northern mouth of the strait were Rear Admiral Jesse B. Oldendorf's battleships *Mississippi* (BB 41), *California* (BB 44), *Maryland* (BB 46), *Pennsylvania* (BB 38), *Tennessee* (BB 43), and *West Virginia* (BB 48) (the latter five were Pearl Harbor veterans) as well as 8 cruisers, 26 destroyers, and 39 motor torpedo boats.

Waiting in the shadows of the mountains that overlooked Surigao Strait, just after 0300 on the black night of 25 October 1944, were the nine destroyers of Captain Roland Smoot's Destroyer Squadron 56. High atop the superstructure of the *Fletcher*-class destroyer *Bennion* (DD 662) sat Lieutenant (j.g.) James L. Holloway III, in charge of the ship's Mark 37 Gun Director, peering through his binoculars. Flashes of gunfire lit up the night in the distance as American PT boats clashed with the Japanese fleet.

One of Holloway's men tugged his uniform sleeve and suggested the officer take a look through the director's high-power optical device. Filling the lens and in its crosshairs was the distinctive "pagoda" mast of a Japanese battleship making 25 knots and firing away at unseen targets. When Holloway reported the sighting to the bridge, the captain, Commander Joshua Cooper, told the lieutenant to get a lock with the fire control radar on the second of now two battleships in column but wait until given the order to launch five of the ship's torpedoes. Meanwhile the Japanese fleet and the American destroyers rapidly closed on one another under the glow of star shells fired by both sides.

Enemy warships opened fire first, their 14-inch and 8-inch rounds sending up towering splashes all around the "tin can" destroyers. All of a sudden, the 16-inch and 14-inch guns of Oldendorf's battle line opened up, and within 15 to 20 seconds their shells roared over the destroyers and slammed into the enemy fleet. Looking through the director optics, Holloway "could clearly see the explosions of the shells bursting on the Japanese ships, sending up

Battleship Tennessee *(BB 43), a survivor of the Pearl Harbor attack, exacted revenge when she helped devastate the Japanese fleet in Surigao Strait during the Battle of Leyte Gulf.*

The officers and men of destroyer Bennion *(DD 662) take part in a crossing-of-the-equator ceremony en route to the Western Pacific. Lieutenant (j.g.) James L. Holloway III is holding a "sword and shield" next to the commanding officer, Commander Joshua Cooper.*

Leyte Gulf: IJN Yamashiro in Surigao Strait *by John Hamilton. Oil on board.*

cascades of flame as they ripped away topside gun mounts and erupted in fiery sheets of molten steel tearing into the heavy armor plate."

When *Bennion* and the other destroyers got within 6,000 yards of the enemy fleet, they turned to starboard for the torpedo attack. The captain ordered "launch torpedoes," and Holloway immediately pushed the "fire" button on the torpedo console. As the American destroyers headed away from the scene at 30 knots, the young officer observed that the Japanese formation had "disintegrated, with ships circling out of control, dead in the water, on fire, shuddering from massive explosions, and unrecognizable with bows gone, sterns blown away and topsides mangled."

The American attack badly hurt the enemy, but the fight was far from over. Holloway spotted another target, identified as a large Japanese warship, only 3,000 yards away. The captain ordered the launch of the destroyer's last five torpedoes and seconds later the lethal weapons leaped from their launch tubes, slapped the water, and headed for the target. Later analysis confirmed that *Bennion*'s torpedoes sank the Japanese battleship *Yamashiro*.

The Seventh Fleet's victory in the Battle of Surigao Strait was a pivotal event in the career of Lieutenant Holloway—a future Korean War and Vietnam War combat veteran, Seventh Fleet commander, and Chief of Naval Operations.

Meanwhile Vice Admiral Jisaburo Ozawa, commanding a group of aircraft carriers and surface warships—the Northern Force—bluffed Admiral Halsey into chasing after him with the U.S. Third Fleet. This action left the Leyte invasion beaches especially vulnerable because Halsey and Kinkaid each believed that the other's major warships would protect the site.

To the horror of the Americans, at dawn on 25 October, Kurita's Central Force emerged from San Bernardino Strait and headed for the assemblage of small escort carriers, transports, and landing vessels—and *Nashville* with General MacArthur on board.

The Battle of Leyte Gulf not only enabled the liberation of the Philippines to proceed but sealed the fate of the Imperial Japanese Navy. U.S. air, surface, and submarine attacks destroyed much of the enemy's remaining combat strength, sinking

Seventh Fleet Warrior

The Seventh Fleet's decisive defeat of the Imperial Japanese Navy at the Battle of Leyte Gulf in October 1944 can be credited to many brave, determined, and self-sacrificing American Sailors. Commander Ernest E. Evans, the commanding officer of the *Fletcher*-class destroyer *Johnston* (DD 557), stood out among them.

Evans, whose mother was Cherokee and father, half-white, half-Creek Indian, graduated from a nearly all-white Oklahoma high school at a time when prejudice was the norm. He enlisted in the Navy and then won an appointment to the U.S. Naval Academy, graduating with the class of 1931. During the 1930s he served on board cruisers and destroyers, taking command of Johnston at her commissioning on 27 October 1943. At that ceremony Evans told his crew, in John Paul Jones's immortal words, "I intend to go in harm's way."

Commander Evans and *Johnston* were clearly in harm's way on 25 October 1944 when Japanese Admiral Takeo Kurita's fleet of 23 battleships, cruisers, and destroyers suddenly appeared through the morning mist off the Philippine island of Samar and headed for the invasion beach at Leyte. All that stood between the enemy force and the virtually defenseless transports landing U.S. Army troops were the escort carriers, destroyers, and destroyer escorts of Seventh Fleet Task Group 77.4, which included Task Unit 77.4.3, or "Taffy 3," under Rear Admiral Clifton A. "Ziggy" Sprague.

Lieutenant Commander Ernest E. Evans and the crew of Johnston *(DD 557) at the destroyer's commissioning in 1943.*

With his destroyer nearest to the Japanese fleet, Evans immediately turned his ship and zigzagged toward the enemy at flank speed. Seeing this maneuver, Sprague directed the destroyers *Hoel* (DD 533) and *Heermann* (DD 532) and destroyer escort *Samuel B. Roberts* (DE 413) to follow suit. The admiral also ordered aircraft from the escort carriers to attack the enemy with whatever ordnance they had on hand.

Evans had his helmsman steer the ship through enemy shell splashes on the assumption that "lightning never strikes twice in the same place." When the destroyer got within range of Kurita's fleet, the commander barked out the order, "fire torpedoes;" one of ten "fish" tore the bow off the Japanese cruiser *Kumano*. But now enemy battleship and cruiser rounds found their mark, riddling *Johnston* and killing and wounding Sailors.

With two fingers blown off and his face and torso cut and bleeding, Evans calmly conned his ship as the 5-inch guns fired rounds that seemed to bounce off the enemy vessels. Only when his destroyer went dead in the water and could no longer fight back did Evans give the order to abandon ship. *Johnston* rolled over and sank taking the commanding officer with her. In a tribute rarely seen in the brutal Pacific war, the captain of a Japanese destroyer saluted as he passed by the surviving crewmen fighting to stay afloat in the ocean.

The hard fight put up by Evans and the other men of Taffy 3 persuaded Kurita that he could not succeed in his mission; he ordered his fleet back through San Bernardino Strait. Taffy 3 and Commander Evans, posthumously awarded the Medal of Honor for his valor, had saved the American forces off Leyte from destruction.

Destroyer Johnston *one year before her date with destiny in the Battle of Leyte Gulf.*

four enemy aircraft carriers, three battleships, eight cruisers, and eight destroyers. Fear of enemy seapower would never again trouble Allied leaders as they engineered the final defeat of Japan.

Securing the Philippines

A new word, however, quickly spread fear among Seventh Fleet Sailors—kamikaze. Japanese pilots, in a desperate attempt to stave off the Allied Pacific advance and ultimate invasion of Japan, deliberating sacrificed their lives by crashing aircraft into fleet vessels. The first large ship to suffer this attack, escort carrier *St. Lo* (CVE 63), went down off the Philippines during the Battle of Leyte Gulf. In October and November 1944, kamikaze pilots operating from airfields ashore sank or badly damaged dozens of fleet carriers, escort carriers, cruisers, destroyers, and other naval vessels.

The Allied conquest of the Philippines continued on 15 December when Seventh Fleet forces under Rear Admiral Arthur D. Struble landed 27,000 Army troops on Mindoro, a strategic island between Leyte and Lingayen Gulf. The Japanese sent waves of aircraft in desperate attacks against fleet units off the island. The experiences of *LST 738* and *LST 472*, deployed off White Beach, were not uncommon. A group of ten enemy aircraft made it through the defensive screen to pounce on the amphibious ships. One plane crashed into *LST 738* commanded by Naval Reserve Lieutenant J. T. Barnett, punching through the hull near the waterline and exploding in the tank deck amid stores of fuel and ammunition. The destroyer *Moale* (DD 693), operating nearby, shot down another plane headed for the LST and then moved close aboard to help fight the fire. The three explosions that rocked the LST killed one Sailor on the destroyer and wounded ten others. Barnett finally ordered the vessel abandoned.

Meanwhile *LST 472* commanded by Lieutenant John H. Blakley attracted Japanese attention off Mindoro. One enemy plane dropped a bomb that holed the landing ship, and then crashed into her, spewing burning engine parts across the deck. Four other planes attacked the LST; nearby ships splashed

Vice Admiral Takeo Kurita, commander of the Japanese naval force that attacked the Leyte invasion ships off Samar until turned back by destroyer Johnston *and the other destroyer-type ships and escort carriers of "Taffy 3."*

two of them. The destroyers *O'Brien* (DD 725) and *Hopewell* (DD 681) and *PCE 851* then moved in close to aid the stricken vessel. Despite the heroic effort, explosions and fire tore through the ship, prompting Blakely to order abandon ship. The attack killed or wounded nine crewmen.

Within a month, Seabees and Army engineers had the airfield on Mindoro up and running to provide air cover for the Lingayen landing on Luzon. Despite fierce Japanese air opposition to the fleet's presence off Mindoro, Navy and Army air units returned the favor during December, destroying hundreds of enemy planes on the ground and in the air.

With the fleet now closer to enemy airfields on Luzon and Formosa, Kinkaid and his task force commanders were especially concerned about the danger of concentrated enemy air attacks. To support the major landing at Lingayen, Halsey's Third Fleet launched devastating air attacks against airfields and ports on Formosa, Hong Kong, and

Destroyer Moale *(DD 693) maneuvers to assist* LST 738, *burning furiously after a kamikaze attack.*

Guangzhou (Canton) and merchant ships in the South China Sea. Army Air Forces and the units of British Lord Louis Mountbatten, Supreme Commander Southeast Asia Command, also hit enemy airfields and conducted diversionary attacks.

Despite this heavy air suppression, Japanese kamikaze and conventional air attacks still sank and damaged Seventh Fleet ships advancing from Leyte to Lingayen for the assault landing. Their attacks sank the escort carrier *Ommaney Bay* (CVE 79) and destroyer minesweeper *Long* (DMS 12) and damaged the escort carrier *Manila Bay* (CVE 61), battleships *New Mexico* (BB 40) and *California*, Australian cruiser *Australia*, and American cruisers *Louisville* (CA 28) and *Columbia* (CL 56). The air assault on *New Mexico* killed Rear Admiral Theodore E. Chandler, a task force commander and grandson of a 19th-century Secretary of the Navy.

On 9 January 1945 an Army-Navy force under Vice Admiral Kinkaid, commander of the Luzon Attack Force (CTF 77) for the operation, assembled off the invasion beach in Lingayen Gulf. Task Force 78 led by Vice Admiral Barbey deployed ashore the Army's I Corps consisting of the U.S. 43rd and 6th infantry divisions. Vice Admiral Theodore S. Wilkinson's Task Force 79 landed the XIV Corps with its U.S. 37th and 40th infantry divisions. The major naval units supporting the landing—six battleships, nine heavy and light cruisers, and numerous destroyers—pounded the enemy-held shore. Escort carriers and submarines established protective barriers around the assault force.

Having learned from previous amphibious assaults the near impossibility of stopping allied combat power coming from the sea, General Tomoyuki Yamashita, in charge of enemy forces on Luzon, ordered his troops to refuse battle on the beaches and withdraw to the mountains so they could fight on longer against the Allies.

At the end of the month Kinkaid's amphibious forces landed additional U.S. Army troops on Bataan Peninsula, site of fierce fighting earlier in the war. The swift Allied advance on Luzon came to an abrupt halt when the U.S. Sixth Army's divisions reached Manila where the local enemy commander had decided to fight to the finish. It took more than a month of hard combat to destroy the Japanese garrison and capture the battered capital city in a battle that cost the lives of 100,000 Filipinos. It took another four months for General MacArthur's ground troops, deployed ashore by the Seventh Fleet's amphibious arm, to defeat Japanese forces on the Philippine islands of Mindanao, Cebu, and Negros. Kinkaid capped his fleet's successful Southwest Pacific campaign with a 16-day bombardment by U.S., Australian, and Dutch warships against enemy troops at Balikpapan on Borneo, followed by the landing there of the Australian 7th Infantry Division.

Seventh Fleet officers and men emerged from World War II as masters of joint and combined warfare, especially amphibious operations. Under

Vice Admiral Kinkaid oversees the Seventh Fleet's amphibious assault at Lingayen Gulf in January 1945.

the sure guidance of Kinkaid, Rear Admirals Barbey and Fechteler led naval forces in one successful assault landing after another. These men interacted well with their U.S. Army and Australian military counterparts as MacArthur's Southwest Pacific Command moved with speed and power from one island to the next in the unrelenting march on Japan. Led by Vice Admiral Kinkaid and Rear Admirals Oldendorf and Sprague, the Sailors of the fleet fought and won the decisive Battle of Leyte Gulf that sealed the fate of the Imperial Japanese Navy. The stellar performance of their World War II predecessors would inspire Seventh Fleet Sailors for many years to come.

Chapter 2

WEATHERING POSTWAR TURMOIL IN ASIA

BEFORE THE END OF WORLD WAR II, the Seventh Fleet embarked on a mission that would take on increasing importance—supporting U.S. foreign policy in the Far East. The defeat of Japan ushered in an era in which the United States faced the rise of Soviet power and militant independence movements, many of them communist in orientation.

The administration of President Harry S. Truman was ambivalent about U.S. goals in Asia after 1945. Most of the millions of American men and women in military service at the end of World War II wanted nothing more than to turn in their uniforms and resume their lives as civilians in a country at peace. Truman also wanted the U.S. economy, for four years the "arsenal of democracy" that produced mountains of war material, to focus anew on overseas trade and domestic commerce. To boost the economy, Truman made fewer defense dollars available to maintain large naval and military forces. A greatly diminished military establishment would be hard-pressed to support an ambitious U.S. foreign policy. Further complicating the situation, Truman and his chief advisors saw their first priority as strengthening the economies of western Europe and deterring the aggressive actions of Joseph Stalin's Soviet Union in eastern Europe.

The administration viewed the situation in Asia as even more chaotic than in Europe and hence harder to deal with. The death and destruction

President Harry S. Truman.

Joseph Stalin, Soviet dictator and spiritual father of the international Communist movement. The USSR's military power and territorial interests in Northeast Asia at the end of World War II concerned U.S. leaders.

On 2 September 1945 Allied leaders and the Sailors of battleship Missouri *(BB 63) witness Japan's surrender in World War II.*

visited by Japanese armies on China from 1937 to 1945 disrupted the central government's control of that nation, leading many observers to predict the outbreak of civil war between Chiang Kai-shek's Republic of China government and Mao Zedong's Chinese Communist Party. With the end in August 1945 of Japan's harsh, 40-year occupation of Korea, various Korean independence movements prepared to fight for control of the country. Japan's march of aggression had also seriously weakened the control of the British, French, and Dutch governments over their Asian colonies of Malaya, Indochina, and the Netherlands East Indies. Native peoples, many of whom who had fought the Japanese, were determined to end their status as "colonials." Postwar Asia seethed with political, social, and economic discontent.

Missions in Korea and China

Well before the Japanese surrender on board the battleship *Missouri* (BB 63) on 2 September 1945, the Seventh Fleet had prepared for a new mission. The wartime Allies faced the need to repatriate hundreds of thousands of defeated, sullen, and potentially hostile Japanese troops. General Order Number 1 provided instructions for the surrender of Japanese forces throughout Asia, and between January 1946 and April 1947, the fleet repatriated from China and Korea more than 400,000 men who had served the Empire of Japan in World War II.

As directed by MacArthur, Vice Admiral Kinkaid organized the transport of the Army's XXIV Corps under Major General John R. Hodge from Okinawa to Incheon (Inchon) on the west coast of Korea. As agreed to by Washington and Moscow, Soviet forces moved into Korea north of the temporary dividing line, the 38th parallel, as American troops occupied the south. Kinkaid's fleet then returned to Okinawa, embarked the 1st Marine Division, and moved the veteran combat unit to Tianjin (Tientsin) southeast of Beijing (Peking) in China. A later operation deployed the 6th Marine Division to North China. During this same period Lieutenant (j.g.) Elmo R. Zumwalt Jr., a future Chief of Naval Operations, conned a captured Japanese minesweeper up the Yangtze River to Shanghai, the first Seventh Fleet officer to enter China's major port.

As laid out in Operation Plan 13-45 of 26 August 1945, Kinkaid established five major task forces to manage operations in the Western Pacific: Task Force 71, the North China Force with 75 ships; Task Force 72, the Fast Carrier Force, directed to provide air cover to the Marines going ashore and discourage with dramatic aerial flyovers any Communist forces that might oppose the operation; Task Force 73, the Yangtze Patrol Force with another 75 combatants; Task Force 74, the South China Force, ordered to protect the transportation of Japanese and Chinese Nationalist troops from that region; and Task Force 78, the Amphibious

Lieutenant (j.g.) Elmo R. Zumwalt Jr. (a future Chief of Naval Operations), second from right, gives instructions to a Japanese army officer in the Chinese port of Shanghai in October 1945.

Force, charged with the movement of the III Marine Amphibious Corps to China.

Kinkaid continued to serve as the naval component commander for MacArthur until V-J Day on 2 September, but the new responsibilities in Korea and China effectively ended the wartime connection. As Kinkaid's ships departed Manila Bay on 28 August, the general graciously recognized the Seventh Fleet's World War II contribution to the success of Allied arms in the Southwest Pacific Area: "I desire to express my admiration and grateful acknowledgement for the magnificent manner in which all its [Seventh Fleet] elements have performed their assigned tasks in the campaigns of this theater. To you and your officers and men who have with great gallantry, resourcefulness, and devotion to duty so fully upheld the highest traditions of our country's naval service, I send Godspeed."

While the purpose of the U.S. troop movements into Korea and China was to establish order and repatriate Japanese troops, both the Soviet and U.S. governments were determined to demonstrate their power to influence the postwar political situation in Asia. The Truman administration expressed concern that Stalin would use the Soviet Red Army to steer Korean political developments and pressure the Chinese government to grant port and railway concessions to the USSR in Manchuria and North China. Even before the emergence of the Cold War between the United States and the Soviet Union, top American officials warned that Moscow had designs on the region. James Forrestal, Secretary of the Navy, and Admiral William D. Leahy, the top military advisor to the President and head of the Joint Chiefs of Staff, forecast that the Soviets would provide military support to Communist groups in Korea and China and work against U.S. interests.

During September 1945 Vice Admiral Kinkaid employed Seventh Fleet ships and aircraft to impress Chinese, Koreans, and Soviets alike of U.S. naval power. Fleet units steamed within clear site of the population of Qingdao (Tsingtao). Carrier planes flew over Korea's port of Incheon and China's Great Wall and the cities of Shanghai, Tianjin, Beijing, and Dalian. At the same time Seventh Fleet ships evacuated Allied prisoners of war (POWs) from the Philippines, China, Taiwan (then called Formosa), and Korea.

A group of 128 POWs to whom Kinkaid spoke in Seoul told a harrowing tale of their captivity. In the latter stages of the war the Japanese had loaded these men and 1,672 fellow Americans, captured during the early 1942 Bataan campaign in the Philippines, on board merchant ship *Oryoku Maru* in Subic Bay. Three hundred men died when Allied pilots, unaware of the passengers on board, sank the ship. The next vessel transporting the survivors went down off Taiwan, killing more men. Starvation, disease, and exposure to the elements had reduced the number of POWs to 600 men by the time they reached Japan. Only 128 of these men remained alive when the Japanese moved them to Korea for imprisonment.

On 9 September Vice Admiral Kinkaid and Major General Hodge accepted the surrender of Japanese forces in Korea. Following the ceremony at a government building in Seoul, U.S. soldiers lowered the Japanese flag from a flagpole out front and ran up the Stars and Stripes.

On 16 September Kinkaid, embarked in minesweeper *YMS 49*, reached Shanghai where he met Rear Admiral Milton "Mary" Miles, Commander, Naval Group China and the top U.S. naval leader in China during the war. Miles arranged for the Seventh Fleet flagship, *Rocky Mount* (AGC 3), to moor at the

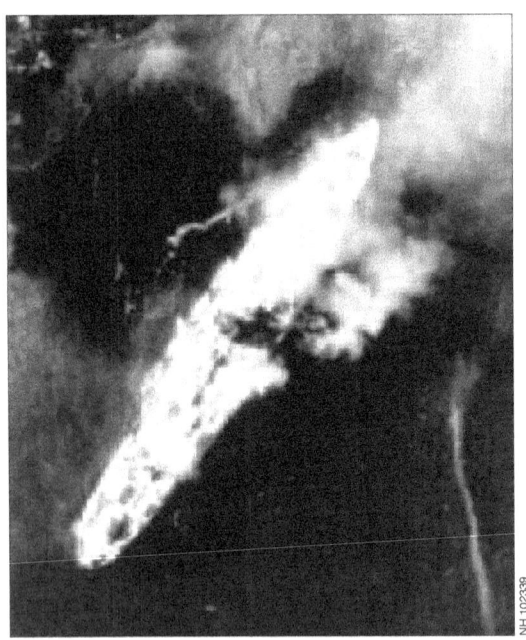

Japanese transport Oryoku Maru *under attack by U.S. carrier aircraft in Subic Bay, Philippines, on 14 December 1944. Unknown to the attackers, many of her passengers were American prisoners of war.*

Vice Admiral Thomas C. Kinkaid and Army Major General John R. Hodge, commander of the XXIV Corps, sign documents in Seoul formalizing the surrender of Japanese forces in Korea. To the left of Kinkaid is a future Seventh Fleet commander, Vice Admiral Daniel E. Barbey.

Seventh Fleet flagship Rocky Mount *(AGC 3).*

harbor's most prestigious buoy, exclusively reserved for the Royal Navy's station ship before the war. In 1945 the Chinese Nationalists had assigned a less desirable site upriver for the British ship. Local officials brushed off British complaints; the Chinese decided there was a new postwar power equation in the Far East.

Kinkaid established Seventh Fleet headquarters in Shanghai and met with the Army's Commanding General, China Theater, Lieutenant General Albert C. Wedemeyer, U.S. Ambassador Patrick J. Hurley, and other chief U.S. and Chinese officials and military leaders. On 20 September Kinkaid flew to Chongqing (Chungking), then the Republic of China's capital, to meet with Generalissimo Chiang Kai-shek and Madame Chiang, his charming and internationally known wife. The American admiral was praised and feted by his hosts who wanted to impress on him that the Seventh Fleet and the U.S. Navy were welcome in Chinese waters.

The Seventh Fleet did not get much of a breather in the months after the war. Kinkaid wrote to his wife that "the Navy out here is like a five-ring circus. The 7th Fleet has been landing the Army in Korea, the Marines at [Tianjin], another Marine force [the 6th Marine Division] will land at another point at an early date, and we are about to start the movement of several Chinese armies from one point to another. At the same time we are in the process of changing the organization of the Fleet . . . and setting up organizations to assist China Theater forces." The fleet also transported service personnel home to America. In Operation Magic Carpet, between October 1945 and May 1946, 369 naval vessels deployed in the Pacific brought more than two million men and women home from war.

The situation in China soon became especially tense. Marines of the III Marine Amphibious Corps, under Major General Keller E. Rockey, deployed by the Seventh Fleet to Beijing, Tianjin, and

Major General Keller E. Rockey, commanding general of the III Marine Amphibious Corps.

other population centers in North China, found themselves in a hornet's nest of political intrigue. Heavily armed and mutually antagonistic forces, including Japanese, pro-Japanese Chinese, Chinese Communist, and Chinese Nationalist staked their claims to overlapping areas.

The Communist-Nationalist dispute, however, caused the most concern. Throughout World War II the Nationalist government of Chiang Kai-shek and the Communist guerrilla movement of Mao Zedong fought the Japanese. Following Japan's surrender, when Chinese Communist forces occupied much of Manchuria and North China, Chiang moved to reassert the national government's authority in those regions. Fighting erupted wherever the two sides made contact.

U.S. foreign policy required Navy and Marine forces to support Chiang's legally constituted government but steer clear of the internal Chinese conflict—an impossible task. The Seventh Fleet deployed Rockey's Marines to some areas already occupied by Mao's troops who did not like the intrusion.

In some cases, Seventh Fleet leaders used common sense to carry out their missions and avoid entanglement in the Chinese civil conflict. For instance, Vice Admiral Daniel Barbey, Kinkaid's amphibious commander, decided that it made no sense to land Marines at the port of Yantai (Chefoo) on the northern coast of the Shandong Peninsula in the face of opposition from local Communist forces. Backed by Major General Rockey, Barbey reasoned that with no POWs or Japanese troops in the area needing repatriation, and the Communists managing the civil administration of the port, there was no need to force the issue. Instead, Seventh Fleet units landed the Marines at Qingdao on the peninsula's south side.

Still, the Seventh Fleet transported entire Chinese Nationalist armies to North China and Manchuria in support of Chiang's effort to reestablish government control of all China. The stated reason for the mission: replace U.S. Marines in North China and Soviet troops in Manchuria with Chinese government troops (as provided for in Allied World War II agreements), take the surrender of Japanese forces, and then transport the latter to Japan. Americans leaders understood, however, that these actions would prevent the Chinese Communists from establishing a foothold in these regions. The Communists understood this too and blocked the debarkation of Nationalist troops at Huludao (Hulutao) and Yingkou, so the fleet landed the units further south at Qinhuangdao (Chinhuangtao).

In October the Navy expanded the Seventh Fleet's area of operations from the waters off China to French Indochina as far south as the 16th parallel. U.S. leaders took this action to enable the transportation of Chinese Nationalist troops from the Tonkin region of Indochina to northern China. In late October and early November, the 136-foot auxiliary motor minesweepers of Mine Squadron 106 (Task Group 74.4), led by Commander Strauss S. Leon, and a number of Japanese minesweepers cleared the waters around Haiphong in French Indochina. Simultaneously, the 28 Liberty Ships, attack transports, and attack cargo ships of

Cold War Admiral

The Navy appointed Admiral Charles M. "Savvy" Cooke Jr. Commander Seventh Fleet to deal with the many challenges facing U.S. foreign policy in a China devastated by World War II and civil strife. The gifted flag officer, Fleet Admiral Ernest J. King's wartime chief of staff and principal planner, saw his mission as preventing Communist inroads in Asia. He and many other Navy leaders advocated robust U.S. military and political support to Generalissimo Chiang Kai-shek's Nationalist government to prevent a Soviet-Chinese Communist victory in the world's most populace nation. Cooke regarded Marine forces in North China and the base at Qingdao as vital deterrents to Communist advances. This position put him at odds with the Truman administration's intention to withdraw the Marines from China and close the base. He carried out his orders, if reluctantly.

With the end of his tour as Commander, U.S. Naval Forces Western Pacific and retirement looming, Cooke on 24 February 1948 made his views public. He joined a chorus of conservative Americans who decried Truman's "loss of China" to the Communists and called for open military support to Chiang's government, now on the island of Taiwan. He backed up his words with action by providing the generalissimo with direct advice on military strategy, tactics, and training and worked to channel U.S. military aid to Chiang. In the months before the Communist invasion of South Korea, the admiral called for the United States to make a stand in the Far East. Cooke's advocacy and that of like-minded military officers influenced President Truman's dramatic decisions in June 1950 to employ U.S. forces in defense of South Korea and the Seventh Fleet in defense of Taiwan.

Vice Admiral Daniel E. Barbey, left, and Admiral Charles M. Cooke Jr. at the Seventh Fleet change of command ceremony in January 1946. The Navy appointed a full admiral to the billet and renamed it Commander, U.S. Naval Forces Western Pacific, in recognition of the position's growing diplomatic responsibilities.

Transportation Squadron 24, under Commodore Edwin T. Short, embarked the 23,000 troops of the Nationalist 52nd Army and delivered them to North China.

Recognizing that naval responsibilities in China and Indochina would hinge more on diplomacy than warfighting in the postwar period, the Navy assigned a full admiral, Charles M. Cooke Jr., as Commander Seventh Fleet on 8 January 1946, and in January 1947 renamed his billet U.S. Naval Forces Western Pacific. To carry out these responsibilities, Cooke's forces normally operated one cruiser division, three destroyer divisions, an amphibious group, and a small number of logistic ships.

The situation of the III Marine Amphibious Corps in North China became increasingly untenable between 1946 and 1948. An attempt by General George C. Marshall, the wartime Army chief of staff, to facilitate a Nationalist-Communist coalition government failed, and civil war broke out soon afterward. Realizing that the U.S. Navy and Marine Corps provided Chiang's forces with training and war material, the Communists retaliated. Mao's troops ambushed III Marine Amphibious Corps guard posts and convoys, killing and wounding Marines. In the face of the Communist hostility and his belief that the United States should openly side with the Nationalist government, Admiral Cooke and other U.S. naval leaders called for increasing the Marine contingent at the port of Qingdao from 2,000 to 5,000 and retaining the base for the Navy regardless of the Chinese civil war's outcome. Cooke considered the base as a strong bar to Soviet advances in the Far East. The Truman administration, especially Secretary of State Dean Acheson, began to see Chiang's cause as lost, so he rejected the admiral's proposals. Washington ordered the reduction of Marine forces in North China and eventual withdrawal from China.

Growing Interest in Southeast Asia

During the five years after World War II, Commander Seventh Fleet served, in essence, as America's naval ambassador to Southeast Asia. With the urging of the State Department, and to carve out an operational area not under General MacArthur's Far East Command, the Navy increasingly dispatched naval vessels on port visits to the region. The aircraft carriers *Antietam* (CV 36) and *Boxer* (CV 21), cruiser *Topeka* (CL 67), and seven destroyers were on hand off Manila for Philippine Independence Day, 4 July 1946. With the support of the newly independent government, the Navy established U.S. Naval Advisory Group Philippines. In March 1947 the two countries signed an agreement allowing U.S. naval forces to

Light cruiser Topeka *(CL 67), one of several Seventh Fleet ships that anchored off Manila to represent the United States at ceremonies marking Philippine Independence Day on 4 July 1946.*

Attack transport Renville *(APA 227) hosted cease-fire negotiations between representatives of the Dutch government and Indonesian independence leaders on 17 January 1948.*

operate bases at Subic Bay and Sangley Point. The Philippines would take on added importance after May 1949 when the fleet left Qingdao. Although the Navy considered the naval base at Yokosuka, Japan, the best place to relocate the fleet, it was loath to have the Seventh Fleet come under General MacArthur's direct control. As a result, most fleet units moved to the Philippines where the Navy retained greater autonomy.

Chief of Naval Operations Admiral Forrest P. Sherman directed Admiral Cooke, commander of U.S. Naval Forces Western Pacific, to begin "showing his flag at Singapore and other points in that direction." On 8 November 1947 Task Group 70.7, with the flagship *Estes* (AGC 12), light cruiser *Atlanta* (CL 104), and destroyers *Rupertus* (DD 851) and *Mason* (DD 852), departed Qingdao for a planned 30-day cruise to Southeast Asia. Cooke's ships made port calls at Hong Kong, Singapore, Brunei Bay (Borneo), Manila, Subic Bay, and Keelung on Taiwan, finally returning to Qingdao in early December.

In late 1947, at Washington's direction, Cooke sent the attack transport *Renville* (APA 227) to the Netherlands East Indies off the island of Java to provide a neutral venue for negotiations between Dutch officials and leaders of an independence movement. On 17 January 1948 the parties signed a document, thereafter called the Renville Agreement, which, while short-lived, demonstrated U.S. interest in securing the peace in Southeast Asia.

Other than diplomatic missions, the Seventh Fleet in this period could handle little else. In 1947 the fleet operated two carriers and 34 other warships, but by 1949 those numbers had been reduced to five small combatants and no permanently deployed carrier. Sherman knew that the Truman administration was increasingly concerned about the situation in the Far East, and he obtained approval to deploy the carrier *Boxer*, a cruiser, and two destroyers "to serve as a stabilizing influence" in the region.

On 16 March 1950 sixty aircraft launched from *Boxer* and conducted an aerial parade over Saigon while the destroyers *Anderson* (DD 786) and *Stickell* (DD 888), with Commander Seventh Fleet Vice Admiral Russell S. Berkey embarked, made a port call at the largest city in southern French Indochina. Seventh Fleet warships would be familiar sights around Saigon in years to come.

China and Korea Heat Up

While dubious about the prospects of Chiang Kai-shek's government and war effort, during 1948 and 1949 the Truman administration actually increased military aid to the Republic of China. As a result of the China Aid Act of 1948 and other programs, the United States government provided $400 million in economic and military assistance, transferred 165 surplus warships to the Nationalist navy, and established programs to train Nationalist forces to use American-made weapons and equipment. The Nationalist navy, however, fought poorly for the mainland. The sailors of many of the vessels provided by the United States and Great Britain eventually defected with their ships to the Communist side.

American support for Chiang's government did little to stem the Communist tide. By mid-1949 Mao's troops had defeated one Nationalist army after another, occupied all Manchuria and northern China, and advanced across the broad Yangtze into southern China. Chiang and his remaining followers fled to Taiwan and numerous other islands along the coast. In light of the Communist advances, the Truman administration finally ordered the Seventh Fleet to evacuate Qingdao. Vice Admiral Badger suggested relocating the fleet's facilities and the Chinese Naval Training Center to Taiwan, but Secretary of State Acheson rejected the proposal. In May 1949 Badger oversaw the redeployment of the Marine defense force in Qingdao to Guam and Japan and moved all naval personnel on board warships in the harbor. On 25 May 1949 the Seventh Fleet steamed seaward, closing this dramatic first chapter of its Cold War history.

The defeat in China was not the only development threatening to undermine America's hard-won power and influence in the Pacific. In July 1949 Mao announced a "lean to one side" (the Soviet side) in the growing U.S.-Soviet confrontation. In September the USSR became the second atomic power after successfully testing an atomic bomb. Having conquered the Chinese mainland, Mao Zedong stood in Beijing's Tiananmen Square on 1 October 1949 and announced the formation of the People's Republic of China (PRC). The Communists took over U.S.-owned properties in China and harassed U.S. diplomats. In February 1950 the PRC and the USSR signed a 30-year Treaty of Friendship, Alliance, and Mutual Assistance. Soviet munitions and military advisors soon flowed into China. During the same period the PRC began supplying Ho Chi Minh's communist-nationalist movement in Indochina with arms and advisors. In April Mao's People's Liberation Army (PLA) defeated Nationalist forces on the large island of Hainan in the South China Sea and prepared to assault Taiwan, Chiang's last refuge.

President Truman, Secretary Acheson, and other administration leaders, despite their anxiety over these developments, could do little in the short term to support a more ambitious foreign policy because of the weakness of the American military. The Navy in general and the Seventh Fleet in particular found it difficult to carry out their responsibilities. Only one aircraft carrier, *Valley Forge* (CV 45), remained in the Western Pacific. The rest of the Seventh Fleet consisted of two destroyer divisions; the submarines *Catfish* (SS 339), *Cabezon* (SS 334), and *Segundo* (SS 398); and a pair of auxiliary ships. An even smaller naval contingent—Naval Forces Far East—operated under MacArthur's Far East Command headquartered in Tokyo.

Congressional actions were underway, however, to bolster the military capability of the United States and that of its Asian friends. In October 1949

U.S. Naval Base, Qingdao, China

During the first four years of the Cold War, the Seventh Fleet called the naval base at Qingdao (Tsingtao) home. The port had served as a Far Eastern outpost of the German navy until a Japanese force seized it at the outset of World War I. Tasked after World War II with deploying U.S. Marines and Chiang Kai-shek's Chinese Nationalist troops to northern China and repatriating Japanese troops, the Navy quickly recognized the port's value as an operating base. On 11 October 1945 fleet ships landed the 6th Marine Division at Qingdao, and shortly afterward Vice Admiral Daniel E. Barbey, Commander Seventh Fleet, established the Chinese Naval Training Center to prepare Chinese Nationalist sailors for operating amphibious craft. By 1946 Seventh Fleet commanders regarded Qingdao as the fleet's primary anchorage in China, with responsibilities for training Chinese sailors, transferring surplus ships and craft to them, and managing an airfield.

During 1947 Mao Zedong's Chinese Communist forces became increasingly hostile toward not only U.S. Marines stationed in North China but also naval units at Qingdao. In June Communist troops fired on the repair ship *Deliver* (ARS 23) working to salvage a pontoon that had gone adrift near the port. Supported by covering fire from *Deliver* and destroyer *Benner* (DD 807), whose purpose was to "discourage and drive off rather than injure the attackers," a landing party from destroyer *Hawkins* (DD 873) recovered the pontoon.

Repair ship Deliver *(ARS 23), fired on by Chinese Communist forces near the U.S. naval base at Qingdao in June 1947.*

Two months later bad weather forced a Marine pilot to land in Communist-held territory near Qingdao. A landing party of Marines from the heavy cruiser *Saint Paul* (CA 73) and Sailors from the destroyer *Tucker* (DD 875) sent to retrieve him traded fire with Mao's troops. To avoid inflaming the situation, the Americans destroyed the plane and withdrew to the ships. The Communists released the young naval aviator but only after protracted and lengthy negotiations with U.S. officials.

In December 1947 the Communists shot and killed a Marine and captured four other men outside the base and only admitted it in February 1948, along with a demand that the U.S. withdraw its forces from Qingdao and stop aiding Chiang's forces. Not until April were the captured men and the body of the slain Marine returned to U.S. custody.

Despite these incidents, Qingdao had become a busy place by the late 1940s. Alternating flagships *Eldorado* (AGC 11) and *Estes* (AGC 12), aircraft carriers *Valley Forge* (CV 45) and *Antietam* (CV 36), hospital ship *Repose* (AH 16), and a host of cruisers, submarines, destroyers, amphibious ships, and auxiliaries operated from the base.

But in line with directives from Washington, during 1947 and 1948 Commander, Naval Forces Western Pacific (formerly Commander Seventh Fleet) Admiral Charles M. Cooke Jr. withdrew the Marines from North China. His successor, Vice Admiral Oscar C. Badger, began closing down operations at Qingdao as Mao's forces stormed across China.

Congress appropriated $75 million for use in the "general area of China." In March 1950 the State Department's Director of Policy Planning, Paul Nitze, authored a study to boost U.S. military and economic power, and that September President Truman approved it as National Security Council NSC-68. Many came to regard NSC-68 as the "blueprint" for America's Cold War military buildup.

Within the State and Defense departments, key officials pressed for increased military and economic assistance to Japan, the Nationalist government on Taiwan, and France, the latter fighting to contain Ho Chi Minh's Vietnamese resistance movement. Top Army and Navy leaders understood that they did not have the forces to defeat an all-out Communist amphibious assault on Taiwan, but they called for everything short of military intervention to assist the Nationalists. If the PRC controlled the island, located strategically between Japan and the Philippines, it would imperil the U.S. strategic position in the Western Pacific. General MacArthur argued that Taiwan would be "an unsinkable aircraft carrier" and a submarine base vital to whichever side held it.

The trigger for a rebirth of U.S. fighting power, however, occurred in relation to another Asian country touched by the sea—Korea. The military occupation of the peninsula by Soviet forces north of the 38th parallel and U.S. forces south of that unofficial dividing line was followed by Moscow's and Washington's support for respective Korean independence movements. Soviet forces withdrew from Korea, but Stalin supplied the Democratic People's Republic of Korea, under Communist leader Kim Il-sung, with hundreds of aircraft, tanks, and artillery pieces. The thousands of repatriated, battle-hardened Koreans who had served in the PLA during the fight for the Chinese mainland formed the core of the Korean People's Army. The late 1940s in Korea was marked by bitter fighting between Communists and anti-Communists who carried out cross-border raids, massacres, and political assassinations. The only U.S. military personnel in South Korea by 1950 were a handful of advisors training the anti-Communist forces of Syngman Rhee's Republic of Korea (ROK) in the use of short-range artillery pieces, small arms, and small naval vessels.

Emboldened by Communist success in China—and mistakenly thinking the United States would not oppose the action—Stalin, Mao, and Kim decided on war to unify the Korean peninsula under Kim's Marxist-Leninist government. During the first six months of 1950, seven North Korean infantry divisions, supported by hundreds of Soviet-made tanks and artillery pieces, concentrated along the 38th parallel, preparing to invade the Republic of Korea.

The U.S. government in Washington and military and naval leaders in the Pacific were unaware of the impending threat to peace and stability in Northeast Asia. As a result, in June 1950 the ships of the much diminished postwar Seventh Fleet rode gently at anchor in Subic Bay in the Philippines. Their idyll would not last for long.

Chapter 3

FIGHTING THE KOREAN WAR

IN LATE JUNE 1950, after a five-year hiatus, the Seventh Fleet engaged once again in its primary mission of defeating America's enemies in combat. For the next three years the fleet's carrier aircraft, surface warships, and amphibious units fought the first armed conflict of the Cold War. The presence in the Far East of this powerful naval force also helped prevent the spread of conflict throughout the region.

On 25 June North Korean armed forces, equipped with Soviet tanks, artillery, and combat aircraft, attacked the Republic of (South) Korea. The communist offensive quickly overran the border defenses and rapidly advanced south. President Truman ordered U.S. air, ground, and naval forces to help South Korean and United Nations forces turn back the Communist invasion. The Seventh Fleet sortied from its base at Subic Bay in the Philippines on the 27th, steamed to Korea via Taiwan and Okinawa, and little more than a week after the invasion, directed naval gunfire and air strikes at targets ashore. The U.S. Navy took full advantage of its control of the sea and the air above it. On 2 July the cruiser *Juneau* (CL 119), British cruiser *Jamaica*, and British frigate *Black Swan* intercepted North Korean torpedo boats and motor gunboats off the east coast of South Korea and destroyed four of the naval vessels. The following day aircraft from *Valley Forge* and British

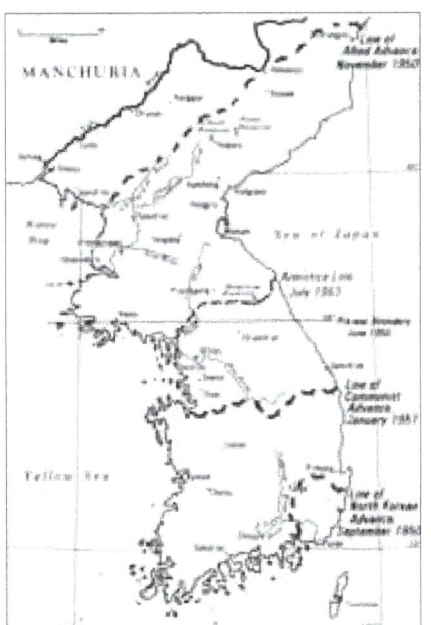

The War in Korea, 1950–1953. *Printed by permission, from Malcolm W. Cagle and Frank A. Manson,* The Sea War in Korea *(Annapolis: Naval Institute Press, 1957).*

President Truman directed carrier Valley Forge *(CV 45), embarking the Navy's first operational squadron of F9F Panther jet aircraft, to steam close to Taiwan as a signal to the new Chinese Communist government of Mao Zedong that the United States would oppose an invasion of the island and consequent widening of the Korean War.*

carrier *Triumph* bombed Pyongyang, the capital of North Korea. The fleet's new jet fighter, the F9F Panther, registered the Navy's first aerial victories in the war when Lieutenant (j.g.) Leonard H. Plog and Ensign Eldon W. Brown Jr. shot down two North Korean YAK-9s.

Seventh Fleet aircraft and warships added their firepower to the UN campaign to halt the North Korean invading forces before they overran the entire peninsula. U.S. and allied cruisers and destroyers bombarded enemy units moving along coastal roads as carrier air units pounded Communist troops and supply convoys heading south on inland tracks. Naval forces from eight other members of the UN coalition fought with the U.S. Navy from the beginning of the war. The Royal Navy contingent (including the carriers *Glory*, *Theseus*, *Ocean*, *Triumph*), and the Australian, New Zealand, Canadian, Colombian,

North Korea's east coast port of Wonsan burns after a strike by U.S. carrier aircraft in July 1950.

The United Nations war effort in Korea involved not only the U.S. Navy but the navies of other UN countries. Tied up at Sasebo, Japan, are, left to right, Royal Australian Navy destroyer Warramunga, *Her Majesty's Canadian Ship* Nootka, *and Royal Navy destroyer* Cockade.

Wartime Fleet Commander

Vice Admiral Arthur D. Struble commanded the Seventh Fleet when it accomplished one of its most decisive Cold War operations—the amphibious assault at Incheon (Inchon). A 1915 graduate of the U.S. Naval Academy, he served during the years before Pearl Harbor in responsible staff positions ashore and in battleships, cruisers, and destroyers at sea. Convinced of Struble's talents in amphibious warfare, after his participation in the 6 June 1944 D-Day invasion of France, the Navy assigned him to the Seventh Fleet. As a battle leader in "MacArthur's Navy," Struble directed amphibious assaults on Leyte, Mindoro, and Luzon in the Philippines, which earned him the Distinguished Service Medal. In the immediate postwar years he gained valuable experience in inshore warfare while directing Pacific Fleet amphibious and mine clearance forces. He polished his interservice cooperation credentials with service in Washington in the office of the Joint Chiefs of Staff.

Newly appointed Commander Seventh Fleet and promoted to vice admiral, Struble directed the fleet's first strikes on North Korea in July 1950. The flag officer also established the air, surface, and submarine patrols demanded by President Harry S. Truman to protect Taiwan from Chinese Communist invasion.

As Commander Task Force 7, Struble led the U.S. and UN forces that executed the masterful September 1950 amphibious assault on Incheon, Operation Chromite. General of the Army Douglas MacArthur's bold plan, executed by the UN coalition under Struble's command, soon liberated South Korea from the northern invaders.

Until his routine relief on 28 March 1951, Vice Admiral Struble oversaw the air interdiction and close air support strikes of Task Force 77 and the bombardment operations of the fleet's surface forces. Under his leadership, the Seventh Fleet demonstrated once again the Navy's unique ability to support and sustain combat operations ashore.

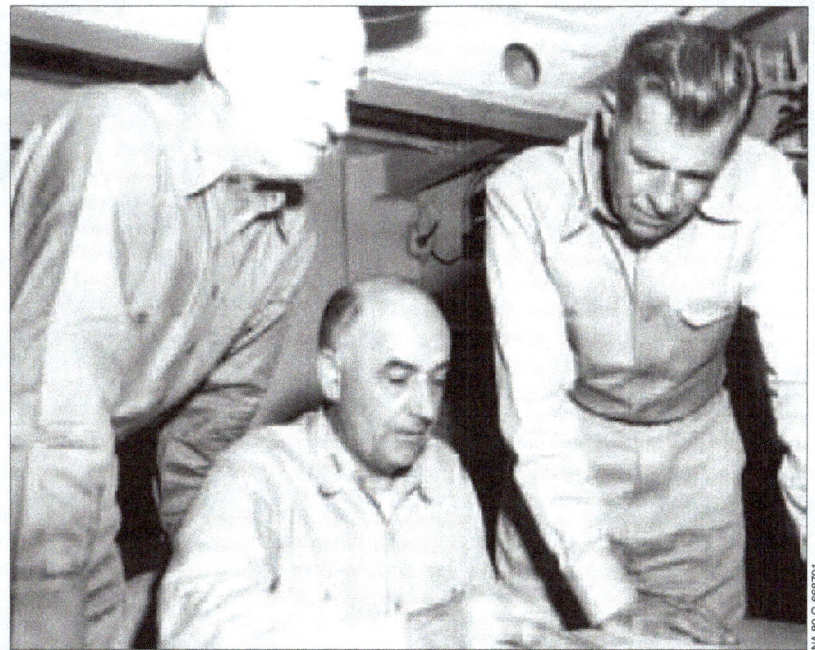

As Rear Admiral James H. Doyle, left, and Rear Admiral John M. Higgins look on, Commander Seventh Fleet Vice Admiral Arthur D. Struble goes over invasion plans.

General of the Army Douglas MacArthur, flanked by Vice Admiral Arthur D. Struble, on the left, and Major General O. P. Smith, commanding general of the 1st Marine Division, come ashore at Incheon after the successful assault landing.

French, Dutch, and Thai naval forces all operated on the seas fronting Korea.

Protected from interference at sea, the ships of the Navy's Military Sea Transportation Service reinforced and resupplied UN troops holding a small toehold on the peninsula near the key port of Busan (Pusan). Without the Seventh Fleet's protection of this oceangoing life line, the UN forces in South Korea would have been forced to make a costly withdrawal from the "Pusan Perimeter."

The fleet's mobility and command of the sea enabled General Douglas MacArthur and his UN command to reverse the tide of battle in Korea.

In mid-September 1950 Vice Admiral Arthur D. Struble, Commander Seventh Fleet and also Commander Task Force 7, led 230 U.S. and allied amphibious and other ships into the Yellow Sea and toward the North Korean-occupied port of Incheon.

As this armada approached the narrow channel leading to Incheon in the early morning hours of 15 September, a lighthouse, which had been out of operation for some time, suddenly illuminated. The man who turned on the light was Lieutenant Eugene F. Clark who had executed a daring intelligence mission behind enemy lines since the beginning of the month. The brave and resourceful naval officer had been operating on a nearby island, Yeongheung (Yonghung), with a small party of South Koreans and another American to learn about local tides, currents, and other information valuable to allied amphibious planners. Clark and his men gathered their intelligence, fought a small naval action with the Communists in which the enemy lost two boats to accurate machine-gun fire, and repaired the light. The enemy overran Yeongheung and caught and executed 50 villagers who had helped the Americans, but the "Blackbeard of Yonghung Do," as Clark would soon be called, avenged them by accomplishing his very important mission for the fleet.

For days Seventh Fleet and UN naval gunfire support ships and carrier aircraft attacked enemy defensive positions ashore at Incheon. Then, at 0633 hours on 15 September, amphibious landing craft disembarked a battalion of the 1st Marine Division's 5th Marine Regiment on Wolmi Do, an island in Incheon harbor. The fight for Incheon had begun.

After several days of hard combat and reinforcement by other Marines, South Korean troops, and elements of the Army's 7th Infantry Division, the allies seized the port and nearby Gimpo (Kimpo) airfield. On the 21st, U.S. Army units that had broken out of the Pusan Perimeter linked up with the Incheon forces. A week later, after bloody, street-to-street fighting, the 1st Marine Division captured Seoul. The amphibious units at Incheon suffered 3,500 killed, wounded, and missing but they inflicted 20,000 casualties on the enemy. More importantly, the successful Incheon assault compelled the North Korean People's Army to flee north in disarray and resulted in the liberation of South Korea.

General MacArthur hoped to destroy the enemy army completely and occupy northeast Korea with another Seventh Fleet amphibious assault, at Wonsan on the Sea of Japan. The Navy was directed to land the Army's X Corps, which included the 1st Marine Division, there; the infantry

Inchon *by Herbert C. Hahn. Colored pencil on paper.*

divisions would then advance overland to the Yalu River and to North Korea's border with the People's Republic of China and the Soviet Union. Fast-moving South Korean troops, however, arrived at Wonsan on 10 October, a week before the planned landing. In addition, the fleet discovered—the hard way—that the North Koreans had emplaced between 2,000 and 4,000 Soviet-made magnetic and contact mines in the approaches to the harbor. Mines sank a number of American and South Korean mine-clearing vessels before the task force opened a safe passage into the port. At long last, on 25 October 1950, the 1st Marine Division began moving ashore from their Seventh Fleet and Naval Forces Far East ships and advancing into the forbidding mountains of North Korea.

The destruction of South Korean minesweeper YMS 516 *by a Soviet-supplied sea mine in the approaches to Wonsan harbor.*

The "volunteers" of the Chinese People's Liberation Army emerged from the snow-covered mountains of North Korea and fell upon overextended Army, Marine, and South Korean units. X Corps had to fight its way back to the coast in bitter cold and howling winds. Marine and Navy attack squadrons operating from Task Force 77 carriers *Philippine Sea* (CV 47), *Valley Forge*, *Princeton* (CV 37), and *Leyte* (CV 32), and several escort carriers hit Chinese troops trying to surround UN units inland. In only one week of operations, naval aviators carried out 1,700 sorties against the enemy.

Tunnel Busting Mission *by Morgan Wilbur. Oil on canvas.*

Meanwhile, most of the UN ground troops had fought their way to the coast, where the battleship *Missouri*, cruisers *Rochester* (CA 124) and *Saint Paul*, and numerous destroyers and rocket vessels put a wall of fire between the infantry and the enemy.

Navy and allied surface ships fired over 23,000 16-inch, 8-inch, 5-inch, and 3-inch rounds and rockets at the Communist units moving toward the port of Hungnam.

The fleet's dominance of the waters off Korea during late 1950 enabled MacArthur to withdraw his forces to the safety of the sea when the battle ashore turned against the UN command. By Christmas Eve the fleet's amphibious task force completed the withdrawal by sea of 105,000 troops, 91,000 civilian

As high-speed transport Begor *(APD 127) stands by, explosives set by Navy demolitions teams destroy the port of Hungnam to deny the enemy use of its facilities.*

refugees, 350,000 tons of cargo, and 17,500 military vehicles. Air Force and Marine planes airlifted another 3,600 troops, 1,300 tons of cargo, and 196 vehicles. Navy explosive demolition teams leveled the port facilities at Hungnam to deny their use to the enemy, and the Seventh Fleet steamed south. Within a few weeks the units withdrawn from North Korea were back in the fight to preserve the independence of the Republic of Korea.

A New Kind of War

From spring 1951 to July 1953, during the so-called static-war phase, naval airpower brought the conflict to the North Korean rear areas to prevent heavy weapons, ammunition, supplies, and construction materials from reaching enemy troops on the front line. Task Force 77 comprising large-deck aircraft carriers (11 ships served in the Korean War) and Task Force 95 (one light and four escort carriers) operated off Korea. Navy combat squadrons operated from the carriers, and Marine aviation units flew from both the escort carriers and shore bases. The naval aviators piloted F9F Panthers, F2H Banshees, and the workhorses of the war, propeller-driven F4U Corsairs and AD Skyraiders.

The fleet's fighter squadrons fought for control of the air against hundreds of MiG-15 jets and other combat aircraft flown by North Korean, Chinese, and Soviet aircrews and shot down 13 of them. Lieutenant Guy P. Bordelon became the Navy's one Korean War "ace" when he downed five enemy aircraft, nicknamed "Bedcheck Charlies," which flew over UN lines at night, dropping bombs to disturb sleeping troops.

The attack squadrons concentrated on enemy locomotives and rolling stock, bridges, tunnels, supply depots, power-generating dams on the Yalu River, and other vital targets. In one of the war's most dramatic and unusual missions, eight AD Skyraiders of Attack Squadron (VA) 195, led by Commander Harold G. "Swede" Carlson and flying from *Princeton*, breached the Hwachon Reservoir dam with air-dropped torpedoes. Thereafter the Navy called the squadron the "Dambusters."

Helicopters also proved especially well suited to retrieving aircrews from the sea. Aviation Machinist's Mate 2nd Class Ernie L. Crawford, crewman of a helicopter operating from heavy cruiser *Rochester*, received the Navy Cross for heroism in saving a downed, unconscious pilot. Crawford got the naval aviator safely into the rescue helicopter and then floated alone for 20 minutes in the freezing ocean while he awaited the helicopter's return.

Carrier and shore-based units carried out another critical responsibility, providing on-call close air support to troops on the front line. By the end of the war naval air crews had flown 275,000 sorties over Korea, which represented 53 percent of the close air support strikes and 40 percent of the interdiction missions flown by Air Force, Navy, and Marine Corps planes. Naval aircraft dropped more than 178,000 tons of bombs, triggered over 274,000 air-to-ground rockets, and fired more than 71 million cannon rounds.

Combat power projected from the sea came from another source—the battleships, cruisers, destroyers, and rocket vessels of the Seventh Fleet. Marines and soldiers facing Chinese "human wave" assaults eagerly sought fire from the 16-inch guns of World War II-built battleships *Iowa* (BB 61), *New Jersey* (BB 62), *Missouri*, and *Wisconsin* (BB 64). The fleet's surface warships also ranged along the Korean coast, shelling railways, roads, supply caches, and troop concentrations. Allied estimates credited U.S. and UN surface warships, which fired 4 million rounds of naval gun ammunition, with killing thousands of enemy troops and destroying an uncounted number of buildings, trucks, bridges, and supply dumps. In contrast, enemy coastal guns failed to sink even one UN warship.

Helicopters made their combat debut in the war and they proved especially useful for rescuing downed pilots in the rugged countryside of North Korea.

The 16-inch rifles of battleship New Jersey *(BB 62) open up against enemy targets in North Korea.*

Without question, the prodigious air effort, with its complementary surface force bombardment operations, denied the enemy vital munitions and saved the lives of thousands of American and allied soldiers fighting to take or hold ground at the 38th parallel—but it did not cut enemy supply lines or prevent the enemy from launching devastating offensives. Tens of thousands of North Korean civilians and military engineers repeatedly put bombed rail lines, bridges, and supply depots back in operation. Nighttime often cloaked supply movements. Moreover, enemy antiaircraft fire brought down 559 Navy and Marine aircraft and MiGs claimed another five. The Korean War experience demonstrated that in a new era of "limited war," airpower would not be a war-winning instrument. That lesson would have to be relearned 15 years later in Southeast Asia.

Throughout the Korean War, U.S. and allied naval forces maintained a tight blockade of North Korean waters, denying the enemy use of the sea to transport troops and supplies. Control of the sea also allowed the Seventh Fleet to threaten other amphibious landings in the rear of the Chinese and North Korean armies arrayed along the 38th parallel. The enemy took the threat seriously and positioned sizable troop units along both coasts and far from the front lines where they were badly needed. To keep the enemy's attention riveted to the sea, the fleet executed a number of naval feints and demonstrations. In Operation Decoy during October 1952, Seventh Fleet carriers and surface ships attacked North Korean defenses around Kojo, and amphibious ships maneuvered as if to land elements of the Army's 1st Cavalry Division near Wonsan. The enemy rushed forces to the coast to defeat amphibious assaults that never came.

The fleet also put special operations forces ashore on the east and west coasts of North Korea and on many of the hundreds of islands that studded those waters. The blockade of Wonsan from February 1951 to the end of the war kept the Communists from using the potentially important port. Ships also landed underwater demolition teams, U.S. Marines, and British and South Korean naval commandos to destroy highway bridges, supply dumps, railroad tracks, and railroad tunnels behind enemy lines.

Some Seventh Fleet warships off Korea used whaleboats to carry the action to the enemy. Commander James A. Dare, the enterprising commanding officer of destroyer *Douglas H. Fox* (DD 779), manned his ship's whaleboat with his most resourceful officers and daring bluejackets and equipped them with a 75-millimeter recoilless rifle, small arms, demolition charges, grenades, a radio, and tools for destroying fishing nets. Every night the boat crew would deploy five to seven miles from the ship (within range of the destroyer's radios and surface search radar) to seize fishing boats and their crews and return both to the ship. By destroying fishermen's nets, impounding their boats, and otherwise disrupting the local fishing activity, the fleet forces denied enemy troops the bounty of the sea. In addition, quite often the prisoners would provide information on where the North Koreans

U.S. and South Korean officers question a captured North Korean fisherman.

had positioned their coastal artillery and the daily routines of the gun crews.

The Sailors also practiced a little psychological warfare on the enemy. The night before May Day 1952—the Communist countries celebrated 1 May as International Labor Day—*Douglas H. Fox*'s whaleboat Sailors planted an American flag on an island at the mouth of Wonsan harbor. So, as the sun rose in the east on the big day, the enemy's first sight was Old Glory flapping gaily in the sea breeze.

The Seventh Fleet's warships and the air units operating from carriers and from shore airfields provided essential support to U.S. and allied troops fighting this first "limited war" of the Cold War. The fleet did not lose a single major warship in the Korean War. More than 1,177,000 Seventh Fleet and Naval Forces Far East personnel served in Korea. Four hundred fifty-eight Sailors were killed in action, 1,576 suffered wounds, and 4,043 succumbed to injury or disease. Without the dedicated service and sacrifices made by Navy men and women, ashore and afloat, the UN would not have been able to preserve the independence of the Republic of Korea or achieve the armistice agreement with China and North Korea that ended the conflict on 27 July 1953.

Keeping the Korean War Limited

As the Seventh Fleet carried out its vital combat mission in Korea, it handled an equally important responsibility—preventing the conflict's spread throughout the Far East. The Truman administration and its UN allies did not want the fighting in Korea to spark a global or a regional war with the Soviet

Pickerel *(SS 524) and other Seventh Fleet submarines, surface ships, and patrol planes carried out the Taiwan Strait Patrol to monitor military activity in the coastal waters of China.*

Union and the People's Republic of China. Indeed, the Seventh Fleet's first action in the war was to deter both a Chinese Communist invasion of Taiwan and Chinese Nationalist attacks on the PRC. Days after the outbreak of the Korean War, President Truman announced that he believed "the occupation of Formosa [Taiwan] by Communist forces would be a direct threat to the security of the Pacific area and to United States forces." He added, "I have ordered the Seventh Fleet to prevent any attack on Formosa" and called on Chiang's government to "cease all air and sea operations against the mainland." He emphasized, "the Seventh Fleet will see that this is done." As they headed for Korea from Subic Bay in the Philippines on 27 June, the carrier *Valley Forge*, heavy cruiser *Rochester*, and eight destroyers made a show of force along the China coast. A formation of *Valley Forge* aircraft flew up the Taiwan Strait on the 29th to signal Beijing that the United States would prevent an attack on Taiwan.

The Seventh Fleet's quick deployment to the Yellow Sea/West Sea (China and South Korea use different names for the same body of water) and reinforcement by surface and air units based in Japan and the United States also sent a strong message to the Communist powers—any involvement of Soviet or Chinese naval forces in the Korean War put the coastal cities and military bases of these countries at great risk from Seventh Fleet retaliation. This understanding helped persuade Stalin to limit the use of his air forces in support of Chinese and North Korean troops and to keep his large submarine force operating close to the homeport of Vladivostok.

Throughout the Korean War, Seventh Fleet submarines, land-based patrol aircraft, and carrier task forces kept watch on the seas and coastal areas of Asia to gather intelligence. In mid-July 1950 the submarines *Catfish* and *Pickerel* (SS 524) sortied from the U.S. naval base at Yokosuka, Japan, for a secret mission. Directed to patrol the Taiwan Strait, approaching no closer than 12 miles of mainland China and six miles to Taiwan, the two submarines patrolled submerged during the day off Xiamen (Amoy) and Shantou (Swatow) for ten days. A Chinese Communist radio news broadcast that 1,500 junks were en route from Shantou to Xiamen initially caused concern, but the report proved to be bogus. Finally, on 30 July *Pickerel* and *Catfish* ended their patrols, returning to Yokosuka. Once in Tokyo, the commanding officers of both submarines reported on their missions to Vice Admirals Struble and C. Turner Joy, the latter commander of U.S. Naval Forces Far East. Their reports helped counter other intelligence that the PRC was about to invade Taiwan.

During the second week of July, Struble and the commanding officers of Patrol Squadrons (VP) 28 and 46 conferred in Taipei with Chinese Nationalist military leaders. On the 16th, aircraft of Fleet Air Wing 1 began reconnaissance missions in the strait. VP-28, which flew nine P4Y Privateers from Naha, Okinawa, inaugurated a daily surveillance of the northern part of the strait. The following day VP-46, with nine PBM-5 Mariner flying boats, kicked off patrols of the strait's southern sector from the Penghu (Pescadore) Islands, where seaplane tender *Suisun* (AVP 53) deployed on the 17th.

American leaders feared a Chinese Communist invasion of Taiwan during July and August. On 17 July the CIA concluded that the PLA could launch a successful amphibious assault on Taiwan despite U.S. opposition. Soon after, crewmen on a British merchant ship spotted a large concentration of junks in the strait. When a P4Y Privateer of VP-28 investigated the report on the 26th, two hostile fighters attacked the patrol plane, which made good its escape. The following day Far East Command officers in Taipei, Taiwan, learned that a Nationalist agent on the mainland had attended a meeting at which Communist leaders discussed an assault in the near future on Taiwan. In response to this perceived invasion threat, the Joint Chiefs of Staff had already directed Commander in Chief, Far East to mount another naval show of force in the strait. The JCS thought that the presence of Seventh Fleet elements in the strait, even for a short time, would demonstrate U.S. resolve and serve as a deterrent.

On 26 July Struble dispatched to the strait Rear Admiral Charles C. Hartman's surface task group, comprising the heavy cruiser *Helena* (CA 75) and three destroyers of Destroyer Division 111. Hartman's group, joined by the light cruiser *Juneau*, reached the northern end of the strait on the 28th and began a sweep southward.

On 4 August Struble established the Formosa Patrol around the ships of this group, which were to operate from Keelung, Taiwan. Hence, for the first time since the evacuation of the mainland naval base at Qingdao in May 1949, U.S. naval forces deployed from a Nationalist port. The Formosa Patrol Force (Task Force 72)—later the Taiwan Patrol Force—would operate in the strait for the next two decades of the Cold War.

These fleet operations were not a bluff. In September 1950, for instance, American carrier planes shot down a Soviet bomber on a reconnaissance mission when it flew too close to the UN fleet in the Yellow Sea/West Sea. The Soviets did not retaliate and indeed did not make the incident public. At least partly because of this UN naval presence, at no time during the war did Beijing or Moscow use the sea or the air above it to support Communist forces fighting hard on the Korean peninsula. But they did on occasion attack fleet patrol units, downing aircraft and killing Navy crewmen. On 6 November 1951, for instance, Soviet fighter planes shot down a Navy P2V Neptune conducting a reconnaissance flight close to the USSR in the Sea of Japan/East Sea.

The Chinese Communists also attacked patrol units that operated off the mainland during the war. Seaplanes and patrol aircraft based on Chinese Nationalist islands, Okinawa, and the Philippines flew along and over the Asian littoral. Photographic reconnaissance planes often flew deep into China. U.S. destroyers of the Taiwan Patrol Force and submarines also made their presence known in Chinese waters.

To give substance to Truman's warning that Chinese Communist forces stay away from Taiwan, Seventh Fleet forces twice left the combat theater off Korea and made a show of force along

Light cruiser Juneau *(CL 119) operating in Far Eastern waters during the Korean War.*

the PRC coast. In April 1951 the carriers *Philippine Sea* and *Boxer* steamed south along the coast and launched aircraft that flew over the coastal cities of Xiamen, Shantou, and Fuchau (Foochow). Chinese antiaircraft fire greeted them. The following year, in July, carriers *Essex* (CV 9) and *Philippine Sea*, along with eight destroyers, set a course from Korea all the way to the island of Hainan in the South China Sea where their aircraft executed low-level photoreconnaissance of Chinese military facilities. Chinese antiaircraft fire and MiG interceptors failed to frustrate the mission. During the latter operation, a spokesman for Admiral Arthur W. Radford, Commander in Chief, Pacific, informed the press that the mission would "show that the Navy could bomb the coastal cities of Amoy, Foochow, and Swatow anytime." The following day Admiral William Fechteler, Chief of Naval Operations, announced during a visit to the Far East that the Navy "could deliver baby atom bombs in Korea [and by implication anywhere else in the region] if it is ordered to do so."

The following January antiaircraft fire from the PRC shot up another patrol plane, killing crewmembers, and forcing the pilot to ditch close to the China coast. While trying to rescue the crew, a U.S. Coast Guard seaplane crashed and sank, with further loss of life. Fire from Chinese Communist coastal guns fell all around the U.S. and Hong Kong-based British ships coming to the rescue.

So these Seventh Fleet patrols could be costly, but they demonstrated to Beijing that U.S. seapower would

A P2V Neptune heads out to sea from Japan to take part in a patrol. Aviation units based in Okinawa and the Philippines routinely monitored oceangoing traffic in the Taiwan Strait.

Carrier Philippine Sea *(CV 47) and other Seventh Fleet units steamed along the coast of China during the Korean War to deter Beijing from attacking Taiwan.*

Army General Mark Clark, Commander in Chief, Far East, signs the Korean War armistice on 27 July 1953 as Vice Admiral Robert P. Briscoe, Commander, Naval Forces Far East, and Vice Admiral J. J. "Jocko" Clark, Commander Seventh Fleet, look on in this painting by Orlando S. Lagman.

oppose an attack on Taiwan. According to one Nationalist spy who attended a high-level meeting of Communist leaders, they were concerned that any invasion fleet would "last only few [hours] against 7th Flt and US Air Force." This fear held throughout the Korean War. Beijing committed a massive ground army and large air forces to the war on the Korean peninsula and, as new scholarship makes clear, the Soviets intervened in the war with hundreds of Russian-piloted aircraft and other air defense units. The presence of the combined UN fleet off Chinese and Russian shores, however, discouraged a comparable naval effort. The Chinese and Soviets never exploited the sea to support the war in Korea.

The Seventh Fleet demonstrated in the Korean War that sea power was critical to success in fighting a conflict far from the United States and on the continent of Asia. The fleet denied the enemy use of the sea; projected naval power ashore in the form of carrier strikes, surface ship gunfire, and amphibious assaults; and ensured troop reinforcement and logistic support to UN forces for the duration of the war. Moreover, the Seventh Fleet symbolized U.S. determination and capacity to prevent the spread of conflict beyond the Korean peninsula. The United States would have been especially challenged to contain this first "limited war" of the Cold War without the presence of strong and flexible naval forces in the Far East.

Chapter 4

DETERRING CONFLICT IN THE FAR EAST

THE END OF THE KOREAN WAR brought no end to hostilities in the Far East and no respite for the Seventh Fleet. The global conflict between the United States and its allies on the one hand and the Soviet Union and fellow Marxist-Leninist nations on the other was especially intense in Asia. During the 1950s the Seventh Fleet faced off with Chinese and Vietnamese Communists in several confrontations that threatened to escalate to nuclear war. To meet these challenges, Washington strengthened the combat power and base structure of its fighting fleet in the Western Pacific.

After the Korean War, Communist military forces continued to attack Seventh Fleet units. Patrol planes conducting intelligence-gathering missions over or near the coast of the USSR faced frequent attacks from Soviet military units. In September 1954 a MiG-15 forced a patrol aircraft to ditch in the frigid waters off Siberia, killing one crewman. Two years later Chinese fighters shot down a P4M Mercator flying near Wenzhou (Wenchow), China, killing all 16 crew members.

After the death of Soviet dictator Joseph Stalin in March 1953, Mao Zedong, the leader of the People's Republic of China, increasingly advertised himself as the leader of the Communist movement, especially in Asia. He championed not only the totalitarian North Korean state but Communist insurgencies and guerrilla movements throughout Southeast Asia, including that led by Ho Chi Minh in French Indochina. Artillery, mortars, small arms, ammunition, military advisors, and a host of other support provided by China enabled the Vietnamese Viet Minh guerrillas to defeat one French military force after another between 1950 and 1954.

Ho Chi Minh, a fervent Communist and Vietnamese nationalist.

The Truman and later Dwight D. Eisenhower administrations were determined to strengthen the French government in its fight with Communists at home in France and in Indochina. Washington provided French forces in Indochina with $2.6 billion in military aid that included two light aircraft carriers, 500 aircraft, 438 amphibious landing ships and river patrol vessels, artillery, trucks, and ammunition. To demonstrate U.S. support for the French war effort, Seventh Fleet ships frequently visited ports in Vietnam. The four "tin cans" of Destroyer Division 30 made a visit to Saigon in October 1953. That same month the transport *General W.M. Black* (APB 5) moved from Korea to Vietnam a French infantry battalion, which had served with distinction

Southeast Asia.

Admiral Felix B. Stump, Commander in Chief, U.S. Pacific Fleet, left, greets Admiral Arthur W. Radford, Chairman of the Joint Chiefs of Staff, on board a U.S. warship. Both men were concerned about Communist activities in the Far East during the 1950s.

during the war as part of the U.S. 2nd Infantry Division. The French soldiers still proudly displayed the American unit's shoulder patch when they disembarked at Saigon.

Because of the Navy's requirement to defend Japan in Northeast Asia and the increasing obligation to promote U.S. interests in Southeast Asia, in 1953 Chief of Naval Operations Robert B. Carney and other naval leaders argued that three carriers should always be forward-deployed with the Seventh Fleet. The Navy also wanted to maintain three carriers in the Far East to justify a budget for keeping 14 carriers in operation worldwide in what the service considered a vital Cold War requirement. President Eisenhower approved the proposal, and Congress authorized the expenditure.

The French Indochina War

Despite American military assistance, by the spring of 1954 French forces were on the verge of defeat at the hands of the Viet Minh army and Chinese Communist arms suppliers. The elite combat forces of France—Foreign Legionnaires and paratroopers—found themselves surrounded and virtually cut off from outside support at Dien Bien Phu, the site of a small, remote airfield on the jungle and mountainous Tonkin border with Laos.

The Eisenhower administration, contemplating military intervention to rescue the French forces at Dien Bien Phu, directed the deployment of carrier task forces to the South China Sea. The Navy assigned command of the deployment to Vice Admiral William K. Phillips, commander of the West Coast-based U.S. First Fleet, rather than Commander Seventh Fleet because the latter served under the Far East Command in Tokyo, led by an Army general. Naval leaders in Washington wanted more leeway to guide Phillips' operations so they assigned at one time or another carriers from both fleets, including *Wasp* (CVA 18), *Essex*, *Boxer*, and *Philippine Sea*.

Some of the aircraft that operated from these carriers were capable of dropping nuclear bombs. A few U.S. leaders, especially Admiral Radford in his new position as Chairman of the Joint Chiefs of Staff, pushed for serious consideration of using nuclear weapons to help the French out of their predicament. In the end Eisenhower decided against intervening to save the French. America's British allies strongly opposed the idea, and the President doubted American air forces, whether using nuclear or conventional weapons, could be decisive. On 7 May Viet Minh forces overwhelmed the last French defenders of Dien Bien Phu. This military defeat spelled the end of French fortunes in Indochina.

Months before the end at Dien Bien Phu, the world's major powers had come together at Geneva, Switzerland, to discuss resolution of the conflict in Indochina. France agreed to the eventual independence of Vietnam, Laos, and Cambodia. The Agreement on the Cessation of Hostilities divided Vietnam into two zones for the separation of Viet Minh and French forces. Ho Chi Minh's troops were to concentrate in the Tonkin region north of the 17th parallel, and French and allied Vietnamese forces would gather to the south of that provisional demarcation line. Vietnamese civilians were allowed to settle wherever they wished.

In answer to the French government's call for assistance, Washington directed the Navy to evacuate French-allied military forces and civilian refugees from Haiphong in the north to Saigon in the south. Rear Admiral Lorenzo S. Sabin, Commander, Amphibious Force Western Pacific, took charge of what came to be known as Operation Passage to Freedom.

His task force included 74 tank landing ships, transports, attack cargo ships, dock landing ships, and other vessels provided by the Seventh Fleet and the First Fleet, and 39 vessels of the Military Sea Transportation Service. Oilers, cargo, provision, repair, salvage, and hospital ships of the Logistic Support Force Western Pacific operated from Danang Bay, located midway between Haiphong and Saigon. Naval medical officers and enlisted Sailors based at the fleet hospital in Yokosuka deployed to Haiphong to provide medical and disease prevention services at the port's refugee camps.

Between August 1954 and May 1955, Sabin's flotilla transported 17,800 Vietnamese soldiers,

In Operation Passage to Freedom, Seventh Fleet and other U.S. naval vessels transported from northern to southern Vietnam more than 293,000 refugees who did not want to live under the Communist government of Ho Chi Minh.

8,135 vehicles, and 68,757 tons of cargo to the southern zone. In a special lift hospital ship *Haven* (AH 12) steamed from Korea to Saigon, embarked 721 French soldiers recently released from Viet Minh prisoner of war camps, and transported them to Marseilles, France. The U.S. Navy also transported to the south 293,000 Vietnamese, many of them Catholics, who opted to live under a separate noncommunist Vietnamese government in southern Indochina rather than under the authoritarian, antireligious regime of Ho Chi Minh.

Taiwan Strait Crisis of 1954–1955

Emboldened by the Communist victory over Chiang Kai-shek's Nationalists in China, the positive showing of the People's Liberation Army during the Korean War, and the Vietnamese-Chinese defeat of French forces in Indochina, Mao Zedong embarked on an aggressive course in the Far East. Aggravated that the Seventh Fleet continued the Taiwan Strait air patrol begun in 1950, the Chinese leader ordered his air forces to attack one of the surveillance planes. On 7 July 1954 Chinese Communist MiGs pounced on a Seventh Fleet P2V in the strait; the patrol plane barely managed to escape its attackers.

A defenseless British Air Cathay passenger plane en route from Bangkok to Hong Kong on the 22nd did not fare as well. PLA fighters destroyed the aircraft and killed 18 passengers 20 miles southeast

Sailors hoist a PBM Mariner from the water after a patrol mission in the Far East.

Hospital Ship Haven *(AH 12).*

of Hainan Island. A Seventh Fleet task force under Rear Admiral Harry D. Felt, which included carrier *Philippine Sea* on an exercise in the South China Sea, immediately deployed to the area and rescued nine survivors. Only four days later a pair of LA-7 Chinese fighters attacked AD Skyraiders from *Philippine Sea*'s Carrier Air Group 5 led by Commander G. C. Duncan. The assailants made head-on firing runs on the ADs piloted by Duncan and Lieutenant Roy M. Tatham but failed to score any hits. The hunters then became the hunted; Tatham and his fellow naval aviators splashed both aggressors.

There would be no let up in hostile Chinese behavior. On 3 September 1954 artillery batteries opposite Jinmen (Quemoy), only a few miles from the port of Xiamen, began a furious shelling of the Nationalist-held island. Beijing announced its ultimate intention to seize all Nationalist islands, including Taiwan itself, and destroy Chiang Kai-shek's government. A direct threat to the Dachen (Tachen) Islands, 200 miles north of Taiwan, developed after midnight on 14 November when a pair of People's Liberation Army Navy (PLAN) vessels attacked Nationalist navy destroyer escort *Tai Ping*, on patrol in nearby waters. *Tai Ping* opened fire with 3-inch and 40-millimeter guns, but before her fire could take effect, a PLAN torpedo slammed into the warship. Destroyer escort *Tai Ho* took *Tai Ping* under tow the following morning, but *Tai Ping*'s hull buckled and she sank before reaching a friendly port.

The assault on the Dachens began in earnest in January 1955 when the PLA air force launched a bombing campaign against Nationalist military facilities on the islands. The 200-mile distance between the Dachens and Taiwan made it especially difficult for Nationalist air units to provide air cover for troops in the island chain. On the 20th, Chinese Communist amphibious forces seized Yijiangshan (Ichiang) Island in a surprise attack.

At the direction of higher headquarters, Commander Seventh Fleet Vice Admiral Alfred M. Pride Jr. deployed his forces to nearby waters prepared for likely contingencies. A flotilla of five carriers—*Kearsarge* (CVA 33), *Essex*, *Wasp*, *Midway* (CVA 41), and *Yorktown* (CVA 10) and their cruiser and destroyer escorts concentrated off the Dachens.

The United States and the Republic of China had signed a Mutual Defense Treaty on 2 December 1954, and on 28 January 1955 Congress passed the Formosa Resolution that empowered the President to use the U.S. armed forces as he saw fit in defense of Taiwan and the Nationalist-held offshore islands. Eisenhower was

Chiang Kai-shek, President of the Republic of China, meets with Commander Seventh Fleet Vice Admiral Alfred M. Pride during the Taiwan Strait Crisis of 1955.

Chinese civilians prepare to board Seventh Fleet landing craft during the evacuation of an island in the Dachen group southeast of Shanghai in February 1955.

prepared to wage war against the PRC to defend Taiwan, but he did not want a fight for the distant and hard-to-defend Dachens. In exchange for the promise of a formal U.S.–Republic of China mutual defense treaty, the President had persuaded Chiang Kai-shek to evacuate the islands. On 6 February the Seventh Fleet amassed a powerful armada within range of the Dachens to signal Beijing that any interference with the evacuation operation by the PLA would be met by overwhelming U.S. force.

The Surface Action Force (TF 75) patrolled around the islands, covered overhead by the carrier air wings of the Attack Carrier Striking Force (TF 77). A hunter-killer group (TG 70.4) managed antisubmarine protection. The Taiwan Patrol Force (TF 72) and U.S. and Nationalist air force units provided additional air cover out to 100 miles. During the next several days the Amphibious Evacuation Force (TF 76) and Nationalist navy units embarked 11,120 soldiers, 8,630 tons of military supplies and equipment, 166 artillery pieces, and 128 vehicles. The fleet units also evacuated to Taiwan 15,627 Dachen Island civilians, most of whom would never see their ancestral homes again.

Just as suddenly as Mao had precipitated an armed confrontation with the United States and the Republic of China in 1954–1955, he ended it. His officials announced on 23 April 1955 that the PRC was willing to negotiate, and on 1 May the PLA ended its shelling of Jinmen and Mazu. During the remainder of 1955 and for the next two years the Chinese chief launched a "peace offensive" to win leadership of the newly independent, "non-aligned" nations of the so-called "third world." At Indonesia's Bandung Conference in April 1955, the PRC showcased itself to Asian and African nations as an international peacemaker, anti-imperialist stalwart, and friend of the dispossessed of the world.

Despite this display of international comity, during these same years Beijing provided diplomatic,

President Dwight D. Eisenhower worked closely with Chief of Naval Operations Admiral Arleigh Burke during the tense 1958 Taiwan Strait crisis.

DETERRING CONFLICT IN THE FAR EAST

economic, and military support to Communist governments and subversive guerrilla movements throughout Asia.

Southeast Asia Beckons

In 1954 President Eisenhower, Secretary of State John Foster Dulles, and friendly leaders in Europe and Asia expressed alarm at Communist advances since 1949. Communist armies had conquered all of mainland China and Tibet, launched a devastating war on the Korean peninsula, defeated French armed forces in cataclysmic battles, and threatened to eliminate Chiang Kai-shek's Republic of China. Marxist-Leninist guerrilla movements attempted to topple legally constituted governments in the Philippines, Indonesia, and throughout Indochina.

In September the United States and its allies gathered in Manila to develop a strategy and organization whose purpose would be to reverse this unwelcome trend in the Far East. The resulting Manila Pact signed by the United States, Great Britain, Australia, New Zealand, the Philippines, Thailand, Pakistan, and France formed the Southeast Asia Treaty Organization (SEATO), headquartered in Bangkok, Thailand, and agreed to oppose the spread of Communist military power and Marxist-Leninist ideology throughout the region. Unlike the North Atlantic Treaty Organization, however, SEATO had no standing forces. Moreover, the Geneva Agreement prohibited South Vietnam, Laos, and Cambodia from entering any military alliance, even though the member states established SEATO with the defense of these countries in mind.

USS Providence in Asia *by John Roach. Oil on canvas.*

Throughout the 1950s the naval forces of the member states carried out combined exercises, exchanged staff visits, and developed plans for the defense of the region. The first SEATO exercise, Firm Link, in February 1956, involved the Seventh Fleet carrier *Princeton* (CVS 37), destroyers *McDermut* (DD 677) and *Tingey* (DD 539), and seaplane tender *Salisbury Sound* (AV 13); British and Australian cruisers and destroyers; and Thai and Filipino troops. *Princeton* helicopters flew an 850-U.S. Marine assault force to Bangkok's Duan Muang Airport while *Salisbury Sound* disembarked Filipino troops at the port. The following day the citizens of the Thai capital toured the warships. The exercise concluded on the 18th with a military parade attended by tens of thousands of people. During Exercise Sea Link in May 1956, Seventh Fleet, Australian navy, and Philippine navy warships practiced naval gunfire support and amphibious operations.

Over the next two years, the Seventh Fleet participated in four SEATO exercises. Exercise Astra, sponsored by the United Kingdom, simulated the defense of a convoy from Singapore to Bangkok against air and submarine attacks in which a trio of Seventh Fleet destroyers, a submarine, and ASW (antisubmarine warfare) patrol aircraft took part. In October Australia sponsored a similar convoy-protection exercise. That same month a Seventh Fleet amphibious task group, a U.S. Marine battalion landing team, and Thai military forces simulated an amphibious assault in Exercise Teamwork. At the end of the year the entire Seventh Fleet Amphibious Force, the Okinawa-based 3rd Marine Division, an antisubmarine hunter-killer task group, and a Philippine navy task group worked together in Exercise Phiblink. Carrier task forces from the United States, the

U.S. Marines storm ashore on the coast of North Borneo in May 1961 as part of SEATO Exercise Pony Express.

United Kingdom, and Australia participated in the multiship Exercise Ocean Link of May 1958.

The member states of the SEATO alliance frequently differed over the nature of the primary threat to the region—whether it was from overt military aggression or internal subversion—but the exercises carried out by U.S., Australian, and New Zealand naval forces enhanced their cooperation. SEATO exercises lasted well into the 1960s.

Development of the Fleet's Far Eastern Bases

The defense of Japan and America's Far Eastern strategic interests during and after the Korean War mandated development of a robust base establishment for the forward-deployed Seventh Fleet. Naval leaders considered supplying the fleet from logistic facilities thousands of miles across the Pacific in Hawaii or on the U.S. West Coast impractical. To be ready for the next Communist invasion of an Asian country or attack on U.S. military forces, the fleet needed close-at-hand, shore-based airfields; stocks of ammunition, fuel, repair parts, food, and other supplies; and ship repair facilities.

The Mutual Security Treaty of 1960 revised and made permanent a 1951 security arrangement

An aerial view of the base facilities at Yokosuka, Japan, in 1962.

had become one of the most modern centers for naval construction in all of Asia.

The Korean War revealed the importance of Yokosuka to the Seventh Fleet. The number of carriers, battleships, cruisers, destroyers, and other naval vessels operating off Korea multiplied almost overnight, and they needed base support. The ship repair facility, which hired thousands of skilled Japanese workers, not only repaired the fleet's warships but reactivated 27 Lend-Lease vessels returned by the USSR shortly after World War II. Yokosuka's facilities provided 85 percent of the repair, maintenance, and resupply of ships that fought in Korea. In December 1952 Commander, Naval Forces Far East shifted his headquarters from Tokyo to Yokosuka, a move which also reflected the growing significance of the base.

Not only American naval leaders but Japanese civilian officials and naval officers saw the great benefit of a U.S. military presence at the base. The pacifist government in Tokyo wanted the U.S. military in the heart of Japan so the war-scarred country would not have to rearm to defend itself. Ironically, Japanese naval officers hoped to keep the U.S. Navy close by so it could help them rebuild a naval force. For whatever reason, Japan's leaders wanted an American military presence in the island nation.

The end of the Korean War did not lead to a downturn in Yokosuka's fortunes. North Korea's continued belligerence, Mao's periodic threats to invade Taiwan, and the growing conflict in Indochina required a ready and forward-deployed Seventh Fleet. During the ten years after the war, in every year but one, more carriers operated in the Pacific than in the Atlantic and Mediterranean combined. Yokosuka routinely serviced the warships of four carrier task groups.

with Japan. The later document stipulated that "for the purpose of contributing to the security of Japan and the maintenance of international peace and stability in the Far East . . . the United States is granted the use by its land, air, and naval forces of facilities in Japan." For their part, the Japanese concentrated on antisubmarine warfare and control of the key Japanese straits. The need for Japanese warships, aircraft, and weapons to carry out these defensive tasks inspired increased defense outlays that, by 1975, not only helped push Japan to the front rank of the world's economic powers, but led to the development of a navy—the Japan Maritime Self-Defense Force (JMSDF)—that ranked fifth in the world in terms of tonnage.

Yokosuka, located 40 miles southwest of Tokyo, was the Seventh Fleet's most strategic base during and after the Cold War. A primary base of the Imperial Japanese Navy since the late 19th century, Yokosuka boasted six large dry docks and extensive ship-repair facilities, numerous warehouses, and administrative buildings. Many of Japan's battleships, aircraft carriers, and submarines slid from the building ways there. By the end of World War II it

The base prospered because the U.S. Navy encouraged and assisted in the development of its major counterpart in Northeast Asia, the JMSDF. Yokosuka's high employment of workers from the city and surrounding region and generally positive interaction between Americans and Japanese kept cultural friction at a minimum.

The former Imperial Japanese Navy base at Sasebo on the southern island of Kyushu became a close second to Yokosuka in importance to the fleet during the Cold War. New base facilities had to be raised literally from the ashes after 1945 when a U.S. bombing attack and a fierce typhoon had leveled the old structures. The outbreak of war on the nearby Korean peninsula in June 1950 marked the rebirth of Sasebo. The naval base proved to be critical to the defense of South Korea, especially during the first six months of the war. In increasing numbers, U.S. and UN carriers, surface warships, amphibious vessels, submarines, and troopships steamed into port for resupply, refueling, and repair before deploying to the battle zone across the nearby Strait of Tsushima.

Repair ship Ajax *(AR 6) and the four destroyers she served at the Sasebo naval base during the Korean War.*

Seventh Fleet ships and base facilities at Sasebo during the early 1960s.

The Korean War also breathed life into the old airfield at Atsugi located near Tokyo and Yokohama. After Seabees and the men of Fleet Aircraft Squadron 11 repaired the runway, the Navy established the naval air station on 1 December 1950 to support fleet carrier operations. The aircraft of three or more carriers and Marine aircraft groups routinely operated from Atsugi during the war. The naval air station, manned by more than 5,000 personnel during the 1950s, became the headquarters of Commander, Fleet Air Western Pacific. Seabees lengthened the base runways at the end of the decade to accommodate new high-performance Navy fighters and attack planes entering the fleet.

The Japanese island of Okinawa, site of bloody World War II battles ashore and afloat, took on added importance in the Cold War because of its proximity to Japan, Korea, China, and Taiwan. In the years after the Korean War, the Seventh

Fleet's amphibious force operated from White Beach on the island, and naval aviation units flew from a naval air station at Kadena. The 3rd Marine Division and 3rd Marine Aircraft Wing were Okinawa's major tenants. Unlike the military bases in Japan proper, those on Okinawa remained under exclusive U.S. control. Despite determined and often heated political action by some Japanese leaders and citizens during the 1950s, Washington refused until 1972 to return the island or the bases to Japanese sovereignty, citing Cold War needs. Some observers referred to Okinawa as "America's Gibraltar of the Pacific."

With Southeast Asia becoming as strategic as Northeast Asia to U.S. interests after the Korean War, Washington considered a change in the Pacific's joint command structure. Naval leaders argued that because of the increasing scope of Navy responsibilities throughout the broad Asia-Pacific region, and its maritime nature, the Seventh Fleet should serve only one unified commander, not two. After deliberating on that concept, in 1957 the Joint Chiefs of Staff disestablished General MacArthur's old Far East Command and assigned responsibility for the entire region to Commander in Chief, Pacific. Henceforth, Commander Seventh Fleet would report only to the Commander in Chief, Pacific/Commander in Chief, Pacific Fleet, until 1958 the same four-star admiral.

Continuing the work begun by Admiral Radford during the Korean War, the new flag officer in charge of the Pacific, Admiral Felix B. Stump, redoubled efforts to develop the Seventh Fleet base at Subic Bay. The naval base had been in existence in one form or another since the Spanish-American War of 1898. During the latter stages of World War II the fleet, then under Vice Admiral Kinkaid, established amphibious and fleet training centers and supply and petroleum storage depots at the site. In 1947 Washington and Manila signed an agreement for a 99-year lease of the land for use by the Navy and the other U.S. armed services, but until the Korean War logistic activity at the base was limited. That conflict, however, spurred the construction of facilities there, and by 1953 more than 7,000 Sailors and Filipino civilians worked on the base. In July 1956 the Navy opened U.S. Naval Hospital Subic Bay, which served the medical needs of fleet Sailors whose numbers swelled during the period.

The naval aviation establishment experienced an even more dramatic growth in the Philippines. By 1953 Seabees had extended the runway at the Sangley Point naval air station to 8,000 feet to accommodate jet aircraft, and close to 4,000 Americans and Filipinos operated the facility. Just three years later four squadrons flew from Sangley Point, and the naval air station boasted plane and fuel storage space to handle fighter, attack, patrol, transportation, training, and seaplane squadrons.

In one of the most remarkable construction projects of the Cold War, Seabees literally carved out of the jungle an air facility at Cubi Point opposite the Subic Bay naval base. From 1951 to 1956, Naval Mobile Construction Battalions 3 and 5 cut a mountain in half at the site and used the fill from the excavation to build a 10,000-foot-long airstrip out into Subic Bay. The Seabees also constructed a pier able to accommodate the largest aircraft carriers. When completed on 25 July 1956, at a cost of $100 million and 20-million labor hours, Naval Air Station Cubi Point stood ready to support fleet air operations throughout Southeast Asia.

Taiwan Strait Crisis of 1958

By 1958 Mao Zedong's "peace offensive" had gone nowhere on the international stage and his disastrous Great Leap Forward domestic economic program had resulted in the starvation of millions of his own people. As often in the past, Mao sparked an international crisis to rally his Chinese citizens against the "foreign devils" and to divert their attention from his colossal domestic failures. He took advantage of the U.S. military's fixation on the Lebanon crisis in the summer of 1958 to once again turn up the heat in the Taiwan Strait. The crisis started in August 1958 when Mao initiated a campaign to see if the United States would back Chiang Kai-shek's government, even at the risk of war. He ordered the PLA to bombard and cut Jinmen Island off from supply. Chiang

The long-time leader of the Republic of China, Chiang Kai-shek, greets Chief of Naval Operations Admiral Arleigh Burke in 1955.

had increased the island's garrison since the earlier 1954–1955 crisis from 30,000 to 86,000 of his best Nationalist soldiers.

Mao believed that loss of Jinmen and the thousands of Chiang's soldiers there would demoralize the Nationalist armed forces on the larger island of Taiwan. In a matter of two hours, on 23 August, some 40,000 shells fell on Jinmen. The men on the heavily fortified island weathered the storm with few casualties, but they would not be able to withstand the bombardment for long unless resupplied with ammunition, food, and other necessities. At the same time, Communist forces shelled more distant Mazu Island and launched an unsuccessful amphibious assault on Tung Ting, a smaller island 18 miles from Jinmen.

Naval units also attacked and sank a Nationalist warship near the island.

Chief of Naval Operations Admiral Arleigh Burke served as Washington's "executive agent" or authorized manager of military operations during the crisis. The Navy's top flag officer and Commander Seventh Fleet, Vice Admiral Wallace M. Beakley, had anticipated the possibility of a U.S. military response in support of Chiang's government, as provided for in the Mutual Defense Treaty of 1954. They deployed the bulk of the Seventh Fleet to waters off Taiwan. At the time the fleet consisted of carriers *Hancock* (CVA 19), *Lexington* (CVA 16), and *Princeton*, 2 cruisers, 36 destroyers, 4 submarines, and 20 amphibious and support ships. Burke also directed the *Essex* carrier task group, then in the Mediterranean, and the *Midway* carrier task group on the U.S. West Coast to reinforce the fleet. By the 28th a host of aircraft carriers, surface warships, and submarines had established a formidable presence in the Taiwan Strait and nearby waters.

The Taiwan Patrol Force deployed a cruiser and four destroyers on surface patrol of the strait and started day and night air patrols over its waters. The aircraft were armed with depth charges and torpedoes. Jet fighters from the carriers flew through the strait but never closer than 20 miles to the mainland—to remind the PLA of the Seventh Fleet's presence and combat power. The demonstration cost the fleet the loss of three naval aviators and four planes to operational accidents.

Given great latitude by Admiral Burke, Admiral Roland N. Smoot, the commander of the Taiwan Defense Command, and Vice Admiral Beakley planned and executed the military operations and deployments off Jinmen. Cautioned by Washington to respond only in self-defense if U.S. or Nationalist ships were attacked, Beakley told his subordinate commanders to "remember, the shot you fire will be heard around the world, maybe [on] the floor of the UN. Be right."

U.S. strategy during this period emphasized nuclear warfare, and plans existed for the use of these weapons in defense of the Nationalists' offshore islands. Since the summer of 1953 Navy carriers had been authorized to carry nuclear bombs, and by 1958 many of the carrier aircraft were equipped to drop them. Eisenhower, however, made it clear that nuclear weapons would only be used as a last resort, and only with his specific authorization.

Contrary to his public assertions, Mao feared America's nuclear arsenal and the Seventh Fleet. The Chinese leader also found out he could not count on the backing of his Soviet allies, who were aghast at Mao's provocative behavior in the crisis. Hence, Mao issued strict orders to even low levels of the Chinese military that U.S. warships were not to be attacked. He even refused permission for PLA units to fire back if fired upon. Throughout the crisis PLA aircraft and torpedo boats hovered menacingly at a distance from U.S.-Nationalist operations but did not come close. Communist artillery fire targeting Nationalist ships ceased when Seventh Fleet destroyer types *Hopewell* and *McGinty* (DE 365) rushed to the assistance of their allies on two separate occasions.

The Nationalist navy, however, proved unable to get its supply vessels through to Jinmen because of the Communist shelling and naval attacks. PLAN torpedo boats sank one Nationalist LST and heavily damaged another. On 5 September Chiang's generals reported that the shelling had prevented three of four LSTs sent to Jinmen from delivering their cargoes; stocks of artillery shells and fuel were becoming alarmingly low on the island.

Chiang wanted to initiate air strikes against PLA targets on the mainland, but Eisenhower shied away from that drastic step. As a less hostile alternative, on 29 August the President authorized the Seventh Fleet to escort Nationalist resupply convoys to within three nautical miles of Jinmen; that is in international waters as interpreted by Washington (the PRC claimed 12 miles off shore as their territorial limit).

On 7 September, in Operation Lightning, heavy cruiser *Helena*, with Beakley embarked, another cruiser, four destroyers, and four Nationalist naval vessels escorted a pair of Nationalist medium landing ships (LSMs) so they could deliver their critical supplies without Communist interference. The next three Lightning operations did not fare so well; PLAN

Destroyer Hopewell *(DD 681) steams through the waters of the Western Pacific.*

A landing craft and a tracked landing vehicle enter the well deck of dock landing ship Catamount *(LSD 17).*

artillery fire destroyed one LSM, damaged another, and frustrated the offloading of supplies. From 14 to 19 September, however, the Nationalists used U.S.-supplied tracked landing vehicles (LVTs) able to move cargoes from the sea directly to fortified storage sites; each convoy delivered 151 tons of supplies.

To drive home the point that the United States would not countenance Mao's seizure of Jinmen, on the nights of 18 and 20 September Nationalist landing craft carried by dock landing ship *Catamount* (LSD 17) delivered six 8-inch howitzers—artillery pieces capable of firing not only conventional but nuclear rounds—to Jinmen. The United States also transferred to the Nationalists the revolutionary heat-seeking, rocket-powered Sidewinder air-to-air missile and trained their pilots in its use. On 25 September a Chinese Nationalist flight of U.S.-built F-86F Sabres engaged MiG-17 jets over the strait and downed four of them with Sidewinders. With these missiles and other weapons to strengthen Chiang's forces, Nationalist jets destroyed 33 opponents during the crisis for the loss of four of their own planes.

Once Mao understood that the blockade of Jinmen would not succeed because the Seventh Fleet protected the resupply convoys, he ended the confrontation. On 6 October Beijing announced a one-week cease-fire on the condition that the Seventh Fleet end its convoy escorts, which it did on the 8th. The PLA temporarily resumed shelling on the 20th to protest the visit to Taiwan of Secretary of State Dulles. Eventually, Mao directed his coastal artillery forces to shell Jinmen only on odd days, which in effect allowed the Nationalists to resupply the island unhindered on the even days. The odd-day shelling went on for years, but only for show. U.S. seapower had called Mao's bluff and won the hand.

Once more, in 1962, Mao triggered a confrontation on the coast of China when he deployed sizable ground forces to Fujian Province across from Taiwan. The ostensible reason was a similar buildup of Nationalist forces in the offshore islands. The action coincided with growing support for North Vietnamese military actions in Laos and South Vietnam and efforts to dissuade the United States from escalating the conflict in Indochina. The fleet's Taiwan Patrol Force kept a wary eye on the waters of the strait, but Mao did not follow up the troop concentration with other provocations.

For the Seventh Fleet, the interlude between the Korean War and the Vietnam War cannot be described as peaceful. To support U.S. foreign policy and deter mainland Chinese aggression, American Sailors conducted air and sea surveillance operations that often tested their endurance and sometimes claimed their lives. Seapower helped resolve the Taiwan Strait crises of 1954–1955 and 1958 but could not reverse French fortunes in Indochina. The fleet's actions and buildup of bases strengthened America's alliances with Japan, South Korea, the Republic of China, the Philippines, Australia, and New Zealand. The fleet became a cornerstone of SEATO's military power. And, as in every era, the Navy's humanitarian operations—evacuation of the Dachens and Passage to Freedom—demonstrated America's concern for people dispossessed by conflict and natural disaster. The fleet and its Sailors were challenged in the political and ideological cauldron of the Far East in the 1950s, but they met that challenge. The deterrence of aggression remains a core function of today's Seventh Fleet.

Commander Seventh Fleet Vice Admiral William A. Schoech, second from left, with American and Chinese Nationalist officers during his 1962 visit to Taiwan.

Chapter 5

COMBAT AND CONFRONTATION

AGGRESSIVE ACTIVITY BY NORTH VIETNAM increasingly drew the Seventh Fleet into Southeast Asian waters during the late 1950s and 1960s. Battle forces deployed to the South China Sea first to limit Communist inroads in Laos and South Vietnam and then to engage in full-scale combat from the sea. Despite its heavy engagement in the Vietnam War, the fleet also responded vigorously when North Korean forces attacked U.S. naval vessels and patrol planes in Northeast Asia.

The conflict for Southeast Asia began in earnest in 1959 when Ho Chi Minh's Communist regime in North Vietnam decided on an armed struggle to overthrow the Ngo Dinh Diem government of the Republic of (South) Vietnam. The People's Republic of China fully supported the Vietnamese Communists in that decision. Frustrated by the Seventh Fleet's successful defense of the Korean peninsula during the 1950–1953 war and the island of Taiwan during the 1954–1955 and 1958 crises, Chinese leader Mao Zedong set his sights on a ground campaign in Indochina to advance Communist regional and international goals. The PRC backed up that support to Hanoi with $100 million worth of small arms, ammunition, and artillery.

The United States was equally determined to frustrate Communist designs. Several times from 1959 to 1963 Washington dispatched Seventh Fleet carrier task forces to the South China Sea and the Gulf of Siam (Thailand) to influence an unstable political situation in Laos. Communist Pathet Lao guerrilla forces, backed by North Vietnam, fought for control of the country with noncommunist Laotian groups. In May 1962, for instance, President John F. Kennedy ordered the fleet to deploy Marine and Army troops to Thailand's land border with Laos. These shows of force convinced Hanoi, Beijing, and Moscow that if their actions continued the United States might position military forces on the very borders of North Vietnam and China—an unwelcome outcome from their standpoint. Consequently, at the 1962 Geneva conference the major world powers agreed to a cease-fire in Laos. In following years none of the powers fully respected either the cease-fire or the sovereignty of Laos; fighting continued but at a lower level than before, and not until 1975 did a major antagonist move to occupy the entire country.

President John F. Kennedy and U.S. Navy flag officers. As a former naval officer, the President understood and used seapower to influence events ashore in Southeast Asia.

53

Southeast Asian Threats

Washington also expressed concern that indigenous Communist groups in the Philippines, Malaya, Indonesia, and other Southeast Asian countries supported by the PRC would overthrow those governments. Unlike Laos and North Vietnam, however, those countries did not border on China or North Vietnam, so the PRC had a much tougher time supplying arms to local insurgents and could not offer them ready sanctuary when noncommunist forces closed in. The Seventh Fleet and the navies of the British Commonwealth dominated the waters of the South China Sea and Indonesian Archipelago, further limiting the material support guerrilla groups could expect from overseas sources. Hence, by 1965 government forces in the Philippines, Malaya, and Indonesia, backed by the United States and its allies, destroyed or suppressed the armed strength of their insurgent groups.

The administration of President John F. Kennedy understood, however, that it would be much more difficult to eliminate the Communist insurgency in South Vietnam. In addition to providing advisors and military assistance to the Saigon government, Washington directed the Pacific Command to take other positive actions. The Seventh Fleet responded with "show-the-flag" demonstrations to bolster the new Saigon government and discourage enemies, both foreign and domestic. Flagships *Saint Paul* and *Oklahoma City* (CLG 5) and other Seventh Fleet warships frequently made port calls at Saigon and hosted onboard visits by President Diem and other South Vietnamese officials.

Guided missile light cruiser Oklahoma City *(CLG 5), flagship of the Seventh Fleet, makes a show-the-flag visit to Saigon in July 1964.*

Seventh Fleet Icon

The quarter-century service of the 13,600-ton heavy cruiser *Saint Paul* (CA 73) paralleled a momentous era in the history of the Seventh Fleet. *Saint Paul* took part in the bombardment of the Japanese home islands at the end of World War II and rode at anchor in Tokyo Bay when Japanese officials surrendered on board battleship *Missouri* (BB 63) on 2 September 1945. The heavy cruiser then operated out of Shanghai and other mainland ports during the tumultuous years of the Chinese civil war.

In the fall of 1950 *Saint Paul* stood ready in the Taiwan Strait to discourage a Chinese Communist invasion of Taiwan. In November she deployed to the Sea of Japan/East Sea off Korea and protected Task Force 77 carriers conducting strike operations. The guns of *Saint Paul*

Commander Seventh Fleet, Vice Admiral Charles D. Griffin, right, welcomes Ngo Dinh Diem, President of the Republic of Vietnam, and U.S. Ambassador Eldridge Durbrow on board the flagship Saint Paul *(CA 73) in October 1960.*

and other Seventh Fleet warships ensured that Communist troops did not contest the UN evacuation of Hungnam in December. Throughout the war the heavy cruiser brought her formidable suite of 8-inch and 5-inch guns to bear against enemy gun emplacements, railway tunnels, troop concentrations, and other military targets ashore, destroying hundreds of them. These successful operations were not without cost; a turret explosion in April 1952 killed 30 Sailors. *Saint Paul* conducted the last surface ship bombardment of the war, firing an 8-inch shell at 2159 on 27 July 1953, one minute before the cease-fire went into effect.

Throughout the 1950s *Saint Paul* accomplished Far East deployments for the Taiwan Strait Crisis of 1954–1955 and numerous diplomatic presence and port call missions. From May 1959 to August 1962, *Saint Paul* became the first U.S. warship home-ported overseas since before World War II, conducting operations from Yokosuka, Japan. During much of this period she served as the flagship of Commander Seventh Fleet. In October 1960, for instance, Vice Admiral Charles D. Griffin visited Saigon, South Vietnam, on board *Saint Paul*.

In great demand during the Vietnam War, the big-gun cruiser earned eight battle stars bombarding roads and railways, bridges, coastal artillery batteries, supply depots, and other lucrative targets in North Vietnam. *Saint Paul*'s 8-inch/55-caliber guns, with a range of 26,000 yards, also supported amphibious assaults and helped defeat enemy attacks on American and allied troops in South Vietnam. The valiant warrior and diplomatic star finally ended her Seventh Fleet service and was decommissioned in 1971.

Heavy cruiser Saint Paul *fires her 8-inch guns at targets in Vietnam during 1966.*

Despite the best efforts of 16,000 American naval and military advisors and the supply of naval vessels, aircraft, artillery, and armored vehicles, by 1964–1965 Communist insurgents called Viet Cong increasingly threatened the survival of the government of South Vietnam. The assassinations of Diem and Kennedy in November 1963 prompted the Vietnamese Communists to redouble their military and political efforts to seize control of South Vietnam. Hanoi increased the flow of munitions to Viet Cong forces via the so-called Ho Chi Minh Trail that wound its way through the panhandle of Laos and into South Vietnam. In addition, the North Vietnamese government began dispatching entire infantry regiments of the People's Army of Vietnam (PAVN) down the trail to reinforce the Viet Cong.

Incidents in the Gulf of Tonkin

President Lyndon B. Johnson, Kennedy's successor, and Secretary of Defense Robert S. McNamara decided to put military pressure on North Vietnam. The American leaders believed that seapower could influence Hanoi to cease its support for the Viet Cong. In 1964 the U.S. Navy provided the Vietnam Navy with Norwegian-built fast patrol boats (PTFs), trained their crews, and repaired the boats in Danang. The PTFs then carried out covert attacks, in Operation 34A, on the coast of North Vietnam. On numerous occasions the patrol boats landed saboteurs to destroy bridges and other military targets and bombarded coastal radar stations and other military sites. The operations were hindered, however, by the lack of good intelligence about enemy defenses.

To correct the deficiency, Washington ordered the Seventh Fleet to use destroyers to collect intelligence on North Vietnam as they had been doing along the coasts of the Soviet Union, China, and North Korea since 1962 in Desoto Patrol operations. In early August 1964 destroyer *Maddox* (DD 731), with Captain John J. Herrick in tactical command, carried out an intelligence cruise in the

Destroyer Maddox *(DD 731) operating in the Western Pacific.*

Captain John J. Herrick, left, the on-scene commander during the Tonkin Gulf incidents of August 1964, and Commander Herbert L. Ogier, commanding officer of Maddox.

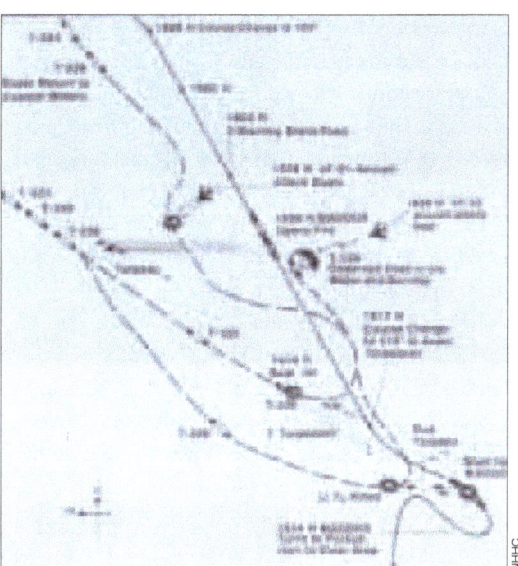

The Naval Engagement of 2 August 1964.

Gulf of Tonkin along the coast of North Vietnam. Shortly before the mission the American-backed South Vietnamese 34A patrol force had bombarded targets further to the south. North Vietnamese naval units were on alert. They had often tried but failed to catch the South Vietnamese boat force. But on 2 August *Maddox* presented the Communists with a slower target, and they sent three Soviet-built P-4 motor torpedo boats to attack the destroyer in broad daylight. The P-4s fired torpedoes that missed their mark, but one round from a deck gun hit the American warship. Planes sent from Task Force 77 carrier *Ticonderoga* (CVA 14) to support *Maddox* strafed the attackers and left one boat dead in the water. *Maddox* steamed safely out of the area and joined the fleet at the mouth of the gulf.

That the North Vietnamese not only failed to back down to U.S. pressure but responded to it in such a hostile manner surprised President Johnson. He and naval leaders in the Pacific, however, decided that they could not retreat from this brazen challenge to the Seventh Fleet. Admiral Thomas H. Moorer, the Pacific Fleet commander, ordered *Maddox* reinforced by destroyer *Turner Joy* (DD

As Commander Seventh Fleet, Vice Admiral Thomas H. Moorer, right, speaks with Commander in Chief, Pacific Command Admiral Ulysses S. Grant Sharp. Both naval leaders advocated strong measures to deter Communist actions in Southeast Asia.

951) and sent the pair back along the coast of North Vietnam to continue the intelligence mission. On the night of 4 August the two warships reported

being attacked by and returning fire on several fast craft far out to sea in the gulf. Signals intelligence and other information convinced Moorer and other officers in the Pacific naval chain of command and leaders in Washington that North Vietnamese naval forces had attacked the two destroyers. It is now clear, however, that the U.S. intelligence analysts erred; no North Vietnamese attack occurred on the night of 4 August.

Sure at least about the 2 August attack, the President ordered Seventh Fleet carrier forces to launch retaliatory strikes, which took place against North Vietnam on 5 August. Aircraft from carriers *Ticonderoga* and *Constellation* (CVA 64) demolished an oil storage site at Vinh and damaged or destroyed about 30 enemy naval vessels in port or along the coast. Of greater significance, on 7 August the U.S. Congress overwhelmingly passed the Tonkin Gulf Resolution, which allowed the President to employ military force as he deemed necessary against the Vietnamese Communists.

Undeterred by the fleet's actions in the Gulf of Tonkin, the Communists stepped up their terrorist attacks in South Vietnam. In late 1964 saboteurs destroyed U.S. combat planes at Bien Hoa airfield north of Saigon, and on Christmas Eve exploded a bomb at a bachelor officer's quarters in Saigon. The blast killed two Americans and wounded more than 100 Americans, Australians, and Vietnamese. In early 1965 insurgents attacked the American embassy in Saigon and U.S. military facilities in Pleiku and Qui Nhon. Convinced these acts demanded a robust response, President Johnson ordered a full-scale bombing campaign against North Vietnam.

North Vietnam did not act alone in its confrontation with the United States. The Soviet Union and the other Communist countries liberally supplied Hanoi with war material. Between 1965 and 1970 the People's Republic of China deployed a total of 300,000 military personnel to North Vietnam. To free North Vietnamese troops for

Commander Task Force 77 Rear Admiral Henry L. Miller and his chief of staff observe carrier operations from the bridge of carrier Ranger *(CVA 61) in early 1965.*

battles in the South, Chinese soldiers operated antiaircraft guns, built coastal fortifications, and repaired damaged bridges, railroads, and roads. Hanoi benefited significantly from this support. For fear of the Seventh Fleet's power, however, Mao expressly forbid any Chinese naval or air action against the Americans, even though the fleet steamed in waters just off his nation's southern coast. PRC air defense units did, however, shoot down several U.S. aircraft that inadvertently strayed into PRC air space.

Carrier Operations from the South China Sea

The Attack Carrier Striking Force, Task Force 77, proved to be the Seventh Fleet's heavy hitter of the Vietnam War's Rolling Thunder and Linebacker bombing campaigns. During 1965 and 1966 some carrier forces operated at Dixie Station southeast of Cam Ranh Bay. Thereafter, the Navy concentrated Task Force 77 in the gulf in an area centered at 17°30'N, 108°30'E. This staging area—Yankee Station—became one of the most recognizable names of the war in Southeast Asia. Carrier planes bombed enemy power plants, fuel and supply facilities, highway and railroad bridges, and rail lines in North Vietnam and Laos.

A carrier's air wing normally comprised two fighter squadrons, three attack squadrons, and smaller fixed-wing aircraft and helicopter detachments. *Enterprise* and the *Forrestal*-class carriers, which had sizable flight decks, could handle as many as 100 aircraft. The smaller *Essex*-class ships routinely operated around 70 planes. The F-8 Crusader and F-4 Phantom II served as the Attack Carrier Striking Force's principal fighter planes. The A-4 Skyhawk, A-6 Intruder, A-7 Corsair II, and prop-driven A-1 Skyraider executed the majority of the air attack sorties.

For photoreconnaissance missions in North Vietnam and Laos, the task force used the RF-8A Crusader, RA-3B Skywarrior, and RA-5C Vigilante. The E-2 Hawkeye provided airborne command control, early warning, and communications support for the multi-aircraft "Alpha strike" groups. Sikorsky SH-3 Sea King and Kaman UH-2 Sea

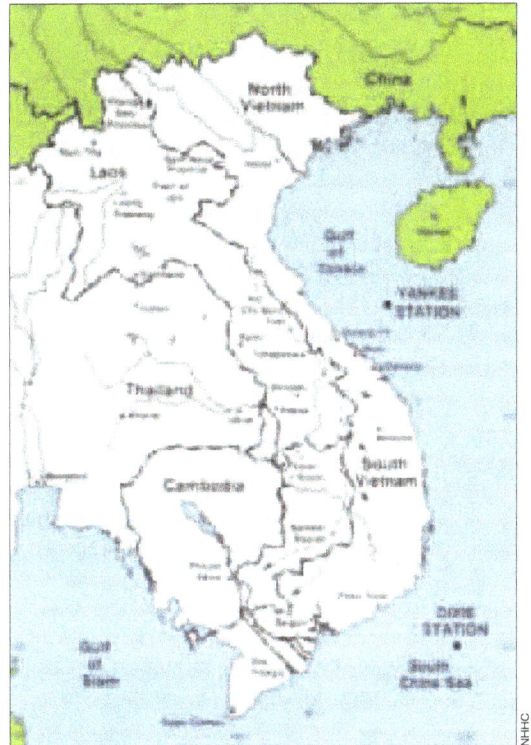

Carrier stations off Indochina.

Sprite helicopters, along with U.S. Air Force aircraft, focused on the land and sea rescue of aircrews shot down or forced to ditch in the ocean during combat operations.

The fleet's fighter and attack planes carried a deadly load of bombs, rockets, missiles, and guns. Strike aircraft dropped 250, 500, 1,000, and 2,000-pound general purpose bombs ("iron bombs)," napalm bombs, and magnetic sea mines; and fired 5-inch Zuni and 2.75-inch "Mighty Mouse" rockets. The "Iron Hand" aircraft responsible for destroying enemy surface-to-air missile (SAM) radars used Shrike missiles, Bullpup glide bombs, and television-guided Walleye bombs. Task Force 77's fighters employed Sidewinder heat-seeking and Sparrow radar-guided missiles and 20-millimeter machine guns to shoot down the enemy's MiG interceptors.

In one action, the air wings from *Coral Sea* (CVA 43) and *Hancock* attacked enemy radar sites on the coast and on Bach Long Vi (Nightingale Island) in the Gulf of Tonkin. The 70 planes in the operation destroyed the mainland targets but had to return to complete the job on the island. During this action North Vietnamese air defense forces directed their fire to the lead aircraft. They hit the planes of three American squadron commanders. Commander Jack Harris, commanding officer of Attack Squadron 155, ejected from his plane and parachuted safely into the sea. To his surprise, the periscope of an American submarine broke the surface near him, and he was soon safely on board. Commander Peter Mongilardi, the leader of VA-153, employed his years of flying Navy aircraft and professional skill to guide his damaged plane home. Fuel streamed from many holes in his shot-up A-4 Skyhawk, so he set up a rendezvous with an A-3 "Whale" tanker en route to *Coral Sea*. The two planes, connected by a refueling hose, then flew together back to the ship for safe recoveries on board.

Sudden Squall *by R. G. Smith. Oil on canvas. The painting depicts the destroyer* De Haven *(DD 727), which is providing antiaircraft and antisubmarine protection for the carrier* Coral Sea *(CV 43) on Yankee Station.*

The commanding officer of Fighter Squadron (VF) 154, Commander William N. Donnelly, had an even more remarkable experience. He "punched out" of his damaged F-8 Crusader fighter but sustained severe injuries in the process. Even though he had a dislocated shoulder and six cracked vertebrae, Donnelly inflated a life raft and managed to climb in. All through the day and night, he floated just off Bach Long Vi under cover of flame and smoke from the carrier strikes. Enemy searchlights traversed the water in search of downed American aviators. Finally, after 45 hours in the water, planes from *Hancock* spotted Donnelly. An Air Force HU-16 amphibian aircraft landed close by, and a paramedic joined Donnelly in the water. With sharks all around, the airman eased the Navy pilot into the plane for the return to his carrier home.

Seventh Fleet aviators were more successful a few months later when four North Vietnamese MiG-21s jumped VF-21 F-4 Phantom II jets flying a combat air patrol over Thanh Hoa. As the MiGs approached the American planes, Commander Louis C. Page and his radar intercept officer (RIO), Lieutenant Commander John C. Smith, destroyed one of the attackers with a radar-guided Sparrow air-to-air missile. Simultaneously, Lieutenant Jack E. Batson and his RIO, Lieutenant Commander Robert B. Doremus, shot down another MiG. The two surviving North Vietnamese fighters then reversed course and beat a retreat for home.

Task Force 77 developed new tactics over the next several years that improved the effectiveness of carrier operations. Instead of multiplane Alpha strikes, operational planners increasingly relied on two or single-aircraft attacks. In one of the latter operations, Lieutenant Commander Charles B. Hunter and his bombardier/navigator, Lieutenant Lyle F. Bull, flew their all-weather, day-night A-6 Intruder attack plane into the "heart of darkness." The men volunteered for an extremely dangerous night attack on a railroad ferry slip near Hanoi, protected by surface-to-air missile batteries, antiaircraft artillery sites, and MiG bases. The Intruder launched from *Constellation* on 30 October 1967 and flew low and fast through the mountain valleys of northeast North Vietnam. The A-6 got to within 18 miles of the target before North Vietnamese radars picked it up. The pilot flew the plane at treetop level and "jinked" left and right to avoid SA-2 Guideline SAMs that the enemy sent up in profusion. As antiaircraft fire and searchlights crisscrossed the sky, Hunter and Bull pressed home their attack and dropped eighteen 500-pound bombs on the railroad ferry slip. As the Intruder banked and headed for the sea, the target exploded in a brilliant display behind the attack plane.

The Seventh Fleet commanded the sea off North Vietnam, even though Hanoi operated about forty motor gunboats and fast attack craft. On a few occasions, however, the North Vietnamese challenged the American fleet's presence in the Gulf of Tonkin. In July 1966 the North Vietnamese sent a trio of P-4 torpedo boats against U.S. warships offshore. In that incident Task Force 77 aircraft used rockets, bombs, and cannon to sink all three fast attack boats, which had the destroyer *Rogers* (DD 876) and the guided missile frigate *Coontz* (DLG 8) in their sights.

Fire posed a much greater threat than enemy naval vessels to the carriers on Yankee Station. In October 1966 a seaman on board carrier *Oriskany* (CVA 34) improperly handled a flare that ignited other munitions and set the ship ablaze, knocking her out of action and killing 44 Sailors. The following year, in July, another carrier fire sent *Forrestal* (CVA 59) home for repairs and resulted in the death of 135 naval aviators and ship's personnel.

From 1965 to 1968 the Navy's carrier squadrons destroyed only two enemy planes for

A pair of Constellation *(CVA 64) A-6 Intruder attack planes en route to North Vietnam for a bombing mission.*

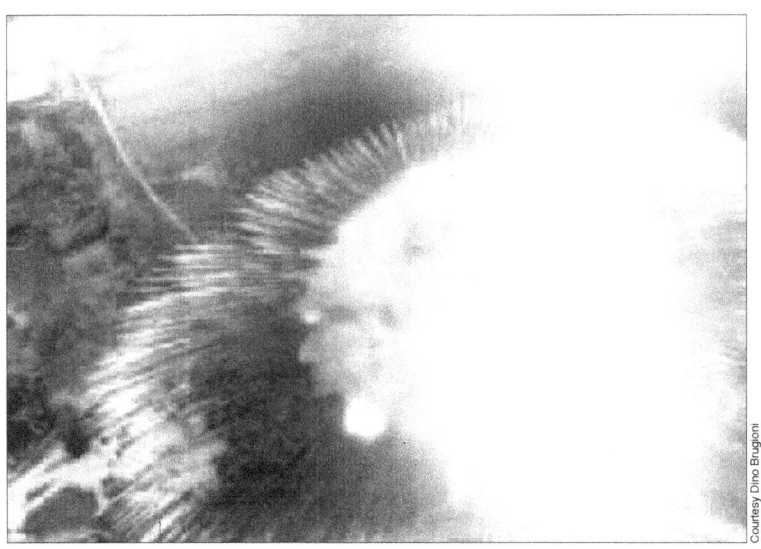

A Soviet-made SA-2 Guideline surface-to-air missile explodes below a carrier plane, sending shards of hot, lethal shrapnel in all directions.

every one they lost in aerial engagements; this was an unacceptable win-loss ratio. Intensive air-to-air combat training at Naval Air Station Miramar, California—the "Top Gun" school—changed all that. During air operations in 1972 and early 1973, the ratio improved to 12-to-1. Lieutenant Randy Cunningham and Lieutenant (j.g.) Willie Driscoll,

Guided missile cruiser Chicago *(CG 11) steaming in the Pacific. The warship often served as the fleet's "Red Crown" ship to monitor and direct U.S. operations in the air over North Vietnam and the Gulf of Tonkin.*

Navy and Air Force aircraft of approaching MiGs and then sent escorting fighters to the rescue. Senior Chief Radarman Larry Nowell, serving on board guided missile cruiser *Chicago* (CG 11) in August 1972, received the Navy Distinguished Service Medal for helping American air units destroy 12 North Vietnamese MiGs.

Despite the best efforts of naval aviators, fleet Sailors, and Air Force fliers, the multiyear Rolling Thunder, Linebacker, and other major air operations did not achieve their primary objective of cutting enemy supply lines. Moreover, the air war cost the death or capture of 881 naval aviators and the loss of 900 aircraft. The campaigns, however, undoubtedly destroyed an enormous amount of war material, delayed and weakened Communist ground offensives throughout Indochina, and finally persuaded Hanoi to negotiate an end to the war.

Bombardment and Amphibious Assault from the Sea

Seventh Fleet surface ships provided invaluable service along the coast on either side of the demilitarized zone (DMZ) separating North and South Vietnam. In Operation Sea Dragon, the 16-inch guns of battleship *New Jersey*, 8-inch- and 6-inch guns of heavy and light cruisers, and 5-inch guns of destroyers bombarded bridges, radar sites, rail lines, and coastal artillery positions in North Vietnam. Royal Australian Navy destroyers *Hobart*, *Perth*, *Brisbane*, and *Vendetta* steamed at one time or another with the Seventh Fleet on the gun line off Vietnam. Communist coastal guns, sometimes fortified in caves, often returned fire and hit allied ships, killing and wounding sailors. The enemy guns, however, failed to sink even one U.S. or Australian combatant during the war.

graduates of the Top Gun school, were exemplars of that training. On 10 May 1972, during the early days of the Linebacker campaign, Cunningham and Driscoll, flying an F-4J Phantom II of VF-96 from *Constellation*, destroyed three MiGs. Combined with two earlier MiG shootdowns, these victories made the Phantom crew the first aces of the Vietnam War.

Surface-ship Sailors were part of the team that reduced the enemy's MiG force. From 1965 to 1973 Task Force 77 positioned a cruiser equipped with advanced radars and communications gear between the enemy coast and the fleet at the PIRAZ (positive identification radar advisory zone) radar picket station. The ship, with the call sign "Red Crown," tracked all planes over the eastern regions of North Vietnam and the gulf. Despite this precaution, in April 1972 two North Vietnamese MiG-17s attacked destroyer *Higbee* (DD 806), one of which dropped a bomb on the ship, wounding four Sailors. A surface-to-air missile fired by cruiser *Sterett* (CG 31) positioned nearby then downed one of the assailants. Red Crown often alerted

Joined by Vietnam Navy, Royal Australian Navy, and U.S. amphibious and patrol vessels, the major Seventh Fleet warships also ranged along the coast of South Vietnam to strike PAVN troop concentrations, supply caches, and fortified bunker complexes. During the Communist Easter Offensive of 1972, the fleet's gunfire support ships savaged North Vietnamese tank and troop units advancing south on the coast road to attack the cities of northern South Vietnam.

Amphibious forces exploited their mobility and flexibility to attack the enemy all along the South Vietnamese coastline, from the DMZ in the north to the Gulf of Siam in the south. During August 1965, in Operation Starlite, the war's most successful amphibious assault, the fleet's amphibious vessels put Marine units ashore, which then linked up with Army of Vietnam troops to destroy the 1st Viet Cong Regiment. In later years large enemy units stayed clear of the coastal areas and employed mostly booby traps and snipers to oppose allied ground operations. Commander Seventh Fleet then used the Navy–Marine Corps Amphibious Ready Group/Special Landing Force as a floating reserve, especially during the hard-fought ground battles of the 1968 Tet Offensive.

Seaborne Supply

The Seventh Fleet had greater success limiting Communist infiltration of supplies into South Vietnam by sea than it had interdicting the Ho Chi Minh Trail. Commander Seventh Fleet directed the destroyer escorts, ocean minesweepers, and patrol planes that formed the blue-water contingent during

A 100-ton North Vietnamese trawler caught trying to land weapons and ammunition on a beach in South Vietnam. Seventh Fleet destroyer escorts, ocean minesweepers, and patrol planes, in coordination with other U.S. Navy, U.S. Coast Guard, and Vietnam Navy units, mounted the successful Market Time anti-infiltration operation along the 1,200-mile coastline of South Vietnam.

Merchantmen such as SS American Corsair, *operated by the Navy's Military Sealift Command, kept U.S. and allied troops well supplied. Minesweepers like the one in the foreground cleared mines from the 45-mile-long river between Saigon and the sea.*

the early days of the Market Time anti-infiltration patrol. Later, Commander, Naval Forces Vietnam took charge and supplemented the warships with Coast Guard cutters and U.S. Navy and Vietnam Navy gunboats, patrol craft, junks, coastal radars, and command centers. The efforts of both commands succeeded in severely limiting North Vietnam's seaborne infiltration. It became almost impossible for the enemy to slip a munitions-laden, 100-ton supply ship past the Market Time patrol.

The Communists did get supplies through by sea to their forces fighting in South Vietnam, however. Soviet and other merchant ships brazenly steamed through the Gulf of Tonkin to deliver their cargoes to the docks of Haiphong. Chinese merchantmen also openly deposited their military cargoes at the port of Sihanoukville in supposedly "neutral" Cambodia. The Communists then ferried the munitions across the nearby Cambodia-South Vietnam border into the Mekong Delta. At least during Johnson's presidency, Washington prohibited

Chairman of the Joint Chiefs of Staff Admiral Thomas H. Moorer assured President Richard Nixon that the Seventh Fleet could cut off North Vietnam from oceangoing supply by mining Haiphong and the nation's other major ports.

the Seventh Fleet from interfering with these enemy sea lines of communication. At the same time the fleet's dominance of the Western Pacific enabled the United States to maintain a half-million-strong expeditionary force on the Asian continent, far from the sources of supply in America. Free from enemy danger at sea, Military Sealift Command ships transported 95 percent of the ammunition, fuel, vehicles, supplies, and other war materials delivered to U.S. and allied forces in South Vietnam.

The Seventh Fleet could have stopped the enemy from using neutral merchant ships to transport war materials into Cambodia or North Vietnam, but President Johnson, who did not want to provoke open Soviet or Chinese intervention in the war, prohibited a blockade. In 1972, however, President Richard M. Nixon knew that because China and the Soviet Union were then at odds, there would be no opposition from Moscow or Beijing, so he ordered the Seventh Fleet to mine the waters of North Vietnam.

On 9 May 1972 Navy and Marine A-6 Intruders and A-7 Corsair IIs from *Coral Sea* dropped hundreds of mines in the approaches to Haiphong and soon afterward that carrier, as well as *Midway*, *Kitty Hawk*, and *Constellation*, mined other major ports and water approaches. With the ports closed to shipping, North Vietnam could not import the huge amounts of fuel, ammunition, and weapons it needed to fight the tank and artillery-heavy battles

Commander Seventh Fleet Vice Admiral James L. Holloway III welcomes aboard his flagship Blue Ridge *(LCC 19) Nguyen Van Thieu, president of the Republic of Vietnam, in June 1972.*

Coral Sea *(CVA 43) Sailors affix sea mines to an A-7E Corsair II of Attack Squadron 94.*

of the period. The Communist war effort quickly lost steam. The mining of North Vietnam's ports in 1972, in conjunction with the Air Force–Navy Linebacker bombing campaign, compelled the enemy to accept reasonable cease-fire terms and release all American prisoners of war. The Paris Agreement of 27 January 1973 ended America's direct involvement in the Vietnam War.

The End in Southeast Asia

Despite the best efforts of American, South Vietnamese, Laotian, and Cambodian fighting men, in the spring of 1975 Communist forces were on the verge of success throughout Indochina. A North Vietnamese offensive in the Central Highlands of South Vietnam soon developed into a rout of Army of Vietnam divisions north of Saigon. In March the Navy's Military Sealift Command dispatched merchant ships and large tugs pulling barges to Danang, Qui Nhon, and other ports. The vessels evacuated thousands of retreating South Vietnamese troops and civilian refugees.

Vice Admiral George P. Steele, Commander Seventh Fleet during the evacuations of Phnom Penh and Saigon and the SS Mayaguez *crisis in the tumultuous spring of 1975.*

As the enormity of the tragedy in northern South Vietnam became apparent, the Seventh Fleet deployed elements of the Amphibious Task Force (TF 76) to a position off Nha Trang. Because of the Paris Agreement restrictions on the use of U.S. military forces in South Vietnam and the availability of MSC resources, however, Washington limited the naval contingent, then designated the Refugee Assistance Task Group (TG 76.8), to a supporting role. For the most part, this involved command coordination, surface escort duties, and the deployment of 50-man Marine security details on board the MSC ships.

Vice Admiral George P. Steele, Commander Seventh Fleet, now directed his attention to Cambodia, which he expected to fall soon to the radical Communist Khmer Rouge guerrillas. Since 1970 the United States had supported the government of President Lon Nol in its battles with Khmer Rouge and North Vietnamese forces operating on the border with South Vietnam. Despite significant U.S. military assistance to the Cambodian government, by early 1975 the Khmer Rouge guerrillas controlled every population center except Phnom Penh and were closing in on the capital.

Vice Admiral Steele directed the updating of relevant evacuation plans and assigned forces to the mission, designated Operation Eagle Pull. On 3 March 1975 Amphibious Ready Group Alpha (Task Group 76.4) and the 31st Marine Amphibious Unit (Task Group 79.4) reached a ready station off Kompong Som (previously Sihanoukville) in the Gulf of Siam. One month later the force consisted of the destroyer types *Edson* (DD 946), *Henry B. Wilson* (DDG 7), *Knox* (DE 1052), and *Kirk* (DE 1087); the amphibious ships *Okinawa*, *Vancouver*, and *Thomaston* (LSD 28); and the carrier *Hancock*. In addition, Marine Heavy Lift Helicopter Squadron 463 deployed on board the carrier for the operation. Expecting as many as 800 evacuees, naval leaders decided that they needed the squadron's entire 25-plane contingent of helicopters as well as the 22 rotary-wing aircraft on *Okinawa*. Naval medical-surgical teams and the 2d Battalion, 4th Marines, slated to

Marines deployed by CH 53 Sea Stallions from Marine Heavy Lift Helicopter Squadron 463 rush to establish a defensive perimeter in Phnom Penh during the successful Eagle Pull evacuation of April 1975.

protect the evacuation landing zone near the U.S. Embassy, embarked in the amphibious group.

Early on the morning of 12 April, Washington ordered the execution of Eagle Pull. At 0745 *Okinawa* began launching helicopters from the Gulf of Siam in three waves to transport the 360-man Marine ground security force to the landing zone. After flying for an hour over hostile territory, the first group of helicopters touched down close to the embassy, and the Marines quickly set up a defensive perimeter.

U.S. officials on the ground assembled the evacuees and directed them to the waiting Marine helicopters. The evacuees, numbering 276, included U.S. Ambassador John Gunther Dean, embassy staff members, the acting president of Cambodia and his senior government leaders and their families, and journalists. Helicopters lifted the evacuees from the landing zone by 1100 and the Marine security force soon afterward. Shortly after noon, all helicopters and personnel were safely on board the ships of Amphibious Ready Group Alpha. Without the loss of a single life and through detailed planning, preparation, and precise execution, the Seventh Fleet Navy–Marine force accomplished their evacuation mission.

With no time to relax, the Seventh Fleet prepared for an even greater evacuation operation—the withdrawal from the Republic of Vietnam. During March and April, Vice Admiral Steele

Drenched by a tropical downpour, South Vietnamese troops and civilian refugees fleeing from the North Vietnamese 1975 spring offensive approach Seventh Fleet ships off South Vietnam.

deployed MSC vessels off Vung Tau southeast of Saigon and reinforced them with Marine security detachments. Naval personnel loaded the ships with food, water, and medicine.

The Seventh Fleet concentrated at Vung Tau, under Commander Task Force 76, Rear Admiral Donald Whitmire, *Blue Ridge* (LLC 19) and 11 amphibious ships. *Hancock* and *Midway*, carrying Navy, Marine, and Air Force helicopters, joined the flotilla, as did flagship *Oklahoma City*, eight destroyer types, and amphibious ships *Mount Vernon* (LSD 39), *Barbour County* (LST 1195), and *Tuscaloosa* (LST 1187). The carriers *Enterprise* and *Coral Sea* stood out in the South China Sea to provide air cover for the evacuation. The 9th Marine Amphibious Brigade (Task Group 79.1), the Marine evacuation contingent, consisted of three battalion landing teams, four helicopter squadrons, support units, and the deployed security detachments.

Army of Vietnam units defending the approaches to Saigon finally collapsed on 21 April, prompting South Vietnamese President Nguyen Van Thieu to resign his office. On the 29th Vietnamese Communist forces surrounded Saigon and began pushing into the city. With the outcome of the war now crystal clear, Washington ordered the evacuation of Saigon—Operation Frequent Wind.

When he received the order at 1108 local time on 29 April 1975, Rear Admiral Whitmire immediately began executing the evacuation plan. At 1244 *Hancock* launched the first wave of helicopters that headed for the primary landing zone in the U.S. Defense Attaché Office (DAO) compound in Saigon. Soon after 2d Battalion, 4th Marines established a defensive perimeter, Task Force 76 helicopters began lifting out American, Vietnamese, and third-country nationals. Two Marines were killed in an earlier shelling of the DAO compound and two helicopters and their crews were lost at sea. A little after 2100 that night, the evacuation force had lifted 5,000 evacuees and the Marine security force from the site.

Chaos ruled at the U.S. Embassy. Hundreds of desperate evacuees pressed the Marine guards and tried to climb over the perimeter fence to board the helicopters. Marine and Air Force helicopters flew at night dodging fire from the ground to lift evacuees out of dangerous landing zones, one atop a building close to the embassy. Nonetheless, by 0500 on 30 April, U.S. Ambassador Graham Martin and the last of thousands of evacuees had been rescued from the closing enemy forces. By the time North Vietnamese tanks smashed down the gates of the Presidential Palace, Task Force 76 had rescued more than 7,000 Americans and Vietnamese.

Not only U.S. but South Vietnamese helicopters and even fixed-wing aircraft loaded with refugees competed for landing space on the flight decks of the evacuation ships. Task force ships recovered 41 Vietnamese aircraft, but American Sailors had

With no room left on board, Sailors push a helicopter over the side.

to jettison another 54 over the side to make room on deck. Navy small craft rescued some but not all of the Vietnamese who bailed out of aircraft that ditched alongside the evacuation ships.

Meanwhile an armada of junks, sampans, and small craft of all types loaded to the gunwales with people headed for the American fleet. MSC tugs pulling barges brought more refugees from Saigon port out to the ships offshore. There, the evacuees were helped on board, registered, inspected for weapons, and given a medical exam. MSC crews and Marine security personnel processed the new arrivals quickly and efficiently. The Seventh Fleet units eventually transferred most of the Vietnamese refugees they had embarked to the MSC ships. Another flotilla, this one consisting of 26 Vietnam Navy warships and support vessels loaded with 30,000 sailors, their families, and other civilians, congregated off the southern coast of the Mekong Delta.

The war over, this former warship of the Vietnam Navy, now under the U.S. flag, rests in peace at the Subic Bay naval base.

Task Force 76 and the MSC ships moved away from the coast on the afternoon of 30 April but for the next 24 hours continued to pick up seaborne refugees. At dusk on 2 May, with the human tide diminishing, TF 76, carrying 6,000

With the assistance of Harold E. Holt *(DE 1074) Sailors, Marines who have just boarded and taken control of merchant ship SS* Mayaguez *return to the destroyer escort.*

passengers; the MSC flotilla with 44,000 refugees; and the Vietnam Navy group set sail for reception centers in the Philippines and Guam. The sun thus set on America's 25-year effort to preserve the independence of the Republic of Vietnam.

The Seventh Fleet had to accomplish one more combat mission in Southeast Asia in the momentous year 1975. On 12 May Khmer Rouge guerrillas seized the U.S. merchant ship SS *Mayaguez* and her crew off Cambodia. Destroyer escort *Harold E. Holt* (DE 1074) intercepted *Mayaguez*, and on 15 May a boarding party of Marines and Sailors retook the ship, which had been abandoned by the Cambodians earlier. Thinking that the Communists were holding the crewmen on nearby Koh Tang Island (they were actually held briefly on the mainland and were soon released by their captors), Air Force Lieutenant

Guided missile destroyer Henry B. Wilson *(DDG 7) provides gunfire support to Marines battling Cambodian Khmer Rouge guerrillas on Koh Tang Island in May 1975.*

General John J. Burns, in charge of the operation, dispatched from Thailand a force of assault helicopters and Marines. Guided missile destroyer *Henry B. Wilson* also steamed toward Koh Tang. Due to complicated command and control procedures, inadequate intelligence, and other factors, a storm of enemy ground fire unexpectedly hit the helicopter landing force, destroying three of the aircraft and pinning down the Marine contingent ashore. Suppressive fire by *Henry B. Wilson* and combat aircraft enabled the extrication of most of the assault party. The Koh Tang operation resulted in the death of 18 servicemen and wounding of another 50, but it showed that the United States would not tolerate the seizure of its ships on the open sea.

Despite this instance of operational success, the Seventh Fleet suffered during the late 1970s from many ills. Washington-mandated budget cuts limited the number of combatants on station, much-needed ship and equipment repairs, and Sailors on duty. Seventh Fleet leaders had to deal with a host of problems such as drug and alcohol abuse among Sailors and antiwar and antimilitary sentiment in the American population that complicated recruitment and retention. Racial unrest especially troubled the fleet. Indeed, racial incidents on board Seventh Fleet ships operating off Vietnam first gained the nation's attention to the problem. Fighting among Sailors, resistance to orders, and other disruptions in October of 1972 hampered the ability of oiler *Hassayampa* (AO 145) and carrier *Kitty Hawk* to carry out their operational responsibilities. The Navy and the fleet took corrective measures that ultimately addressed Sailors' grievances and improved the racial atmosphere afloat and ashore in subsequent years.

Seventh Fleet Far Eastern Bases

The demands of combat in Vietnam and deterrence operations in the waters of Northeast Asia resulted in the development of Seventh Fleet bases that became the Navy's largest military-industrial enterprises in the world.

Even though the naval base at Subic Bay ran sizable ship repair, ordnance, and supply facilities during the 1950s, they were a pale reflection of the mammoth logistic establishment that operated at the site during the Vietnam War. After the Tonkin Gulf incident of August 1964, there was a four-fold increase in the number of U.S. warships that entered the bay for fuel and munitions and a 300 percent increase in supply issues. Construction began on a crash basis to establish additional magazines, warehouses, fuel storage tanks, piers for major warships and to stockpile ship and aircraft parts, weapons, and general supplies. Soon, the ship repair facility had to recondition destroyers hit by the fire of enemy shore batteries and repair aircraft carriers *Oriskany* and *Forrestal* badly damaged by accidental fires. The Navy deployed tenders and floating dry docks to the site, increased the naval contingent to more than 4,000 Sailors, and employed 15,000 Filipino workers. The naval supply depot handled more than four million barrels of fuel oil for the fleet each month and pumped aviation gas to Clark Air Base via a 41-mile-long pipeline. During the Tet Offensive of 1968 and in the months afterward, the naval ordnance depot at Subic supplied Seventh Fleet warships on the gun line off Vietnam with 600,000 rounds.

Equally busy during the Vietnam War, the naval air station at Sangley Point handled air operations over the South China Sea. In Operation Market Time, P2V Neptune and P-3 Orion patrol planes flying from Sangley Point helped find, fix, and destroy North Vietnamese trawlers trying to deliver war materials to Communist forces in South Vietnam. Sangley also handled the air delivery of supplies to the naval air facility at Cam Ranh Bay across the South China Sea in South Vietnam. With the drawdown of U.S. forces in Vietnam, the Seventh Fleet transferred much of the workload at Sangley Point to Cubi Point and disestablished the former naval air station on 31 August 1971.

Cubi Point became another focal point during the Vietnam War for land-based naval air operations over the South China Sea and Indochina. Aerial photographic and electronic intelligence, air early warning, and other specialized squadrons operated from the naval air station. Cubi served as the primary site in the region for stocking aircraft repair parts and equipment and for aircraft repairs. Much of the ordnance, aviation fuel, mail, and general cargo destined for naval aviation units afloat and

An A-7 Corsair II heads skyward from the naval air station at Cubi Point in the Philippines.

ashore in Southeast Asia reached there via Cubi. In 1967, on 172,000 occasions, naval aircraft involved in wartime operations landed or took off from Cubi. To handle the traffic in the peak year of 1969, Seabees lengthened the airfield to 9,000 feet. With the closure of Sangley Point in 1971, Cubi took on the extra work, servicing that year 45 aircraft carrier and amphibious landing ship visits. During the evacuation from Vietnam and Cambodia in the spring of 1975, Cubi facilitated the airlift from the Philippines of more than 40,000 Vietnamese, Cambodian, and Laotian refugees.

Almost as important as the Philippines bases to Seventh Fleet operational responsibilities during the war was the base at Yokosuka, Japan. The ship repair facility, for instance, worked on over 800 naval vessels in 1967 alone. The base's naval supply depot and naval ordnance facility managed a similarly heavy work load.

Yokosuka and Sasebo not only provided logistic support to the war effort in Vietnam but served as symbols of the enduring U.S.-Japan alliance. The visit of U.S. nuclear-powered warships during the 1960s, while generating loud demonstrations by antinuclear and antimilitary parties, had the effect of solidifying support by the Japanese people for the Seventh Fleet's long-term deterrence and stability responsibilities in Northeast Asia.

With only nuclear-powered submarines entering service with the Navy early in the 1960s, Washington understood that the boats would need to use the logistic services of the Seventh Fleet bases in Japan. After approval by the Japanese government, on the morning of 12 November 1964 *Seadragon* (SSN 584) became the first nuclear-powered warship to enter a Japanese port when she proceeded into Sasebo. Because of its horrific experience with the atomic bombings of Hiroshima and Nagasaki in World War II, Japan was said to have a "nuclear allergy." Despite noisy protest demonstrations in Sasebo and elsewhere in Japan, however, the event passed peacefully. The submarine returned three months later followed by *Snook* (SSN 592), *Permit* (SSN 594), *Plunger* (SSN 595), and *Sargo* (SSN 583) in later years.

Attack submarine Seadragon *(SSN 584), in 1964 the first nuclear-powered warship to enter a Japanese port, steams in the Western Pacific during the early 1960s.*

Bonhomme Richard in Hong Kong Harbor *by Louis Kaep. Watercolor.*

Snook's visit to Yokosuka on 31 May 1966 also generated heated opposition by some segments of the Japanese population, but Japanese political leaders stepped forward to stress the benefit of the submarine and other U.S. Navy warships to Japan's security and prosperity. Japan's oil imports and overseas trade depended on the protection afforded by the Seventh Fleet. As historian Roger Dingman has observed, the words of these Japanese leaders "put flesh on the concept of commitment to alliance with America." Between May 1966 and January 1968, nine more "nuke boats" visited Yokosuka without major incident.

The strength of the alliance was tested on 19 January 1968, however, when *Enterprise*, then the world's only nuclear-powered aircraft carrier, and

Nuclear-powered carrier Enterprise *(CVAN 65) surrounded by her battle group.*

whose aircraft were equipped to drop nuclear bombs, made port at Sasebo, accompanied by nuclear-powered guided missile cruiser *Truxtun* (CGN 35) and guided missile frigate *Halsey* (DDG 23). Tens of thousands of protestors thronged Sasebo's streets, fought with one another and the police, and threatened to break into the base. Once again Japanese leaders stepped forward to remind the populace that the Seventh Fleet provided vital security in the seas around the island nation. This message became especially clear as the Soviet Pacific Fleet began menacing Japanese interests in Northeast Asia in the 1970s. So, despite the brief furor over the nuclear carrier's visit, between 1968 and 1973 nuclear-powered submarines made 100 visits to Japan, and *Enterprise* herself returned for a port call in 1978. The U.S.-Japan alliance only grew stronger in the coming decades.

Countering Chinese, Soviet, and North Korean Hostility

Although the fleet was heavily committed to fighting the war in Southeast Asia from 1965 to 1975, it had to continue deterrence, sea control, presence, and intelligence-gathering missions throughout the Far East. Naval leaders had to contend not only with Chinese diplomatic measures to drive a wedge between the United States and Great Britain over Hong Kong but with overt Soviet and North Korean military actions.

The supreme irony of the Cold War in Asia was that while Task Force 77 mounted combat operations against enemy forces in North Vietnam, including Chinese Communist antiaircraft and railroad repair units, every year hundreds of Seventh Fleet warships anchored peacefully in Hong Kong harbor only a few miles from the People's Republic of China. The visit of *Enterprise* to Hong Kong in January 1966, after bombing operations against North Vietnam, prompted outrage in the PRC's official press but little else.

Mao Zedong often railed against the Seventh Fleet, which he regarded as a symbol of the Western seapower that had dominated China for centuries and continued to frustrate his foreign policy objectives in Asia. He told a visiting delegation from Syria that "the U.S. has four fleets altogether: The Seventh Fleet is the biggest [and it] surrounds us."

In contrast to the *Enterprise* visit to Japan a few years later that generated huge left-wing and antiwar demonstrations, no outcry from the Hong Kong populace greeted the ship's 1966 visit. Indeed, many Hong Kong residents appreciated America's commitment to the defense of South Vietnam.

American Sailors considered the British Crown Colony one of the best rest and recreation (R&R) sites in the Western Pacific. In 1966, 180,000 Sailors and other Americans visited Hong Kong and 390 U.S. naval vessels entered the harbor. Money spent by military personnel on liberty in addition to other economic activity generated by the 400 U.S. commercial firms made Hong Kong a rich city.

Seventh Fleet Sailors and the residents of Hong Kong got along famously. The September 1966 rescue of 46 Hong Kong fishermen in distress by helicopters from carrier *Oriskany* earned much positive comment from the local press. Moreover, according to historian Chi-kwan Mark, "they contributed to the local economy and social stability at a time of political unrest. In the eyes of the Hong Kong Chinese, the "Vietnam War tourists were not 'ugly Americans' but beautiful imperialists."

Seventh Fleet warships visit the British colony of Hong Kong in the 1960s.

In another example, in December 1968 the Seventh Fleet headquarters issued a letter of appreciation to local entrepreneur Mary Soo, whose company sold food and drink to American Sailors and provided the ships with painting services. With British power in Asia on the wane during the 1960s, the People's Liberation Army could have seized Hong Kong with relative ease. But, the port city also served as China's window on the world for overseas trade, and the PRC reaped huge profits by trading with and through the British colony.

In support of Asian allies, Soviet naval vessels—called AGIs (from auxiliary, general, intelligence)—routinely trailed U.S. task forces operating in the Gulf of Tonkin or elsewhere in the vast Pacific. These vessels tried to get as close to U.S. ships—even inside carrier task group formations—to snoop and disrupt combat operations. American commanders discouraged this activity by maintaining course and speed even when AGI's crossed in front of their warships. As a captain in command of the carrier *Enterprise*, James L. Holloway III maintained this approach when an AGI moved into the path of his 90,000-ton carrier. The admiral observed that rather than continue the challenge, the AGI "got the hell out of the way."

U.S. and Soviet ships did not always steer clear of collisions, however. From November 1965 to June 1966, *Banner* (AGER 1), an intelligence-gathering ship, ranged up and down the coast of the Soviet Far East in waters considered territorial by the USSR but not the United States. Soviet destroyers and other warships harassed the U.S. vessel to force her away from those waters but to little avail. Finally, on 24 June 1966, *Banner* and Soviet AGI *Anemometr* collided in the Sea of Japan/East Sea, each commanding officer blaming the other man's actions for the mishap. A similar occurrence took place in the spring of 1967 when destroyer *Walker* (DD 517), then in the protective screen for carrier

U.S. Sailors of destroyer Walker *(DD 17) and Soviet bluejackets of a* Krupnyy-*class destroyer stare in amazement after their two ships collided in the Sea of Japan/East Sea in May 1967.*

Hornet (CVS 12), worked to prevent the Soviet destroyer *Besslednyy* from interfering with the carrier's flight operations. After several especially close and dangerous approaches, the Soviet vessel hit and lightly damaged the American warship. The next day another Soviet destroyer maneuvered dangerously close to the U.S. task force and this ship also hit *Walker*. With both sides recognizing the danger in these close ship and aircraft encounters, the United States and the Soviet Union finally exhibited good sense in May 1972 when they signed the Incidents at Sea Treaty that laid out clear instructions on how the two navies should safely operate while in proximity to one another.

North Korean Belligerence

With the war in Southeast Asia drawing heavily on the resources of the U.S. and South Korean military (two infantry divisions and a brigade served in South Vietnam), the Seventh Fleet spent the 1960s and early 1970s working to prevent hostilities on the Korean peninsula. That was no easy task since the North Korean regime of Kim Il-sung acted aggressively throughout the period. In April 1965, one month after the Seventh Fleet deployed U.S. Marines ashore at Danang in South Vietnam, a pair of North Korean MiG fighters attacked and damaged a U.S. Air Force reconnaissance plane in the Sea of Japan/East Sea. In January 1967 North Korean coastal batteries sank a Republic of Korea Navy (ROKN) patrol vessel protecting fishing craft on the east coast. That year numerous spies and North Korean guerrilla teams infiltrated the south across the DMZ and from the sea with the objective of destabilizing the Republic of Korea.

The year 1968 proved to be especially challenging as the United States concentrated on defeating the Tet Offensive in Vietnam and dealing with domestic and international antiwar sentiment. In January a 31-man special forces team intent on killing the president of South Korea, Chung Hee Park, infiltrated South Korea and headed for his Seoul residence, the "Blue House." South Korean forces intercepted and destroyed the assassination team. North Korean-sparked ambushes, raids, artillery exchanges, and other combat in the DMZ cost the lives of more than a thousand Koreans on both sides.

In a bolder action, two days after the Blue House Raid, combat vessels of the North Korean navy attacked Pueblo (AGER 2), a U.S. ship gathering signals and other intelligence in international waters in the Sea of Japan/East Sea. The North Koreans fired on the U.S. ship, killing Fireman Apprentice Duane Hodges and compelling Commander Lloyd Bucher, the commanding officer, to order an end to resistance. The North Koreans took the ship and her vital intelligence gear into Wonsan harbor and imprisoned the 83 surviving crewmen. For the next year the Communists tortured the men to gain "confessions" for political purposes and released them only when the Johnson administration agreed to a written apology for spying.

As the North Koreans were bringing Pueblo into port, the Seventh Fleet prepared to take whatever action Washington directed. The President, however, recognized that with the United States fully committed to the war in Vietnam, it could not risk another major conflict in Asia. North Korea had one million highly trained and motivated men under arms and could count on support from the Soviet Union. To back up their Communist ally,

Intelligence-collection ship Pueblo *(AGER 2) seized by North Korean naval forces off Wonsan in January 1968.*

the USSR deployed into the waters around Korea a naval task force whose ships in the following weeks shadowed the carrier task force. At one point an AGI compelled the U.S. carrier to stop and reverse engines lest she collide with the Soviet ship. U.S. naval leaders believed that the aggressive behavior was deliberately intended.

North Korean aggression continued. In April 1969 a pair of North Korean MiG-21 fighters shot down a U.S. Navy EC-121 reconnaissance plane in the Sea of Japan/East Sea, killing all 31 crewmen on board. In June 1970 a North Korean fast attack vessel seized a ROKN ship and her 20 crewmen in the Yellow Sea/West Sea. From 1973 to 1976 North Korean naval vessels and combat aircraft frequently crossed the Northern Limit Line (NLL), a maritime border in the Yellow Sea/West Sea between the mainland and five South Korean islands. The United Nations command had established the NLL after the armistice agreement of 1953 to make clear South Korea's sovereignty over the islands. In reaction to Pyongyang's provocative actions in the Yellow Sea/West Sea, South Korea fortified these islands and deployed there strong ground, air, and naval forces.

Then on 18 August 1976, responding to their officer's orders to "kill them all," North Korean guards used axes to bludgeon and kill two U.S. Army officers, Captain Arthur Boniface and 1st Lieutenant Mark Barrett, who had led a team of American and South Korean soldiers into the Joint Security Area of the DMZ to trim the branches of a poplar tree that impeded observation between two UN posts. This barbarous act related to contemporary anti-U.S. rhetoric by Kim Il-sung.

With the war in Vietnam over for more than a year, Washington reacted much more robustly to this aggressive North Korean action than it had over Pyongyang's seizure of *Pueblo*. U.S. General Richard Stillwell, commander of United Nations and U.S. forces in Korea, recommended that strong U.S. and South Korean forces be directed to reenter the area and cut down the tree. The general believed it important to demonstrate to the Communists that their heinous actions would not be tolerated.

A Navy EC-121 electronic intelligence plane in company with a carrier-based A-3 Sky Warrior.

Admiral James L. Holloway III, Chief of Naval Operations and acting Chairman of the Joint Chiefs of Staff when U.S. forces launched Operation Paul Bunyan in August 1976.

President Gerald R. Ford knew that U.S. forces in Northeast Asia were now fully capable of protecting American and allied interests. He also understood that world opinion solidly opposed the brutal Pyongyang-sanctioned murders. At the President's direction, Admiral Holloway, now the acting Chairman of the Joint Chiefs of Staff, raised the defense condition (DEFCON) in the Pacific from 5 to 3 and initiated a "show of strength" in Northeast Asia.

Midway *(CV 41) in 1974.*

The Pacific Command ordered the Seventh Fleet's *Midway* carrier task force to sea from Yokosuka. The carrier, with Commander Carrier Group 7 embarked, and accompanied by the guided missile cruiser *Gridley* (CG 21); guided missile destroyer *Cochrane*; frigates *Kirk* (FF 1087), *Meyerkord* (FF 1058), *Lang* (FF 1061), and *Lockwood* (FF 1064); and oilers *Ashtabula* (AO 51) and USNS *Mispillion* (T-AO 105), immediately steamed into the Sea of Japan/East Sea ready to launch strikes against North Korea.

Commander in Chief, Pacific Command (CINCPAC) also deployed B-52 bombers close enough to North Korean air space to be picked up on Pyongyang's radar and dispatched Air Force tactical aircraft to South Korean airfields. General Stillwell raised the DEFCON in Korea to 2—the highest readiness condition short of war—and readied U.S. and ROK infantry divisions for action. On 21 August 1976, in Operation Paul Bunyan, engineers armed with chain saws and axes and protected by infantrymen skilled in martial arts and helicopter gunships entered the DMZ and reduced the tree to a stump. Faced with the armed might of the United States and the Republic of Korea, the Communist regime in the north did nothing to counter the action. Indeed, the only thing that Kim Il-sung did was release a personal statement expressing regret that "an incident occurred in the Joint Security Area."

Throughout the Vietnam era, the Seventh Fleet accomplished its mission of fighting to defend U.S. treaty alliances, deterring Communist aggression throughout the Far East, and bringing humanitarian assistance to tens of thousands of people in need. Seventh Fleet Sailors, many of whom sacrificed their lives in Vietnam and elsewhere, carried out their duties with courage, perseverance, and above all dedication to the basic principles held dear by the citizens of the United States.

Chapter 6

OLD ENEMIES AND NEW FRIENDS

AS THE SEVENTH FLEET FOUGHT the Vietnam War it tended to its deterrence, presence, and other security responsibilities in Asian waters. The Soviet navy was never more powerful than during the post-Vietnam period when it challenged the Seventh Fleet's presence in the Indian Ocean, the South China Sea, and Northeast Asia. The challenge forced the Seventh Fleet to work with renewed vigor to strengthen cooperation with allies and the formerly antagonistic People's Republic of China. The end of the Cold War found the Seventh Fleet once more in firm control of its maritime domain.

The Soviet navy served as the tip of the spear for the USSR's global expansion during the 1970s and 1980s. Embarrassed by the inability of their naval forces to counter the U.S. quarantine of Cuba during the missile crisis of 1962, Khrushchev's successors invested enormous resources to develop a first-class navy. Admiral Sergei Gorshkov, a gifted and influential strategic thinker, championed and directed this massive Cold War building effort. The world took notice in 1970 when hundreds of Soviet naval units mounted a coordinated global exercise. Demonstrating an ability to operate far from the USSR in 1971, a Soviet Pacific Fleet battle group of cruisers, destroyers, submarines, and auxiliaries operated in the Gulf of Alaska before steaming to within 25 miles of Hawaii's Diamond Head. OKEAN 75, an exercise that involved 200 warships worldwide, including 28 Soviet Pacific Fleet nuclear and conventional submarines, displayed a significant capacity to challenge the U.S. Navy for dominance of the world's oceans.

Admiral Sergei Gorshkov, the father of the modern Soviet fleet, led the Soviet navy from 1956 to 1985.

During and after the Vietnam War, the Soviet Pacific Fleet also deployed operational squadrons into the South China Sea and beyond. Between 1966 and 1991 its surface units and submarines carried out 2,304 deployments, and naval aircraft completed 21,220 sorties. According to historian Alexey Muraviev, these were "the golden years for Russian naval power in the Pacific." In support of USSR foreign policy, in the late 1960s and early 1970s Soviet Pacific Fleet warships made numerous port calls to countries in East Africa and South Asia, including Ceylon (Sri Lanka), India, Iran, Iraq, Pakistan, Somalia, the People's Republic of Yemen, and South Yemen.

Enterprise *(CVAN 65) with her combat aircraft aligned on the flight deck.*

Admiral Thomas H. Moorer, top left, President Lyndon B. Johnson, and Secretary of Defense Robert S. McNamara on board the Navy's first nuclear-powered carrier.

During the latter years of the Vietnam War, the Soviet Pacific Fleet increasingly deployed strong naval units into the distant Indian Ocean in support of the USSR's activities in the Horn of Africa, the Arabian Gulf, and South Asia. The number of days spent by individual Soviet warships in the Indian Ocean increased from 1,200 in 1968 to 11,800 in 1980. In 1983 the helicopter carrier *Minsk* made a port visit to Bombay, India.

Soviet involvement in the Indo-Pakistan War of 1971 directly challenged America's commitment to Pakistan and the Seventh Fleet's once preeminent status in the Indian Ocean. The war broke out when armed independence groups in East Pakistan (today's nation of Bangladesh) rebelled against the government located in West Pakistan (today's Pakistan). India came to the assistance of the rebels, its armed forces crushing the government forces in the east.

President Richard Nixon and Secretary of State Henry Kissinger called for UN-sponsored cease-fires, but the Soviet Union twice vetoed these UN measures. To show its strong support for India, Moscow ordered a destroyer and a minesweeper transiting the Strait of Malacca to reinforce two similar ships already on station in the Indian Ocean. Then, on 6 December 1971, the Soviet Pacific Fleet sent from Vladivostok a task group comprising a missile cruiser and two other warships. On the 16th the Soviets dispatched from Vladivostok a second task group consisting of a missile cruiser, missile destroyer, and two other combatants.

Nixon and Kissinger expressed concern that if the war continued, Indian armed forces would attack West Pakistan and activate a U.S. commitment to defend the Southeast Asia Treaty Organization ally. With American forces still fully engaged in the Vietnam War, the United States could not take on another major conflict. Nixon and Kissinger thought that if the United States did nothing in response to Soviet moves, its inaction would jeopardize the diplomatic effort underway to end more than twenty years of enmity between the United States and the People's Republic of China. In short, they believed American credibility was on

Enterprise on Yankee Station *by R. G. Smith. Oil on canvas, 1968.*

Admiral Elmo R. Zumwalt Jr., Chief of Naval Operations from 1970 to 1974.

the line with Pakistan, China, the Soviet Union, and other countries watching the crisis unfold.

To create a better balance of forces in the region, on 9 December Washington ordered the Pacific Command to dispatch a Seventh Fleet task group centered on the carrier *Enterprise* from the Gulf of Tonkin to waters off East Pakistan in the Bay of Bengal. Steaming with *Enterprise* as part of Task Group 74 during late December and early January 1972 were the amphibious assault ship *Tripoli* (LPH 10), a submarine, ten destroyer types, and five logistic support vessels.

The ostensible and publicly given reason for the deployment: oversee the evacuation of Americans from the war-torn region. But the real reason was to mount a show of force, since there would be no American citizens there by the time the task group arrived. Of relevance, Washington told the commander of Task Group 74 to proceed through the Strait of Malacca during daylight "in full view of the world." U.S. leaders approved a recommendation from Admiral Zumwalt, Chief of Naval Operations, to deploy the task group southeast of the island of Ceylon instead of to a more vulnerable position in the northern Bay of Bengal. Soon afterward, on the 16th, Pakistani forces in East Pakistan surrendered, and the next day India established a unilateral cease-fire throughout the war zone. Washington understood that since India did not intend to conquer all of Pakistan, the crisis was over.

The two Soviet task forces reached the Indian Ocean only on the 18th and 24th of December, but the U.S.-Soviet competition continued. Zumwalt related that even in January 1972, the "American and Russian ships circled around each other warily, much as their counterparts had been doing in the Mediterranean for years." Zumwalt's comment that "the American ships were put at a disadvantage," with the concentration of Soviet naval forces in the Indian Ocean covered by warplanes in Yemen, showed significant concern. The United States returned its warships to the fight off Vietnam, but the Soviet Union solidified its connection both to India and the new country of Bangladesh, providing India with weapons and other war materials and clearing mines from the Bay of Bengal.

The island of Diego Garcia in the Indian Ocean.

Diego Garcia

Washington eased some of the Seventh Fleet's problems from operational stretch when the United States and the United Kingdom agreed to develop a jointly run naval base on the island of Diego Garcia in the Indian Ocean. With the logistic facilities at Subic Bay in the Philippines some 3,550 miles away, Diego Garcia would be vital to fleet operations in the Indian Ocean, North Arabian Sea, and Arabian Gulf. American and British officials signed an executive agreement on 30 December 1966 establishing joint administration of the military facilities to be built there. The withdrawal of the Royal Navy from "east of Suez" in 1971, however, made it clear that the United States would bear the cost of base development, and the Seventh Fleet, the responsibility for controlling the Indian Ocean. Backed by $53 million from Congress, between 1970 and 1974 Seventh Fleet Seabees built communications facilities, shops, quarters, and warehouses; lengthened the existing airfield to handle P-3 Orion patrol planes and Air Force long-range bombers; and dredged the lagoon to accommodate warships as large as an aircraft carrier. In 1976 London agreed to the expansion of the naval facilities on the island, and the following year Washington established the U.S. Naval Support Facility, Diego Garcia.

Diego Garcia took on added importance in 1979 with the overthrow of the Iranian government by a radical, anti-American revolutionary movement and the massive Soviet invasion of Afghanistan. By 1980, 25 Seventh Fleet warships operated in the Indian Ocean securing the vital sea lines of communication between the oil-rich Middle East and the waters of the Western Pacific. Diego Garcia kept these naval vessels refueled and resupplied. Washington also deployed to the site four ships of Maritime Prepositioning Squadron 2, which contained equipment and 30 days' worth of supplies for a Marine expeditionary brigade of 16,500 men. The Army, Air Force, Navy, and Defense Logistics Agency stowed material in 11 other prepositioning ships at Diego Garcia.

The Soviet invasion of Afghanistan in 1979 had a maritime dimension. As a deterrent to a possible U.S. military reaction, the Soviet Pacific Fleet deployed amphibious ships and naval infantry to the Red Sea and executed combined exercises with the naval forces of Yemen on Socotra Island in the Indian Ocean. The Soviet Union also established an air and naval base at Berbera in Somalia.

Forward Basing of Seventh Fleet Ships

With the decline of non-Vietnam-related Navy budgets during and after the war, the Navy looked for ways to cut costs but maintain the combat readiness of its operational forces. In the early 1970s Washington considered reducing the fleet from 15 carriers to 12. At the same time, however, the Seventh Fleet's responsibilities were increasing with deployments to East Asia and as far away as the Indian Ocean. One proposal: maintain ships and crews at forward bases rather than periodically return them to the United States for repair and overhaul and the reunion of Sailors and their families. There would be no need for the latter if families lived close to the Sailors overseas. Because of the vast distances between the U.S. West Coast and the Far East, Navy planners considered Seventh Fleet ships as likely candidates for forward-basing in Japan.

The Japanese government and populace reacted positively to the proposal. Japanese political leaders, foreign policy officials, and military leaders believed that a U.S. aircraft carrier stationed in Japan would strengthen the Mutual Security Treaty and reverse a widespread public perception that the United States would not risk war for Japan. The Japan Maritime Self-Defense Force, hoping to benefit from a closer USN–JMSDF connection, enthusiastically endorsed the concept as did Yokosuka politicians anticipating an economic boon to their district. Another plus, the U.S. offered to share the base's dry docks and other facilities with commercial interests. In 1972 Prime Minister Kakuei Tanaka had word passed to U.S. diplomatic officials that Japan supported the forward-basing of a carrier at Yokosuka. Tokyo's predictions that domestic opposition to the deployment would be minimal proved accurate. *Midway* task groups, which included Destroyer Squadron 15, operated out of Yokosuka from October 1973 to August 1991.

The base at Sasebo on the island of Kyushu eventually gained amphibious and mine warfare squadrons after having lost some U.S. Navy business in the immediate post-Vietnam years. The citizens of Sasebo demonstrated their friendship with America in July 1976 when thousands of local residents poured through the gates to help celebrate the U.S. Bicentennial. The forward-basing of Seventh Fleet ships brought economic prosperity to Yokosuka and Sasebo, reaffirmed to the Japanese people the strength of the Mutual Security Treaty, and improved the operational readiness and mobility of the fleet.

A New Power Equation

Moscow supplanted Beijing as North Vietnam's chief sponsor in the last years of the war and in November 1978 concluded a mutual security agreement with Hanoi. During a short war between the People's Republic of China and the Socialist Republic of Vietnam in 1979, the USSR supported the Vietnamese by deploying naval forces off China's coasts. One battle group, headed by a guided missile cruiser, operated in the East China Sea, and another battle group steamed in the South China Sea. Beijing expressed particular concern about the Soviet naval menace to China's Hainan and Paracel islands.

In 1984, when Chinese and Vietnamese forces again clashed briefly on their mutual border, the Soviet Pacific Fleet and naval units of Vietnam executed a joint amphibious exercise off Danang involving the Soviet helicopter carrier *Minsk*, the amphibious ship *Ivan Rogov*, six other ships, combat aircraft, and naval infantry. In the words of historian Alexey Muraviev, "the significance of this exercise lay not just in the fact that it was the Soviet navy's first amphibious exercise in the South China Sea or that it highlighted the extent to which Soviet-Vietnamese military solidarity had evolved during the early 1980s. More important was its timing; it was staged during the heaviest fighting since 1979 along the Sino-Vietnamese border." In addition, the USSR provided the Vietnamese navy with corvettes, fast attack boats, and antisubmarine aircraft.

At the invitation of Vietnam, Soviet warships and aviation units operated from the American-built base at Cam Ranh Bay. For the first time since the turnover of Lushun (Port Arthur) to China right after the Korean War, Soviet naval forces could now operate from a base on China's maritime flank.

The USSR had become so powerful and menacing that its former ally, the People's Republic of China, sought foreign help. In 1969 Soviet and Chinese troops had fought pitched battles along the Ussuri River border between these two huge countries. The PRC's Mao Zedong then and later feared that the Soviet Union planned to attack his nation, perhaps with nuclear weapons. The Chinese also feared that the Soviet navy would destroy China's large merchant fleet as well as launch amphibious assaults on Manchuria and other northern territories.

To gain support from another anti-Soviet world power, Mao hosted visits to China by U.S. Presidents Nixon and Ford. To facilitate a closer relationship, the United States recognized the PRC as the sole government of China. Washington ended the Seventh Fleet's 22-year Taiwan Strait Patrol that had defended the people on Taiwan against a Communist invasion. At the same time the United States made clear to Beijing that it would not tolerate the use of force by the PRC to recover Taiwan. On 1 January 1979, two months after the USSR and the Socialist Republic of Vietnam signed their security agreement, the United States and the PRC established diplomatic relations.

The U.S.-PRC rapprochement continued under Mao's successor, Deng Xiaoping, during the 1980s. President Ronald Reagan visited China in 1984, which prompted the visit to Washington in June 1985 of PRC Minister of Defense Zhang Aiping to discuss military cooperation. One year after Secretary of the Navy John Lehman's 1984 trip to the PRC, his Chinese counterpart Liu Huaqing traveled to the United States.

Going beyond reciprocal visits, in the mid-1980s the United States approved commercial sales to China that included Sikorsky transport helicopters (unarmed versions of the UH-60 Black Hawk), General Electric gas turbine engines for new Chinese destroyers, and Mark 46 antisubmarine torpedoes (later cancelled).

In 1983 and 1984 Chinese Communist Party General Hu Yaobang and Japanese Prime Minister Yasuhiro Nakasone exchanged visits. By the mid-1980s Japan, only a few years before China's most bitter enemy, had become its largest trading partner. During Hu's visit, he indicated support for Japan's military buildup and close defense relationship with the United States. Indeed, analyst Kenneth Weiss concluded that the United States was the "'glue' in a (very) loose anti-Soviet grouping in the Pacific that includes Japan, China, South Korea, the ASEAN, and ANZUS nations."

Seventh Fleet Operational Concerns

In addition to menacing China, the Soviet navy's presence at Cam Ranh Bay posed an operational problem for the Seventh Fleet. From the excellent, American-built port, the Soviets could stretch U.S. maritime resources in the entire Pacific and threaten the Seventh Fleet's large naval and air facilities around Subic Bay. By the mid-1980s, 20 to 30 Soviet surface ships; 3 to 5 submarines; fighters, attack planes, and special mission aircraft; and naval

Ready for Action

The Navy service of *Midway* (CVA 41, CV 41 after 30 June 1975), the lead carrier in her class, spanned the Cold War era. *Midway* made her Seventh Fleet debut during the Taiwan Strait Crisis of 1954–1955, during which her air wing provided cover for the evacuation of Chinese Nationalist troops and civilians from the Dachen Islands off China. Following modernization with the addition of an aft deck-edge elevator, angled flight deck, steam catapults, and an enclosed bow, the carrier operated in the South China Sea during the Laos crises of the early 1960s.

Midway *operating in the Western Pacific in 1964 on the eve of the Vietnam War.*

Midway steamed at Yankee Station in the Gulf of Tonkin during the spring of 1965 when Seventh Fleet and U.S. Air Force units inaugurated the three-year Rolling Thunder bombing campaign against North Vietnam. *Midway* aircraft were among the first carrier units to strike targets in South Vietnam when they bombed a Viet Cong base near Nui Ba Den ("Black Virgin Mountain") northwest of Saigon in April. And naval aviators from the ship's Carrier Air Wing 2 registered the first air-to-air victories of the war when they downed four MiG-17s in June.

After further modernization in the states, *Midway* returned to fight in Southeast Asia during 1971 and 1972, taking part in the Linebacker I and II operations that stymied North Vietnam's Easter Offensive in South Vietnam and helped bring about an end to the war. Marine and U.S. Air Force helicopters embarked in *Midway* were among those in Operation Frequent Wind that rescued Americans and Vietnamese fleeing the Communist conquest of South Vietnam in April 1975.

Even as *Midway*'s operations in Southeast Asia were coming to a close, developments in other Asian waters demanded her attention. After an agreement between the U.S. and Japanese governments, in October 1973 *Midway* became the first carrier forward-deployed to an overseas base. For the next 18 years the ship and her escorts, as well as their Sailors and families, called Yokosuka, Japan, home. Proximity to likely trouble spots enabled *Midway* to mount a show of force in August 1976 when North Korean soldiers in the Demilitarized Zone brutally murdered two U.S. Army officers. Aggressive Iranian and Soviet actions increasingly drew *Midway* to the Indian Ocean and North Arabian Sea during the late 1970s and 1980s.

Midway *steaming in the Arabian Sea in 1991 shortly after participating in the defeat of Saddam Hussein's armed forces in Operation Desert Storm.*

Along with the flagship *Blue Ridge* (LCC 19) and other Seventh Fleet ships and units, *Midway* deployed to the Arabian Gulf in 1990–1991 to counter Iraqi leader Saddam Hussein's aggression against Kuwait. As part of Battle Force Zulu, *Midway* launched bombing strikes against targets in Iraq and Kuwait. In March 1991, following the Gulf War victory, the battle-tested carrier returned to Japan. That fall *Independence* (CV 62) relieved *Midway* as the Yokosuka-based carrier; the Navy decommissioned *Midway* in April 1992, thus closing her illustrious career with the Seventh Fleet.

infantry operated from the Cam Ranh base, which had also become a "vast storage area" for weapons and equipment. As U.S. Pacific Fleet commander Admiral James A. "Ace" Lyons observed, in the ten years after the Vietnam War the Cam Ranh base had quadrupled in size. He intimated that this military presence in Vietnam put the Soviets "astride the key lines of communication in the South China Sea, in the Strait of Malacca, and the Eastern Indian Ocean." He noted that if the U.S. Navy did nothing to counter this presence, it would be akin to "turning over our friends and allies to Soviet political and military intimidation and eventual domination."

Naval forces from both the USSR and the Socialist Republic of Vietnam posed a threat to Seventh Fleet ships. In June 1982 a naval vessel believed to be Vietnamese fired a machine gun round that pierced the wardroom bulkhead of destroyer *Turner Joy* operating in the South China Sea with guided missile cruiser *Sterett* and guided missile destroyer *Lynde McCormick* (DDG 8). When *Lynde McCormick* closed with the perpetrator of the attack, she too came under fire, prompting return warning shots that persuaded the Vietnamese unit to desist.

While coping with the growing Soviet and Vietnamese naval presence in the South China Sea, the Seventh Fleet carried out other responsibilities, including the rescue of people in distress on the open ocean. In the early 1980s tens of thousands of refugees, the so-called "boat people," fled from economic deprivation and political persecution in Vietnam by taking to the sea in crowded, often unseaworthy junks and fishing boats. In just a

After surviving many grueling days at sea, Vietnamese "boat people" fleeing harsh Communist rule in Indochina prepare to board Seventh Fleet flagship Blue Ridge *for eventual resettlement somewhere in Asia.*

five-day period during May 1982, for instance, the U.S. guided missile cruiser *Fox* (CG 33) and frigates *Brewton* (FF 1086) and *Ouellet* (FF 1077) rescued 378 Vietnamese refugees.

The USSR also strengthened its military forces in the land and sea approaches to Japan. In 1968 the Soviets enlarged their naval infantry force in the Far East from regimental to divisional size. In 1978, to put pressure on Japan, for the first time the Soviets fortified and positioned troops on the southern Kurile Islands (referred to as the Northern Territories by Japan) seized at the end of World War II. The following year Moscow deployed the antisubmarine carrier *Minsk*, the large amphibious ship *Ivan Rogov*, and advanced antiship Backfire bombers to Vladivostok. In 1982 the fleet carried out a large-scale nighttime exercise in the Soviet Far East with amphibious ships and naval infantry units employing night vision devices. Soviet naval forces held live-fire exercises in the Sea of Japan/East Sea, and Backfire bombers practiced mock attacks on Seventh Fleet units. The Soviet Pacific Fleet conducted submarine and antisubmarine warfare exercises in the broad expanse of the Pacific Ocean. The exercises showed the Soviet Pacific Fleet's greater capability for open-ocean operations far from the Russian heartland.

The heightened menace from Soviet military forces in the Far East took concrete form in September 1983 when a Soviet SU-15 Flagon fighter shot down a Korean Air Lines 747 jumbo jet near Sakhalin Island, killing all 269 passengers and crew on board, including a U.S. congressman. Soviet aircraft and naval vessels used aircraft "buzzings" and aggressive ship maneuvers to impede the salvage operation by Japanese and U.S.

Soviet antisubmarine carrier Kiev *during the early 1980s.*

A Sovremenny-*class guided missile destroyer in the port of Vladivostok.*

The buildup in the Far East of Soviet military forces, including these naval infantrymen armed with Kalashnikov AK-47s, concerned U.S. naval leaders.

units dispatched to the scene. In one instance, a Soviet ship closed to within 30 feet of the *Sterett*'s stern and only turned away at the last minute to avoid a collision.

The Soviet Pacific Fleet increasingly operated in waters near Japan and South Korea. During the spring of 1985 a carrier battle group consisting of helicopter carrier *Novorossiysk*, four cruisers, two frigates, and two logistics ships exercised near Okinawa and points north in the Sea of Japan/East Sea. The following year carriers *Minsk* and *Kiev*, a dozen other surface ships, and 16 submarines took part in a major exercise near the Kuriles. Throughout the 1980s Soviet combat aircraft intruded into the air defense zones of Japan and even approached Alaskan air space. Vice Admiral David Jeremiah, Commander Seventh Fleet, commented in 1987 that there had been "more aggressive air activity [and] a much more aggressive posture in air defense" than the year before.

Between 1976 and 1986 the Soviet Pacific Fleet increased from 775 to 840 naval vessels, including 120 attack and missile-launching submarines and 85 cruisers and other major surface combatants. By 1984 almost half of the naval vessels in the Soviet navy operated in the Pacific. According to Muraviev, by 1985 the Soviet Pacific Fleet "was possibly the strongest of the four Soviet naval fleets" that enabled the Soviet Union "to engage confidently in the Cold War strategic naval confrontation." Admiral Lyons observed that by the mid-1980s, the Soviet Pacific Fleet operated 500 warships and submarines, including the advanced *Kirov* nuclear-powered cruiser, *Sovremenny* and *Udaloy*-class guided missile destroyers, and *Akula*-class attack submarines. One thousand six hundred Soviet aircraft and one-third of the USSR's intermediate-range ballistic missile force operated in the Far East. By the mid-1980s Soviet military strength in Northeast Asia was formidable.

The Japan Maritime Self-Defense Force Fills the Breech

On top of reductions in U.S. fleet strength in the wake of Vietnam, developments in the Middle East in 1979 put additional strain on Seventh Fleet resources. At a time of troubling growth in Soviet Far Eastern military and naval capability, and other regional concerns, the Seventh Fleet had to divert a significant portion of its strength to operations in the Indian Ocean and the Arabian Gulf, thousands of miles from the bases in Japan and the Philippines. Indeed, by 1979 the Joint Chiefs of Staff had expanded the Seventh Fleet's area of operational responsibility to include the entire Indian Ocean.

In the late 1970s the administration of President Jimmy Carter considered a "swing strategy" that would remove Seventh Fleet forces from the Pacific in the advent of a major war. Admiral Zumwalt, the former Chief of Naval Operations, observed in his post-retirement memoir *On Watch* that in much of the Indian Ocean and the Pacific, the United States had no "relevant power."

The United States did take an approach during and after the Vietnam War to redress this security imbalance, calling on Asian allies to increase their share of the military burden in the Far East. On Guam, in July 1969 President Nixon announced that henceforth the United States would provide military support to allies but expected them to take on the primary responsibility for their own defense. Key noncommunist Far Eastern nations, especially Japan, increased their contribution to joint defensive efforts. Thanks to the security shield provided by the Seventh Fleet since 1945, Japan, South Korea, and Taiwan were now much better prepared to share strategic responsibilities and provide their own military resources. Their market-oriented economies had prospered even as those of the Communist states fell apart. Historian Michael Howard has cogently observed that by the 1980s, capitalism was "transforming global society in a manner that made Marxist-Leninist regimes look like dinosaurs surviving in a kind of Jurassic Park; dinosauric in their size, their ferocity, their inability to adapt themselves and, not least, their tiny brains."

In November 1978 U.S. and Japanese officials developed "Guidelines for Japan–United States Defense Cooperation." The guidelines provided for combined operations planning and exercises. It is perhaps overstated, but according to Japanese analyst Tetsuo Maeda, the guidelines "implemented the security treaty as though it were a two-nation version of NATO." In May 1981 Prime Minister Zenko Suzuki visited Washington and announced that "since the United States Seventh Fleet is in charge of security in the Indian Ocean and the Arabian Gulf, it cannot be in the environs of Japan." Suzuki pledged that his country's naval and air forces would defend the area around Japan out to several hundred miles and the sea lanes out to 1,000 nautical miles.

Reaffirming Maritime Supremacy in the Pacific

In the last years of the Cold War, leaders of the U.S. Navy were determined to counter aggressive Soviet naval activity around the globe, especially in the Western Pacific. A new Maritime Strategy guided this effort. It emphasized the forward deployment of powerful U.S. naval forces, in conjunction with the other armed forces, on what U.S. naval leaders considered the vulnerable maritime flanks of the Soviet Union. The concept assigned that mission in Northeast Asia to the Seventh Fleet. The Navy also took action to ensure a nearly continuous presence of fully capable carriers in the waters of the northern Pacific. In the Global Naval Force Presence Policy, the service staggered or delayed maintenance and training cycles for those carriers not deployed forward.

The naval leader who inspired the global Maritime Strategy first explored the concept while considering the power balance in the northern Pacific. Admiral Thomas B. Hayward, Commander Seventh Fleet, and then Commander in Chief, Pacific Fleet from 1975 to 1978, advocated a

President Nguyen Van Thieu of the Republic of Vietnam and President Richard M. Nixon of the United States meet on Guam in July 1969. At that time, Nixon announced a new U.S. policy of encouraging regional allies to assume greater responsibility for ground combat.

new approach for dealing with Soviet power. He concluded that plans by the Carter administration to concentrate U.S. military power in Europe and the Atlantic in the event of a war with the Soviet Union would surrender the Pacific to the enemy and compromise America's Asian alliances. Japan and other Asian allies were concerned that Washington might "sacrifice the East to save the West." Hayward affirmed that an offensive-minded strategy in the Pacific would better serve U.S. and allied interests. It was not lost on Hayward or other strategists that Japan's failure to attack the USSR's Far Eastern flank in World War II enabled the Soviets to concentrate forces in front of Moscow and then defeat Hitler's invading legions. The insightful flag officer also recognized that a proactive strategy would help rebuild the Navy and bolster the morale of America's Sailors after the debilitating Vietnam experience. Such an approach would also reassure Japan and South Korea about U.S. treaty commitments to their defense.

Hayward based his concept on an understanding that the Soviet navy, then operating throughout the Western Pacific and in waters as distant as the Indian Ocean, depended on Vladivostok and Petropavlovsk and a few other vulnerable naval bases on the USSR's remote North Pacific coast for logistic support. He proposed that in the event of war, the U.S. Navy destroy the bases and defenses on the Kamchatka Peninsula. He also reasoned that the

Admiral Thomas B. Hayward, Chief of Naval Operations from July 1978 to June 1982, inspired development of what became known as the Navy's Maritime Strategy. Hayward stressed dealing with the Soviet threat in Asia because of the Pacific Ocean's importance to America and the U.S. commitment to its Asian allies.

U.S. threat to the Soviet Far East would compel the Russian fleet to withdraw from the broad Pacific and concentrate for defense in Northeast Asia. Studies at the Naval War College bolstered this appraisal. Hayward championed the concept that under his successor, Admiral James B. Watkins, became the new global Maritime Strategy.

In March 1984 Secretary of the Navy John Lehman stated that one tactical objective of Pacific naval operations in the event of war with the Soviet Union would be to "catch the Backfires [Soviet antiship bombers] on the ground." Admiral Watkins elaborated on this topic that same year when he observed: "In the Northwest Pacific . . . if we are swift enough on our feet we would move rapidly into an attack on Alekseyevka [Backfire base on the Kamchatka Peninsula]. We might put a carrier strike in there along with the Air Force. We know how to do that. . . . We tested our ability with the Air Force to coordinate strikes at Petropavlovsk or Alekseyevka."

But U.S. naval leaders did not see warfighting readiness as the only good reason for deploying Seventh Fleet and other forces into the Soviet Union's "back yard." They also wanted to make abundantly clear, through shows of force and capability, the maritime advantage that would be enjoyed by the United States and its Asian allies in any conflict; that a display of strength stood the best chance of preventing war. In 1986 Admiral Lyons commented that if the Soviets take "that message back [of U.S. and allied military strength in the region], which is one we want him to take back, we've raised deterrence without firing a shot." Naval leaders also wanted to acquire critical intelligence of the best warships, aircraft, weapons, and equipment in the Soviet arsenal by stimulating a response to U.S. operations close to their most vital bases.

Seventh Fleet Buildup

Operating close to the Pacific coast of the Soviet Union would not have been possible if the Seventh Fleet had not been strengthened during the late 1970s and early 1980s with advanced ships, aircraft, and weapons systems. The Navy armed the fleet with Tomahawk land attack missiles (TLAMs) able to carry nuclear or conventional warheads. The cruise missiles enabled fleet submarines and surface ships to eliminate Soviet command posts and radar installations prior to an attack by carrier planes. Harpoon antiship missiles enhanced the surface fleet's ability to take out opposing warships. Also introduced to the fleet were advanced versions of the all-weather, day-night A-6 Intruder attack plane, the F/A-18 Hornet strike fighter, and the EA-6B Prowler electronic countermeasures plane. The Prowler could jam enemy communications and fire high-speed anti-radiation missiles (HARMs) to destroy enemy radars and missile batteries.

Since the Maritime Strategy anticipated amphibious operations on the USSR's flanks, the Navy recommissioned the four *Iowa*-class battleships,

Chief of Naval Operations Admiral James Watkins, along with Secretary of the Navy John Lehman, were the driving forces behind the Reagan administration's support for the Maritime Strategy and a larger, "600-ship Navy."

with their 16-inch naval guns, and armed them with the new Tomahawk cruise missiles. The new *Whidbey Island* (LSD 41) and *Wasp* (LHD 1) classes of amphibious ships and landing craft air cushion (LCAC) strengthened the fleet.

Operating in waters close to the USSR, however, meant that task force defenses had to be strong and far-seeing. The Navy introduced to the fleet advanced shipboard radars and E-2C Hawkeye early-warning aircraft that could discover enemy aircraft and missiles at great distances. Once these systems spotted hostile approaching aircraft it was critical to destroy them before they could launch their antiship missiles, or in the words of Admiral Watkins, "shoot the archer before he releases his arrows." F-14 Tomcat air superiority fighters armed with

DN-ST-9109302

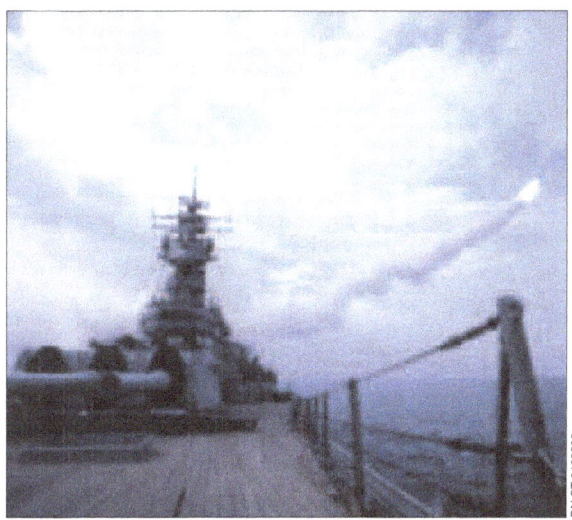

World War II-era battleships armed with Tomahawk land attack missiles strengthened the Seventh Fleet during the late Cold War.

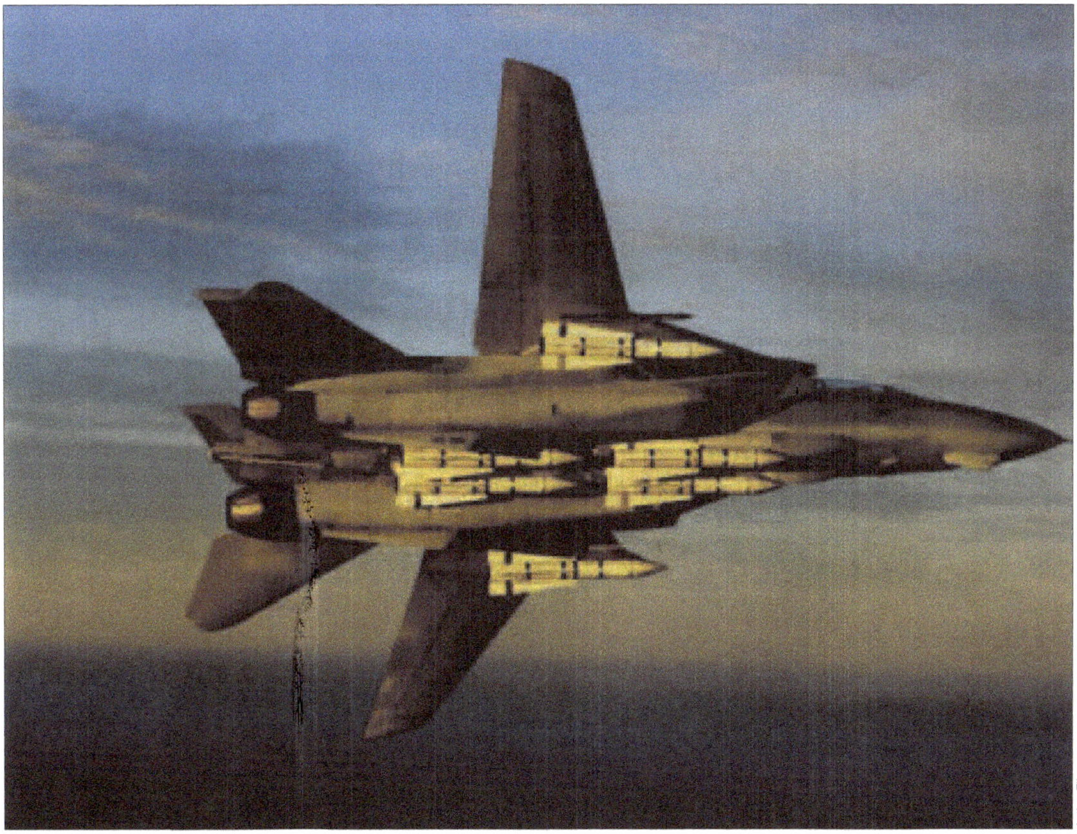
Author File

An F-14 Tomcat fighter loaded with long-range AIM-54 Phoenix air-to-air missiles.

Los Angeles *(SSN 688), the lead ship of a formidable class of nuclear-powered attack submarines, proceeds through waters off Guam.*

An advanced Harpoon surface-to-surface missile fired from just below the ship's Phalanx close-in weapon system.

new AIM-54C Phoenix air-to-air missiles prepared the fleet to destroy multiple attackers hundreds of miles away. Guided missile cruisers of the *Ticonderoga* (CG 47) class equipped with the revolutionary Aegis battle management system, destroyers, and frigates formed the next line of defense. Surviving attackers would then face the ship-mounted Phalanx close-in weapon system (CIWS) that fired 3,000 depleted uranium rounds per minute.

One of the Seventh Fleet's greatest concerns was the Soviet Union's large and capable attack and ballistic missile submarine force operating from the Kamchatka Peninsula. To cope with the threat, the Navy deployed to the Pacific a succession of large, stealthy *Los Angeles* (SSN 688)-class attack submarines that came off the building ways in the late 1970s. The Navy Department also added to its Far East fleet *Spruance* (DD 963)-class destroyers and *Oliver Hazard Perry* (FFG 7)-class frigates embarking SH-60B Seahawk Light Airborne Multipurpose System, or LAMPS, helicopters. These rotary-wing aircraft boasted search radars, underwater sonobuoys, and torpedoes. With an even more sophisticated suite of detection and data processing equipment, the fixed-wing S-3 Viking could be armed with Harpoon antiship missiles, bombs, mines, and torpedoes.

Guided by the Maritime Strategy, bolstered by Secretary Lehman's "600-ship" navy, and armed with a lethal array of new weapons and equipment, the Seventh Fleet made its presence known in Northeast Asia during the last years of the Cold War.

Assertive Seventh Fleet Operations

As the Navy Department refined the Maritime Strategy in Washington, Pacific Fleet commanders began using Seventh Fleet operations, naval exercises, and "freedom of navigation" (FON) ship cruises to gauge how the Soviets would react to an

Underway Replenishment *by Walter Brightwell. Oil on canvas.*

increased allied naval presence in Northeast Asia. During May 1981 Seventh Fleet and JMSDF units for the first time in ten years conducted a naval exercise in the Sea of Japan/East Sea. At the same time a task group composed of *Wadell* (DDG 24), *Richard S. Edwards* (DDG 950), *Harry W. Hill* (DD 986), and USNS *Mispillion* carried out a two-day FON mission in the Sea of Okhotsk to "demonstrate freedom of the seas in this area." That September the guided missile cruiser *William H. Standley* (CG 32) and frigate *Lockwood* observed the naval activity off the Soviet submarine base at Petropavlovsk.

If the Soviets were unsure that the U.S. had inaugurated a new operational approach in the Asia-Pacific region during 1981, they would have no doubt the following year when U.S. attack submarines began operating in the Sea of Okhotsk. In February *Coral Sea* and 13 other naval vessels conducted a large-scale exercise in the Sea of Japan/East Sea. Several months later *Lockwood* again operated near Petropavlovsk in what the U.S. considered international waters, but which the Soviets contended were their territorial waters. Soviet ships and planes harassed the frigate and communicated that the U.S. naval vessel should depart the area. That autumn, in the largest concentration of U.S. naval vessels off Alaska since World War II, the *Enterprise* and *Midway* carrier battle groups conducted flight operations 450 miles east of Kamchatka. At the end of the year, in another Cold War first, U.S. Navy and Marine and Canadian forces practiced amphibious assaults on Amchitka in the western Aleutian Islands in Exercise Kernal Potlatch.

To ensure that not only Soviet but North Korean leaders recognized the combat power and capability of the allied forces facing them in Northeast Asia, in 1983, 190,000 U.S. and South Korean military forces conducted the annual Team Spirit exercise on the Korean peninsula and offshore. Units under the operational control of Commander Seventh Fleet included the *Midway* and *Enterprise* battle groups.

In March and April these carriers plus *Coral Sea* and 39 other U.S. combatants exercised near the Aleutians in FleetEx 83. Naval leaders wanted to reaffirm the fleet's presence in the region and see how the Soviets reacted to it. Commander in Chief, Pacific Fleet Admiral Sylvester R. Foley observed, "I'm sure we surprised the Soviets once again, sending them a message that our deployments are not going to be easily predicted."

The Seventh Fleet kept just as busy in 1984. In May frigate *Lockwood* patrolled close to Soviet territory in the Sea of Japan/East Sea. During the last months of the year U.S. and Japanese naval and marine forces conducted amphibious training on Hokkaido, Japan's large northern island close to Soviet-held territory; the U.S. Navy and the JMSDF conducted a large exercise near Okinawa; the *Midway* and *Carl Vinson* battle groups operated within 50 miles of Vladivostok in the Sea of Japan/East Sea; and cruiser *Sterett* and destroyer *John Young* (DD 973) entered the Sea of Okhotsk on a FON mission.

Starting in February 1985, more than 200,000 American and Korean sea, air, and ground troops took part in the annual Team Spirit 85 exercise, during which the Navy's Military Sealift Command deployed a brigade of the U.S. Army's 7th Infantry Division to South Korea. In 1986 U.S. naval forces began conducting more frequent operations and exercises in the North Pacific and other waters near the Soviet Far East. In the first half of the year frigates *Kirk* and *Francis Hammond* (FF 1067) steamed in proximity to Vladivostok.

To determine if a carrier task force could operate without being detected near the Soviet Union—a key factor of the Maritime Strategy—in May the *Ranger* (CV 61) battle group made the transit from San Diego to the Western Pacific under a condition of EMCON (emissions control). The Soviets lost track of the battle group when every ship in the formation ceased electronic transmissions. In August and September the carrier *Carl Vinson* (CVN 70) steamed for nine days through Japanese waters, the North Pacific, the Bering Sea, the Sea of Okhotsk, and the Sea of Japan/East Sea apparently without being detected by the Soviets.

Ranger *(CV 61)* sorties from San Diego, California, in February 1987. The year before, the carrier steamed from the United States to Northeast Asia without communicating to keep the Soviets in the dark about her whereabouts.

For the first time in the Cold War, a battleship, *New Jersey*, accompanied by guided missile cruisers *Vincennes* (CG 49) and *Long Beach* (CGN 9), entered the Sea of Okhotsk and operated between Kamchatka and the Soviet island of Sakhalin. While under close observation by Soviet air and surface units, the battleship's commanding officer, Captain W. Lewis Glenn Jr., slowed the ship to 20 knots and carried out a routine underway refueling of *Vincennes*. Immediately afterward, *New Jersey* joined *Ranger* and *Constellation* in the Bering Sea for the Cold War's first two-carrier exercise in those waters. During the last half of 1986, Japanese and U.S. naval forces then carried out extensive exercises off Hokkaido and Honshu. Simultaneously, on the other side of the globe, NATO navies carried out Northern Wedding, one of the largest exercises of the Cold War. The U.S. Navy and its naval allies thoroughly tested the global viability of the Maritime Strategy.

In November 1986 Admiral Lyons, the hard-charging Pacific Fleet commander, tasked his Third Fleet with directing North Pacific operations. From 1987 to 1989 Marine and Navy units returned to the frigid waters and barren islands of the Aleutians and Bering Sea to test their ability to operate in these harsh environs. On a number of occasions, Navy F-14s operating out of Adak in the Aleutians intercepted Soviet patrol planes in the Bering Sea and escorted them away from surface units. In Operation Shooting Star, A-6E Intruder attack planes on two dozen occasions flew directly toward the Kamchatka Peninsula and turned away only when they were 100 miles from the Soviet Pacific Fleet base at Petropavlovsk. By the end of the 1980s the Navy had accomplished a critical goal of the Maritime Strategy: compel the Soviet navy to withdraw from Asian-Pacific waters and concentrate for defense in the Sea of Japan/East Sea and Sea of Okhotsk.

Furthering U.S. Alliances and Overseas Interests

The execution of the forward strategy also achieved the Navy's goal of improving allied cooperation and stimulating a buildup of their naval resources. At the beginning of the 1980s U.S. naval leaders had expressed concern that the Japanese were not sufficiently alarmed about the growth of Soviet military power in Northeast Asia and consequently were not devoting enough of their own resources to meet the threat. In 1981 Commander in Chief, Pacific Admiral Robert L.J. Long informed Secretary of Defense Caspar Weinberger that there needed to be "greater threat awareness in Japan . . . vital for obtaining the force improvements."

By the end of the decade the Japanese had a much clearer appreciation of the threat and had responded accordingly. Japan increased its defense spending by more than 5 percent annually during the 1980s and increasingly joined the U.S. Navy in multinational exercises. The U.S. and Japanese navies became quite adept at combined antisubmarine warfare. The two naval services were especially effective in confining the Soviet navy to the Sea of Japan/East Sea and Sea of Okhotsk. By the end of the Cold War the JMSDF operated 81 technologically advanced warships and submarines, and hundreds of aircraft, and was, in every sense of the term, a blue-water navy. Chairman of the Joint Chiefs of Staff Admiral William J. Crowe Jr. observed in 1986 that the "Japanese Self Defense Force [has] arrived. They are good and they know it."

In line with its own economic "miracle," during the 1980s the Republic of Korea strengthened its navy to defend the maritime flanks of the Korean peninsula and to operate with the U.S. and allied navies against potential aggressors. In keeping with U.S. treaty commitments, the Seventh Fleet on many occasions deployed forces near the Korean peninsula to support the Republic of Korea. For instance, the *Midway* and *Nimitz* (CVN 68) battle groups made their presence known in the Sea of Japan/East Sea to discourage any North Korean thoughts of disrupting the 1988 Olympics held in Seoul.

The Soviets recognized the growing cooperation between the U.S. Navy and its Northeast Asian allies. In 1988 Admiral Vladimir Sidorov, the deputy commander in chief of the Soviet navy, observed, "it is significant that the troops of US allies, Japan and South Korea, are increasingly . . . involved in manoeuvres [in the Sea of Japan/East Sea]."

With the assignment of North Pacific duties to the Third Fleet and the growing capability of Japanese and South Korean naval forces, the Seventh Fleet looked to other weighty responsibilities in Asia-Pacific waters and the Indian Ocean. In 1986, 100,000 U.S. and Thai army, navy, and marine forces; 30 ships; and hundreds of aircraft mounted near the Cambodian border Cobra Gold 86, the largest combined exercise since the end of the Vietnam War. That same year U.S. and Philippine naval forces accomplished a 15-day amphibious exercise in the Philippines.

Improving U.S. Relations with Asian Nations

Unlike the previous decades, the Seventh Fleet did not show concern about a military threat from the People's Republic of China in the 1980s. Beijing feared a Soviet invasion of the country, perhaps involving nuclear weapons, and courted American support. Indeed, in January 1986, Seventh Fleet and People's Liberation Army Navy warships steamed together in the Western Pacific. In April, Chief of Naval Operations Admiral Watkins met with PLAN Chief of Staff Admiral Liu Huaqing. That November the guided missile cruiser *Reeves* (GG 24), with Admiral Lyons embarked, and accompanied by destroyer *Oldendorf* (DD 972) and frigate *Rentz* (FFG 46), made an official port call at Qingdao (homeport of the Seventh Fleet in the late 1940s). Lyons later remarked that "the Chinese clearly made every effort to make this visit a success. They made us feel like members of the family." In 1989 the midshipman training ship *Zheng He* (named for the famous 15th-century admiral whose fleet sailed in the South China Sea and the Indian Ocean) became the first PLAN vessel to visit the United States when it made port in Hawaii.

After 1979, when the United States and the People's Republic of China established diplomatic relations, Washington freed the Seventh Fleet of its previous responsibility to defend Taiwan from mainland attack. But the previous 22-year interaction between the United States and Taiwan, in which the Seventh Fleet figured prominently, had well prepared the Chinese on the island to defend themselves. The government on Taiwan exploited the country's considerable economic wealth to domestically produced combat aircraft, tanks, and missiles and purchased more of these weapons systems overseas. By the 1990s the Chinese Nationalist navy operated almost 500 combat aircraft and

Admiral James A. "Ace" Lyons, Commander in Chief, U.S. Pacific Fleet, receives a gift from an officer of the People's Liberation Army Navy at Qingdao in November 1986 during the first visit to China since the late 1940s of Seventh Fleet warships.

During the Seventh Fleet's port call at Qingdao, China, in November 1986, American and Chinese sailors tour a warship of the Chinese navy.

180 naval vessels. Taiwan and the offshore islands still bristled with long-range antiship missiles, antisubmarine aircraft, and integrated air defenses. Harkening back to the earliest days of Taiwan's independence from Chinese Communist control and General Douglas MacArthur's memorable phrase, analyst Gary Klintworth observed that Taiwan was then, "metaphorically speaking, still an unsinkable aircraft carrier."

Much the same occurred in Southeast Asia. With the development of stronger economies and relatively stable political systems during the 1970s, Australia, Malaysia, Singapore, Indonesia, and Thailand supported stronger defense establishments and blue-water flotillas. By the end of the Cold War these noncommunist countries of Southeast Asia boasted 43 surface warships and submarines and more than 500 combat aircraft.

Support for the Philippines Government

As the Seventh Fleet dealt with the Soviet threat in Northeast Asia, it also maintained peace throughout its vast area of responsibility. When a 3,000-man Philippine armed forces group led by Colonel Gregorio Honasan launched a coup against the government of Corazon Aquino on 1 December 1989, the Pacific Command readied U.S. forces for likely contingencies. The rebels attacked military bases around Manila, stormed the capital's financial district, and seized an airfield in Cebu.

Soon after the Aquino government asked for U.S. help, Washington established Joint Task Force (JTF) Philippines under the commanding general of the 13th Air Force headquartered at Clark Air Base northeast of Manila. Under the operational control of Commander JTF Philippines, carriers *Midway* and *Enterprise* entered the Philippine Sea with aircraft on deck-alert and dispatched E-2C Hawkeye aircraft for 24-hour surveillance flights over Manila. Commander Seventh Fleet Vice Admiral Henry H. Mauz Jr. put Navy and Marine units at Subic Bay on alert to execute JTF orders. Marines from the Seventh Fleet's Special Purpose Marine Air-Ground Task Force reinforced the U.S. Embassy in Manila. And two amphibious ready groups prepared to evacuate noncombatants from the troubled capital. To communicate the extent to which the United States would support President Aquino, the joint task force commander had Air Force F-4 Phantom II fighters mount combat air patrols over the bases of the Philippine air force. Convinced that the Aquino government had strong U.S. support, on 6 December the rebels agreed to a cease-fire and life in the Philippines gradually returned to normal.

In summary, the 1970s witnessed the rise of Soviet naval power and influence in the Asia-Pacific region that paralleled a decline in Seventh Fleet strength due to heavy operational commitments off Vietnam and in the Indian Ocean. The United States countered the Soviet threat, however, by establishing closer ties with the People's Republic of China and encouraging America's Asian allies to take on more responsibility for unilateral and multilateral defensive efforts. In the 1980s the United States went over to a full-court press on the USSR's power base in Asia, adopting the Maritime Strategy, strengthening the battle fleet, conducting comprehensive multinational exercises, and deploying U.S. naval forces in waters right off the coast of the Soviet Far East. The end of the Cold War in 1989 found the United States and its naval forces in the Pacific never more powerful, and the Soviet Union only two years away from its ultimate demise.

Chapter 7

FROM THE ARABIAN GULF TO MOUNT PINATUBO

STARTING IN THE 1940s THE SEVENTH FLEET protected U.S. interests in the Western Pacific and later the South China Sea and the Indian Ocean. In the 1990s that responsibility spread to the Arabian Gulf where Commander Seventh Fleet directed the Gulf War and his forces helped liberate Kuwait from the Iraqi dictator Saddam Hussein. Even while engaged in the Middle East, the fleet carried out its humanitarian and disaster relief mission in Bangladesh and the Philippines.

When the armed forces of Iraqi dictator Saddam Hussein invaded the Arabian Gulf sheikdom of Kuwait on 2 August 1990, the call again went out for help from America's distant fighting fleet—the Seventh. On 16 August 1990 the Joint Chiefs of Staff directed the Seventh Fleet commander, Vice Admiral Henry Mauz to take charge of U.S. naval forces even then heading toward the Arabian Gulf to defend Saudi Arabia and America's other friends in the region from Iraqi attack. Washington wanted a three-star flag officer with experience heading a combat fleet to handle maritime matters as Commander, U.S. Naval Forces Central Command (COMUSNAVCENT). Mauz kept his Seventh Fleet hat as well.

One of the Navy's top leaders, "Hank" Mauz graduated from the U.S. Naval Academy in 1959

U.S. Central Command Theater.

Vice Admiral Henry H. Mauz Jr., commander of the U.S. Seventh Fleet and U.S. Naval Forces Central Command, during Operation Desert Shield.

and then served in destroyers *John A. Bole* (DD 755) and *Blue* (DD 744). As a river patrol boat officer in Vietnam with River Squadron 5, he earned a Bronze Star with Combat V. He continued to impress his superiors with his performance in the surface warfare community and in various billets in the Office of the Chief of Naval Operations. After a stint in Supreme Headquarters, Allied Powers Europe, he served on the staff of the Pacific Fleet. As Commander, Battle Force Sixth Fleet in 1986, he planned and executed carrier strikes against Libya in Operation El Dorado Canyon. Mauz took the reins as Commander Seventh Fleet in 1988.

That Washington tapped Commander Seventh Fleet to head naval operations in the Arabian Gulf and surrounding waters reflected the Navy's Cold War mindset that had the battle commander directing major naval forces brought in from either the Pacific or the Mediterranean/Atlantic. Lower-ranking naval officers commanded the small number of ships in the Arabian Gulf, then considered a secondary theater. The Navy had also resisted permanently assigning peacetime forces to Central Command, normally headed by an Army general headquartered in Florida. As a result, Vice Admiral Mauz did not gain the benefits of prewar interaction with General Norman Schwarzkopf, Commander in Chief, U.S. Central Command, and the opportunity to familiarize himself with the general's plans for dealing with Saddam's aggression.

The inadequate Cold War command structure also delayed Mauz from taking on his new duties in the Middle East. The Pacific Command told the admiral to delay his arrival in the Central Command theater until the JCS officially cut an order appointing him COMUSNAVCENT. Mauz spent 14 August, one week after the start of Operation Desert Shield, on Diego Garcia. He flew forward to Bahrain in the Arabian Gulf only on the 15th. He had to exercise his leadership from the command ship *LaSalle* (AGF 3) tied up there because his own flagship, *Blue Ridge*, would not arrive in-theater from Japan until 1 September.

Despite these complications, Mauz acted at Schwarzkopf's direction to coordinate seaborne protection for the maritime prepositioning ships deploying from Diego Garcia and for the U.S. carrier and amphibious groups en route to the operational area. The admiral also established contact with the leaders of the British, Dutch, Canadian, Australian, and other naval forces of the United Nations coalition then forming.

By 1 October Mauz commanded a powerful flotilla that included the *Saratoga* (CV 60), *John F. Kennedy* (CV 67), and *Independence* carrier battle groups, each with an air wing of 75 aircraft and five to seven cruisers and destroyers; the battleship *Wisconsin*; the Sasebo-based amphibious transport dock *Dubuque* (LPD 8); and 17 other amphibious ships loaded with Marine infantry, helicopters, and Harrier vertical/short take-off and landing aircraft. *Midway*, with the guided missile cruiser *Bunker Hill* (CG 52) and destroyers *Oldendorf* and *Fife* (DD 991), sortied from Yokosuka on 2 October.

The admiral immediately concentrated on his most pressing duty, coordinating the embargo—a blockade in all but name—of Iraq's imports and exports. As detailed in United Nations Security Council Resolution (UNSCR) 661 of 6 August, the goals of the embargo were to degrade Iraq's

Independence *(CV 62) at sea on the eve of the 1990–1991 Gulf War.*

A guided missile destroyer Goldsborough *(DDG 20) Sailor trains his .50-caliber machine gun on Iraqi merchant ship* Zanoobia *prior to her boarding and inspection for contraband by UN coalition naval forces in September 1990.*

military capabilities by cutting off access to foreign munitions and to compel Saddam to withdraw his troops from Kuwait. On 17 August U.S. naval forces began maritime interception operations. After passage of UNSCR 665, warships from 12 nations took part in the embargo patrol. Vice Admiral Mauz took the lead in organizing the international effort. At monthly meetings, participating navies established common interception procedures, delineated patrol sectors covering more than 250,000 square miles of ocean, and handled rules of engagement, boarding techniques, and intelligence sharing.

A typical maritime embargo action occurred on 8 October 1990 when the U.S. frigate *Reasoner* (FF 1063), British destroyer *Battleaxe*, and Australian frigate *Adelaide* intercepted the Iraqi merchantman *Al Wasitti* in the Gulf of Oman. Despite radioed demands from naval commanders and shots fired by UN warships across the bow of his ship, the Iraqi master refused to slow or stop the vessel. Finally, British Lynx helicopters hovered over the merchantman and Royal Marines "fast-roped" onto the deck to take charge of the ship. A U.S. Coast Guard law enforcement detachment then boarded and ensured that the ship held no contraband. Only then did the task force commander allow *Al Wasitti* to proceed into port.

Mauz's forces also protected the ships transporting the armored fighting vehicles, ammunition, fuel, equipment, and supplies of the UN coalition to the sands of Saudi Arabia. The U.S.-based Ready Reserve Force ships, fast sealift ships, maritime prepositioning ships, and chartered merchant vessels controlled by the Military Sealift Command required unhindered access to three key Arabian Gulf ports: Damman, Dhahran, and Jubail. Guarded by the 60 U.S. warships controlled by Mauz, a fleet of 173 ships delivered more than one million tons of equipment, 135,000 tons of

Vice Admiral Stanley R. Arthur, commander of the U.S. Seventh Fleet and U.S. Naval Forces Central Command, led U.S. and allied naval forces in Operation Desert Storm (January–March 1991), one of the most successful campaigns in U.S. military history.

supplies, and 1.8 million tons of petroleum products to the operational theater during the first phase of Operation Desert Shield.

In late fall the UN coalition decided on a military campaign to oust Saddam's forces from Kuwait. In a monumental operation 111 ships employed by MSC transported the Army's tank-heavy VII Corps from Germany to Saudi Arabia and additional troops and equipment from the United States. Mauz believed that the carriers in his Arabian Gulf-based Battle Force Zulu could deal with any air threat from Iraq so he deployed *Independence* and her escorts into the gulf. The *Midway* task force, after a month-long voyage from Yokosuka, relieved *Independence* on station in the gulf on 1 November. For the next two and one-half months, the squadrons of *Midway*'s air wing trained in the skies over Saudi Arabia and Oman and completed a number of multicarrier, "mirror-image" strike exercises with Air Force and coalition units. *Midway* also took part in Imminent Thunder, a multinational amphibious landing exercise on the Saudi coast.

When Vice Admiral Stanley R. Arthur became Commander Seventh Fleet and COMUSNAVCENT on 1 December 1990, in a routine rotation, he understood that he would lead the fleet to war. Arthur had flown numerous combat missions in Southeast Asia, in the process earning the Distinguished Service Medal, Legion of Merit, Distinguished Flying Cross, and other decorations. The naval aviator had served during the 1980s as COMUSNAVCENT so he was familiar with the region.

Arthur, like Mauz, considered how Navy and Marine forces would fight the war, and one of the options they ruled out was an amphibious assault on the coast of Kuwait. The difficult geography in the northern gulf, the presence of offshore minefields, and the concentration there of strong Iraqi armored and Republican Guard forces dissuaded Arthur, as did the fear of likely heavy Navy and Marine casualties. They did think, however, that the amphibious task force and embarked troops of the 4th and 5th Marine expeditionary brigades under Vice Admiral John B. "Bat" LaPlante could act as a strategic reserve afloat and would be key to diverting Saddam's attention from his desert flank. From that direction would come the killing blow from the Army's VII Corps.

Combat in the Arabian Gulf

In the early morning hours of 17 January 1991, the UN coalition launched a devastating air assault on Iraq. Tomahawk land attack missiles fired from U.S. battleships, cruisers, destroyers, and submarines deployed around the Arabian Peninsula entered Iraqi air space and slammed into targets in Baghdad and elsewhere. In the largest air strike since World War II, attack planes launched from *Midway* and five other carriers stationed in the Arabian Gulf and Red Sea unleashed ordnance against the foe in Iraq and Kuwait, as did Air Force, Marine, and coalition squadrons. Allied fighters made short work of Saddam's air force; Navy Lieutenant Commander Mark I. Fox and Lieutenant Nick Mongillo of *Saratoga*'s Strike Fighter Squadron (VFA) 81 each shot down an Iraqi MiG-21 with Sidewinder and Sparrow air-to-air missiles.

Enemy antiaircraft weapons took a toll of coalition aircraft during the first 48 hours of Operation Desert Storm, shooting down ten planes, including three Navy aircraft, most of which approached their targets at low levels. Vice Admiral Arthur, remembering his experiences as an attack pilot in Vietnam, wisely advised his naval air commanders to seek higher altitudes for their bomb runs; losses dropped almost immediately thereafter.

One of Arthur's greatest attributes as a battle leader was his ability to work out differences with superiors and counterparts and accomplish the overall mission. Even though the admiral wanted naval aircraft to keep close watch over Iraqi mine-laying activity during Desert Shield, he understood General Schwarzkopf's desire to avoid sparking hostilities before coalition forces were fully prepared for combat. He also did not press Air Force Lieutenant General Charles A. Horner, the coalition's "air boss," to carve out a separate air defense zone over Iraq for Navy fighter aircraft, as advocated by his carrier commanders. Arthur was persuaded that the IFF (identification friend or foe) equipment on his F-14 Tomcats might not be good enough in the combat theater's crowded air environment. The Navy did have disagreements with the Air Force over the target selection process, aerial refueling priorities, and other issues, and Arthur upheld the Navy's interests. The admiral, however, never let disagreements hinder the joint effort to defeat the enemy.

Midway, Ranger, and later in the war *Theodore Roosevelt* (CVN 71) and *America* (CV 66) would not have been able to operate in the confined space of the Arabian Gulf without robust defenses against air and surface attack. Iraqi forces posed the greatest threat, but only two years before Desert Shield, Iranian antiship missiles and naval vessels had

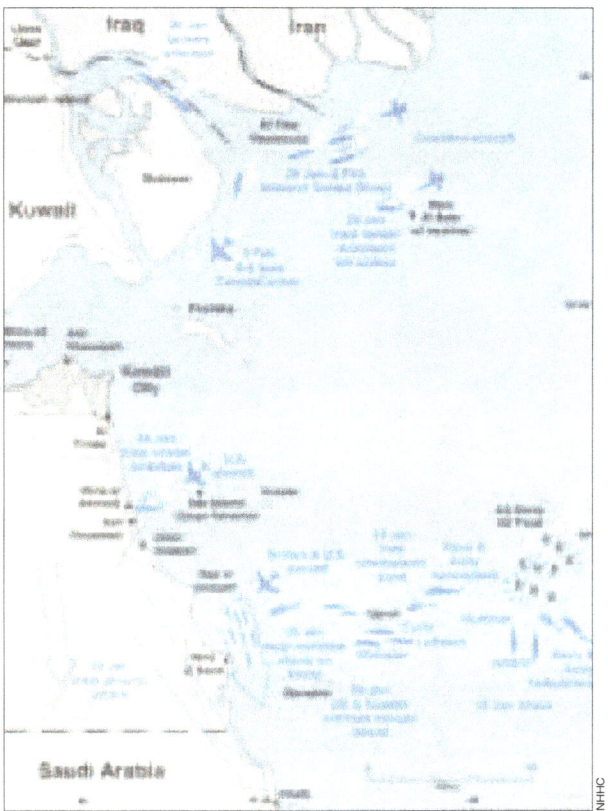

Naval Operations in the Northern Arabian Gulf during Operation Desert Storm.

attacked U.S. warships. The carriers and other ships operating in the gulf were protected from attack by multiple layers of defense. Carrier and shore-based fighter and early warning aircraft maintained combat air patrols over the gulf night and day, seven days a week. A force of nine U.S. cruisers and 12 U.S., British, Australian, Dutch, and Italian destroyers and frigates, most armed with surface-to-air missiles and Phalanx CIWS complemented the defenses.

Because the *Ticonderoga*-class guided missile cruisers provided the world's most advanced battle management system, Rear Admiral Daniel March, Commander, Battle Force Zulu, made the Yokosuka-based warship *Bunker Hill* the command ship for fleet defense. He designated her commanding officer, Captain Thomas Marfiak, the antiair warfare commander for Battle Force Zulu. Marfiak employed *Bunker Hill*'s radars and communications

The Yokosuka-based Oliver Hazard Perry-*class guided missile frigate* Curts *(FFG 38) was a star performer during the Gulf War.*

To divert Saddam's attention from allied forces in the desert on the Saudi border, Vice Admiral Arthur conducted powerful air and surface combat operations in the northern gulf beginning in mid-January. On the 18th the U.S. guided missile frigate *Nicholas* (FFG 47) and two Kuwaiti guided missile patrol boats, in conjunction with U.S. Army and Royal Navy attack helicopters, seized two Iraqi gulf oil platforms, taking 23 prisoners.

On the 24th A-6 Intruders from *Theodore Roosevelt* discovered and attacked a Soviet-built Iraqi minesweeper near Qaruh, an island off the coast of Kuwait. The naval command dispatched the Yokosuka-based guided missile frigate *Curts* (FFG 38), with an SH-60B and two U.S. Army OH-58D helicopters embarked, to capture the boat. After the aircraft strafed the enemy vessel, Commander Glenn H. Montgomery, the commanding officer of *Curts*, ordered a party of SEALs and Sailors to board the minesweeper, where they took 22 prisoners. Montgomery deployed other SEALs on Qaruh to accept the surrender of 29 more Iraqis. The SEALs raised the Kuwaiti and U.S. flags over the island, the first territory liberated from Saddam Hussein's forces in Desert Storm. The Seventh Fleet guided missile frigate received a Navy Unit Commendation for her performance in the action.

Meanwhile the aircraft and surface ships of Battle Force Zulu attacked Iraqi naval vessels off Kuwait and in waters between Iraq and Iran. By 2 February allied units had destroyed or badly damaged all 13 missile boats and most of the other combatants in the Iraqi navy. As one commander observed, the campaign had driven

equipment to coordinate the entire air defense picture in the gulf. The only time Saddam tested the air defense umbrella in the gulf, on 24 January, he lost two of his F-1 Mirage fighters to coalition air defense forces.

Command ship Blue Ridge (LLC 19) *during Operations Desert Shield and Desert Storm.*

The 16-inch guns of battleship Wisconsin *(BB 64) open up on Iraqi fortifications along the coast of Kuwait in January 1991.*

"Saddam's navy into Neptune's soggy arms." On 8 February Arthur declared that the allied coalition had established sea control in the Northern Arabian Gulf. By now his forces included command ships *Blue Ridge* and *LaSalle*, 6 aircraft carriers, 2 battleships, 12 cruisers, 11 destroyers, 10 frigates, 4 mine warfare ships, 31 amphibious ships, 32 auxiliaries, 2 hospital ships, 3 submarines, numerous military sealift ships, and the 4th and 5th Marine expeditionary brigades.

By 23 February 1991 the air campaign launched against Iraqi forces in Kuwait on 17 January had destroyed 1,772 enemy tanks, 948 armored personnel carriers, and 1,477 artillery pieces. Of equal significance, the massive air attacks by *Midway*, the five other U.S. carriers, and allied warplanes based in Saudi Arabia had thoroughly demoralized Iraqi ground forces in Kuwait.

In preparation for the final coalition assault on Saddam's occupation army, Arthur's naval forces edged closer and closer to the enemy-held coast of Kuwait. The sea mine, an enemy weapon that had dogged Seventh Fleet ships in World War II, Korea, and Vietnam, also complicated naval operations in the Gulf War. On 18 February the amphibious assault ship *Tripoli* struck a mine, sustaining severe damage. That same day, not far from *Tripoli*, the Aegis cruiser *Princeton* (CG 59) set off two mines that buckled the keel and badly injured three Sailors. As damage control parties fought to keep both warships afloat, the Guam-based salvage and rescue ship *Beaufort* (ATS 2), despite the obvious

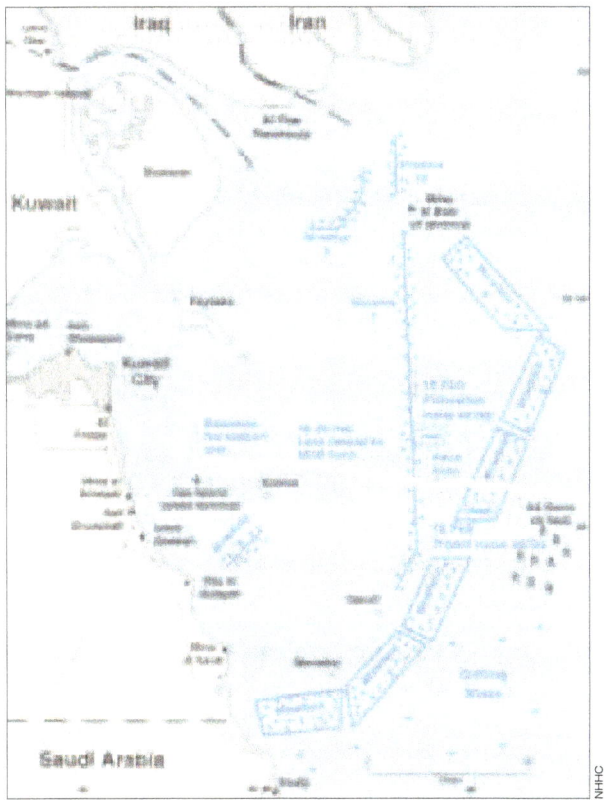

Mine Warfare in the Arabian Gulf.

danger, made her way to the stricken warships. *Beaufort*'s expert salvage officers decided that *Tripoli* could steam on her own power out of the minefield.

At the request of *Princeton*'s commanding officer, Captain Edward B. Hontz, however, *Beaufort* took the cruiser under tow and brought her safely out of the minefield and into Bahrain for repairs.

On 24 February the UN coalition opened the long-awaited ground, air, and naval campaign to liberate Kuwait. To keep Saddam's eyes focused on the sea, Arthur's fleet intensified operations on the coast and among offshore islands. SEALs and other special operations forces attacked targets ashore, and the battleships *Wisconsin* and *Missouri* moved in close to bombard Iraqi coastal fortifications and troops facing the Marines. The Guam-based combat stores ships *Niagara Falls* (AFS 3) provided logistic support to these ships in the northern gulf. Aircraft from *Midway*, *Theodore Roosevelt*, and *America* dropped tons of bombs on Iraqi troops on Faylaka Island.

In a lightning campaign, U.S. Marine and Arab coalition forces stormed Kuwait City while the U.S. Army's VII Corps and XVIII Airborne Corps and other allied forces smashed the Iraqi army in the desert of western Kuwait and southern Iraq. Carrier aircraft pummeled fleeing enemy troops on the so-called "highway of death" north of Kuwait City. By 0800 on 28 February it was over. Washington announced a cease-fire and directed Saddam to dispatch subordinates to the Iraqi village of Safwan to learn the terms of a permanent cease-fire spelled out in UN Security Council Resolution 687.

Despite the end of hostilities, Arthur's naval forces still had much work to do. For much of 1991 allied salvage and explosive ordnance disposal teams cleared Kuwait's ports of unexploded bombs and sunken vessels. An international flotilla with vessels from 11 navies cleared 1,288 sea mines from the approaches to Kuwait and Iraq. Not until 24 April 1991 did Arthur relinquish control of U.S. Naval Forces, Central Command and returned to Yokosuka to resume his Seventh Fleet duties in the Far East.

Washington recognized that even with Saddam's defeat, the Middle East would remain in turmoil. Iraq's internal situation remained unsettled, Iran still posed a threat to U.S. interests, and the Arab-Israeli conflict showed no signs of abating. Naval

The volcanic eruption of Mount Pinatubo on the Philippine island of Luzon in June 1991.

leaders decided they needed to create a permanent three-star billet to serve as Commander in Chief, Central Command's naval component commander and to handle maritime affairs in the waters around the Arabian peninsula. This measure would relieve Commander Seventh Fleet, fully engaged with the never-ending confrontation on the Korean peninsula and China's military rise, of those responsibilities. Hence, on 19 October 1992, the Navy established COMUSNAVCENT as a permanent three-star billet, assigning the duty to Vice Admiral Douglas Katz, and on 4 May 1995 Secretary of Defense William J. Perry approved establishment of the U.S. Fifth Fleet to defend America's interests in the region.

Seventh Fleet to the Rescue

The evacuation of people in distress and humanitarian relief constituted important Seventh

Collapsed and ash-covered buildings at Subic Bay Ship Repair Facility.

Fleet responsibilities. Operation Fiery Vigil, the fleet's response to the eruption of Mount Pinatubo on the Philippine island of Luzon in June 1991, brought these missions to the fore. On 4 June American and Filipino scientists determined that the mountain's seismic activity had increased dramatically and warned that a massive eruption was a distinct possibility. The lives of the thousands of Filipinos and Americans in the vicinity were at great risk, as were Clark Air Base and the Subic Bay naval base lying within a few miles of the mountain.

By Sunday, 8 June, the seismic activity had increased to such a high degree that Commander in Chief, Pacific Command Admiral Charles R. Larson established Joint Task Force Fiery Vigil and ordered the closure of Clark and evacuation of all 21,000 American service personnel and dependents there. This prescient decision enabled the Seventh Fleet to deploy ships and planes to Subic 24 hours before the volcano blew its top. The Air Force airlifted out some evacuees but transported most by vehicle to the Subic naval base. The following morning hundreds of vehicles snaked down the 50-mile-long road between Clark and Subic. Under the direction of the naval base commander, Rear Admiral Paul E. Tobin, chapels, classrooms, a day care center, and other buildings opened their doors to accommodate many of the tired but grateful evacuees. Service families willingly shared their homes with the families from Clark. In addition, Seabees and 3,000 Marines provided engineering, construction, and medical support to the evacuees.

On the 13th a deluge of ash forced closure of Manila International Airport and Naval Air Station Cubi Point, from which 29 fixed-wing aircraft had already departed. On Friday, 14 June, the ash mixed with the heavy rain brought by Typhoon Yunya to form a wet concrete-like mixture that covered every structure at the Subic base. By the following day, "Black Saturday," the situation had become desperate. A massive explosion that rocked the volcano sent an enormous cloud high in the sky. The heavy ash mixture continued to fall, shutting down the power, water, and emergency medical systems and blocking out the sun. The weight of the ash and ground tremors collapsed 50 buildings in and around Subic. Earthquakes caused by the eruption shook the ground. The collapse of one building killed an Air Force dependent and a Filipino. The combined Clark and Subic populations were at great risk.

The Seventh Fleet came to the rescue. The destroyer tender *Cape Cod* (AD 43) immediately supplied the naval base with electrical power, food, fresh water, repair support, and an emergency space staffed by medical personnel. The base, however, could not long sustain the 30,000 Americans concentrated there, so the Seventh Fleet mounted a massive seaborne evacuation of Navy and Air Force military personnel and their dependents from Subic to Cebu Island, 350 miles away. On 16 June, 900 evacuees boarded the guided missile cruiser *Arkansas* (CGN 41) and the frigates *Rodney M. Davis* (FFG 60) and *Curts* for the transit. The following day 1,700 embarked in *Long Beach*, *Lake Champlain* (CG 57), *Merrill* (DD 976), *Gary* (FFG 51), and USNS *Passumpic* (T-AO 107). The amphibious assault ship *Peleliu* (LHA 5), augmented by staff members of the Subic Bay naval hospital, provided an emergency medical facility that accommodated seriously ill patients and pregnant women, a number of whom gave birth while underway. One mother on board carrier *Abraham Lincoln* (CVN 72) even named her newborn boy Abraham. Hundreds of evacuees filled the cavernous spaces of *Abraham Lincoln* and

Seventh Fleet guided missile frigate Rodney M. Davis *(FFG 60)*.

Midway. For over a week 28 Seventh Fleet and other units transported to safety close to 17,000 men, women, and children.

Seventh Fleet Sailors earned the gratitude of their fellow Americans. One naval officer observed that "many evacuees visibly wept as they boarded the ships because of the genuine concern, warm welcome, and gracious hospitality exhibited by the Sailors. . . . Once on board the ships, the evacuees enjoyed their first cold drink, hot meal, shower, or working toilet facility in many days."

He added a vivid description of life on board: "Sailors gave up their racks for the evacuees; ships' menus changed to hot dogs and potato chips for the children; first-class lounges became playrooms; cartoons played continuously over the ships' televisions; razor blades were replaced by diapers in ships' stores; games of jump rope were common on the helicopter decks; pet motels were created out of boxes; rubber gloves were used as baby bottles."

Once the ships arrived at Cebu, after a 19-hour passage, Navy and Marine helicopters transported the evacuees to Mactan International Airport for Air Force flights to Guam and on to the United States. Throughout Operation Fiery Vigil, Seventh Fleet units and personnel demonstrated exceptional professional skill and concern for the well-being of their fellow Americans.

End of an Era for Subic Bay

During 1991 American and Filipino government representatives negotiated a Treaty of Friendship, Peace, and Cooperation that would have allowed another three-year occupation of Subic, but the Philippine Senate refused to ratify the agreement. Despite once favoring a pact, the administration of President Cory Aquino announced on 27 December 1991 that the Subic Bay naval base must be evacuated by the end of 1992.

Subic Bay had figured prominently in U.S. naval history since the Spanish American War of 1898. The fight against Japan for control of the area during World War II had been intense and bloody. The Seventh Fleet steamed from Subic Bay into battle in the opening days of the Korean War. The naval base, along with the naval air stations at Cubi Point and Sangley Point, proved critical to the Seventh Fleet's operations afloat and ashore during the Vietnam War. And the Subic Bay naval base provided substantial support to the Navy during the conflicts in the Arabian Gulf and numerous crises.

Naval leaders were not only conscious of Subic's legacy but concerned that the loss of the base would severely constrain their ability to support operations in the South China Sea, the Indian Ocean, and beyond. The Seventh Fleet would no longer have access to facilities and services offered by Subic for "one-stop shopping." In 1991 Subic's ship repair facility handled 60 percent of the Seventh Fleet's repairs; the naval magazine held 40,000 tons of ordnance; the supply depot was the Navy's largest overseas depot; and the training facility could accommodate live-fire naval gunfire, close air support, and jungle training available nowhere else in the Western Pacific. Without Subic, naval vessels operating in distant waters would have to steam almost 2,000 miles or more to reach the ship repair, supply, ammunition, and training facilities at Yokosuka and Sasebo in Japan and Guam in the Marianas.

Some might have considered the eruption of Mount Pinatubo and resulting evacuation of the Subic Bay Naval Base as signals from the gods that the time was right for the United States to vacate one of largest U.S. naval bases in the world. More down-to-earth observers, however, understood that changes in the international scene, American global interests, and most important, Filipino desires mandated Subic's closure.

By 1991 neither the Soviet Union nor the People's Republic of China posed an immediate threat to Southeast Asia; Washington needed to divert considerable military resources to Middle Eastern contingencies; and the people of the Philippines were determined to assert full sovereignty over the bases on their soil. Moreover, Singapore, located on the strategic Strait of Malacca, had stepped in to improve the Seventh Fleet's ability to operate in the Indian Ocean and Arabian Gulf. In November 1990 the United States and Singapore had signed an addendum to a memorandum of understanding, enabling U.S.

warships, later including *Nimitz*-class aircraft carriers, to use the naval facilities at Changi Naval Base for logistics support. During 1992 the Navy moved mountains of material to other Pacific bases and turned over the facilities to Filipino authorities. On 24 November 1992 the last U.S. naval personnel left the Philippines by air from the naval air station at Cubi Point and by sea on board the amphibious assault ship *Belleau Wood* (LHA 3).

Fortunately for the Seventh Fleet, the Gulf War had ended when natural disasters in South and Southeast Asia demanded rapid and sustained action to help thousands of people in distress. Humanitarian assistance to the victims of a cyclone in Bangladesh and the eruption of Mount Pinatubo in the Philippines received the fleet's attention for much of that summer.

Still the combat operations in the Arabian Gulf and humanitarian operations in the Pacific stretched the fleet's resources. Separate naval leaders and forces were required to handle the continuing turmoil in the Middle East and perennial U.S. responsibilities in the Far East. The turnover of the Subic Bay naval base and the naval air stations in the Philippines during 1991–1992 impeded the Seventh Fleet's ability to operate in the far reaches of the Indian Ocean and North Arabian Sea. Assignment of a permanent three-star flag officer as COMUSNAVCENT and creation of the Fifth Fleet finally enabled the Seventh Fleet to tackle the weighty challenges it would soon face in the Far East.

Amphibious assault ship Belleau Wood *(LHA 3) and other U.S. naval vessels tied up at the Subic Bay Ship Repair Facility in 1987.*

CHAPTER 8

SAFEGUARDING THE PEACE

A CONFRONTATION OVER TAIWAN and military incidents sorely tested but did not torpedo the U.S. relationship with the People's Republic of China during the years from 1995 to 2001. The Seventh Fleet strengthened that connection and U.S. alliances throughout the area of responsibility with ship visits, military-to-military exchanges, and disaster relief operations. The fleet assisted in the international effort to restrain North Korea's aggressive behavior and to bring peace to East Timor.

As it had throughout the Cold War, the confrontation over Taiwan continued to trouble American-Chinese relations during the mid-1990s. The U.S.-PRC relationship had been formalized with the establishment of diplomatic relations in January 1979. That same year the Seventh Fleet's Taiwan Patrol Force, which began operations at the start of the Korean War, officially ceased to exist. U.S. military personnel also withdrew from Taiwan, home to the government of the Republic of China, a bitter enemy of the People's Republic of China. Washington and Beijing exchanged ambassadors that same month. The increasing global threat posed by the Soviet Union in the early 1980s continued to warrant close U.S.-PRC ties.

But when the USSR began to disintegrate late in the decade, Beijing had less to fear from a Soviet attack and hence less need for a close connection to the United States. Further damage to U.S.-PRC relations occurred after the People's Liberation Army massacred hundreds of students and other demonstrators in Beijing's Tiananmen Square in June 1989. Americans and others around the world watched in horror as Communist tanks and troops crushed the pro-democracy movement. Troubling actions by the People's Liberation Army continued to roil the waters. In October 1994, for instance, when the *Kitty Hawk* carrier battle group trailed a *Han*-class attack submarine operating dangerously close to the U.S. ships, Beijing dispatched fighter aircraft toward the American ships, and a PLA leader later warned that if another such incident occurred the planes would open fire.

In February 1995 PLAN units occupied Mischief Reef in the Spratly Islands some 620 miles from China's Hainan Island, but only 150 miles west of the Philippines, an American ally and another claimant to the Spratly Islands. The following month, for the first time since the 1989 Tiananmen Square upheaval, a U.S. Navy warship visited China when the Seventh Fleet Aegis cruiser *Bunker Hill* put in at Qingdao, but it did little to warm the chill between the two nations.

PRC determination to put pressure on Taiwan in 1995–1996 led to a confrontation with the United States, similar to the crises of 1954–1955 and 1958. During the 1970s U.S. presidents had recognized that "China" included both the mainland and Taiwan, but in January 1979 the United States shifted diplomatic recognition of China from Taipei to Beijing. Later that year Congress passed the Taiwan Relations Act, which included this statement: "[The] United States decision to establish diplomatic relations with the People's Republic of China rests upon the expectation that the future of Taiwan will be determined by peaceful means." The United States was not about to abandon Taiwan, its faithful Cold War ally.

Several developments in the early 1990s inspired the PRC to threaten military action against Taiwan. First, to Beijing's disappointment, democracy had flourished on the island after the death of President Chiang Kai-shek and the retirement from public office of his son and successor Chiang Ching-kuo. All voting-age citizens would elect a chief executive in 1996. Lee Tung-hui, the first native-born Taiwanese president, began openly discussing independence for his island nation. In addition, Taiwan was known as one of the "Asian Tigers" for the wealth of its booming free-market economy. When the people of Taiwan compared the benefits of life on their island with the lack of political freedoms and widespread poverty in the PRC, they were decidedly unenthusiastic about a union with the mainland.

The planned May 1995 visit of Lee Tung-hui to the United States, for which he needed a U.S. government-approved visa, sparked the Taiwan Strait Crisis of 1995–1996. Even though President Lee intended only to give the commencement address at his alma mater, Cornell University, as a "private individual," the leaders in Beijing objected vehemently. Chinese Communist Party hard-liners charged that the move was evidence of U.S. intent to "split" Taiwan from China and was part of a secret plan to "contain China" as the United States had done during the Cold War. Chinese leaders demanded that the U.S. government deny Lee's request for a visa. Determined not to buckle under this pressure from the PRC, the U.S. House of Representatives voted 396 to 0 and the Senate 96 to 1 for a resolution in support of a U.S. visa for Lee. President Bill Clinton wanted to diffuse the conflict, but reluctantly endorsed Congress' resolution.

In response, Beijing cancelled already-planned visits of its officials to the United States. During July and August 1995 the PLAN conducted missile and live-fire tests in waters only 80 miles from the northern coast of Taiwan and close to the air and sea lanes between the island and Japan. Other PLAN and air force units carried out strike maneuvers. The exercises were meant to demonstrate that the PLA could not only devastate Taiwan with its ballistic missiles but cut off the island from outside support.

Secretary of Defense William J. Perry warned China against threatening Taiwan during the PRC-U.S. confrontation of 1996.

Hoping to defuse the crisis, Washington avoided officially condemning the military provocations or warning Beijing to refrain from further such actions. President Clinton came away from a meeting in October 1995 with Chinese Premier Jiang Zemin confident the PRC wanted good relations with Washington. Just in case, State Department officials expressed to Chinese officials in later months that use of force by the PRC against Taiwan "would be a serious mistake." As another signal, in December the *Nimitz* carrier battle group, en route from Japan to the Arabian Gulf, transited the Taiwan Strait, the first time in 17 years a carrier had entered these waters. The next month the amphibious assault ship *Belleau Wood* also transited the strait. If these measures were intended to deter aggressive Chinese behavior, they did not work, as the Chinese interpreted the response as weak and half-hearted.

In anticipation of a national election on Taiwan scheduled for mid-1996, the PRC decided to influence the vote indirectly by military pressure. Chinese leaders also envisioned an opportunity to demonstrate to the Taiwanese and others in Asia that the United States would not risk war with China over the island. The Clinton administration bent over backwards to convince Beijing that the United States had no "contain China" plan, secret or otherwise. Nor did it encourage Taiwan's independence, or consider Lee's visit to Cornell as official in any way. PRC leaders found none of these explanations convincing and concluded that the weak response by the United States indicated a lack of resolve to support Taiwan. Indeed, Secretary of Defense William Perry admitted that "our diplomatic approach, although uncommonly blunt, had not been effective."

Beginning in February 1996, nuclear and conventionally powered submarines, destroyers, frigates, patrol craft, and amphibious vessels from each of China's three fleets converged on the coast of Fujian Province across from Taiwan as did 150,000 ground troops. Hundreds of high-performance aircraft, including fighters, bombers, and attack planes, deployed to airfields in range of Taiwan. The Chinese military planned to demonstrate in various exercises that if war came, PLA forces would isolate Taiwan from outside support by attacks on sea and air lanes and destroy Taiwan's ports and airfields, power generation facilities, transportation centers, military command-and-control sites, and air defenses. After air and naval bombardments, special forces carried in aircraft and amphibious landing craft would then launch the ground assault. The PLA did not consider the difficulty of the operation or expected heavy losses as a deterrent to an invasion.

From 8 to 15 March 1996—during the Taiwan presidential campaign—the PLA conducted live-fire and missile exercises in two areas only 22 and 32 miles respectively from Taiwan. China's official news agency reminded readers that the exercises were being held on the 17th anniversary of China's 1979 war with the Socialist Republic of Vietnam when Beijing acted to teach the former Communist ally "a lesson" for opposing China's policies in Indochina.

This time the U.S. response was unequivocal. Concerned that the Chinese were preparing to put enormous pressure on Taiwan's electorate to vote the "right" way, Washington took action. On 7 March Secretary Perry publicly called Beijing's actions "reckless" and "could only be viewed as an act of coercion." Within days he announced that the Seventh Fleet aircraft carrier *Independence*, guided missile cruiser *Bunker Hill*, destroyers *Hewitt* (DD 966) and *O'Brien* (DD 975), and frigate *McClusky* (FFG 41) had deployed near Taiwan. Vice Admiral Archie R. Clemins, Commander Seventh Fleet, cancelled a port visit to Thailand and monitored developments from his flagship *Blue Ridge* in contiguous waters.

The Chinese upped the ante, announcing the next phase of exercises—live-fire demonstrations southwest of Taiwan by ground, air, and naval forces. The PRC's defense minister made a broadcast in which he quoted Zhu De, a founder of the PLA: "As long as Taiwan is not *liberated*, the Chinese people's historical humiliation is not washed away; as long as the motherland is not reunited, our people's

Los Angeles-*class attack submarine* Columbus *(SSN 762).*

armed forces responsibility is not fulfilled." Alarm bells went off in Washington that the Chinese might actually be planning to invade Taiwan.

On 10 March Secretary of State Warren Christopher told the Chinese that the U.S. viewed their actions as "reckless" and "risky" and an obvious attempt to coerce Taiwan. He announced that if the PRC resorted to force to resolve the Taiwan issue, there would be "grave consequences," adding, "we have real interests in Taiwan, and I don't want the Chinese to misunderstand about that."

The next day the U.S. government announced that a second carrier battle group, comprising the carrier *Nimitz*, guided missile cruiser *Port Royal* (CG 73), destroyers *Callaghan* (DD 994) and *Oldendorf*, frigate *Ford* (FFG 54), attack submarines *Columbus* (SSN 762) and *Bremerton* (SSN 698), and two auxiliary ships, operating in the Arabian Sea, to join the *Independence* battle group off Taiwan. Washington stated that the purpose of the deployment was to "make sure there is no miscalculation on the part of the Chinese as to our interest in that area" and "reassure our friends in the region that we will maintain an interest in both the peace and stability in that region."

The Chinese government's reaction to the U.S. naval deployment was both strident and sustained. Official and unofficial media outlets condemned the action as provocative and interference in China's internal affairs. Spokesmen alluded to U.S. plans to "contain" China and solidify its "hegemonic" designs on the world. Beijing, however, did not send additional air and naval forces into the Taiwan Strait or concentrate in south China the enormous number of troops, amphibious ships and craft, or civilian merchant vessels it would need to execute and sustain an invasion of Taiwan. In addition, PLA air and naval units did not approach U.S. naval vessels or aircraft in the vicinity.

In reality, the Beijing government expressed surprise at the U.S. reaction to its pressure campaign against Taiwan. Given the tepid American response to the PRC's 1995 exercises, Chinese leaders expected Washington to voice mild displeasure but refrain from stronger measures over the threatening but bloodless military movements and weapons demonstrations. Chinese leaders understood that the PLA navy and air force, much improved since Mao Zedong's days, were still no match for the combat power of the two carrier battle groups and the U.S. national security establishment backing them. The Chinese recognized the technological superiority of the U.S. military, which only five years before had quickly and decisively destroyed Saddam Hussein's Iraqi armed forces in Operation Desert Storm.

An invasion of Taiwan in 1996, with or without U.S. opposition, would have been a herculean task for which the PLA was ill prepared. Executing an operation across 100 miles of some of the most storm-tossed waters on the globe posed great risks. Premier Jiang Zemin knew that an invasion attempt on Taiwan, even a "limited" conflict (if that was possible) with the United States, would put China's coastal cities and industrial centers at risk and jeopardize the country's booming export-based economy. The PRC's foreign policy would suffer as the other Asian nations once again witnessed aggressive Chinese military behavior. If the invasion failed, the people on Taiwan could hardly be expected to favor union after being attacked by their "brothers." And finally, a fiasco in the strait might even cause the people on the mainland to question the Chinese Communist Party's ability to rule.

Impact of the Crisis

While cool heads prevailed in Beijing, the PRC did suffer consequences for its threat to the democratic process in East Asia. The U.S.-PRC relationship, on a generally even plane since President Richard Nixon visited Beijing in 1972, experienced a dramatic downturn. From Beijing's standpoint, the crisis wrought one undesirable result—the previously ambiguous U.S. commitment to the defense of Taiwan became explicit

The crisis also forged closer ties between the United States and Japan, a historic and potential future antagonist of China. One month after the 1996 crisis, President Clinton and Japanese Prime Minister Ryutaro Hashimoto boarded the aircraft carrier *Independence* docked at the Seventh Fleet's Yokosuka naval base. The two leaders signed the

Carrier Independence *(CV 62) turns to port in Asian waters.*

Joint Declaration on Security Alliance for the Twenty-first Century. The Taiwan Strait crisis, while not explicitly identified in the document, clearly influenced it. The joint declaration affirmed the goal of the two nations to achieve a "more peaceful and stable security environment in the Asia-Pacific region [and] the importance of peaceful resolution of problems in the region." It affirmed the two nations' "commitment to the profound values that guide our national policies; the maintenance of freedom, the pursuit of democracy, and respect for human rights." At the ceremony President Clinton observed that the Seventh Fleet's presence in the region had helped "calm a rising storm," "prevent war's return," and reassured "nations all around the Pacific."

As a follow up to the joint declaration, the Guidelines for Japan-U.S. Defense Cooperation, agreed upon in September 1997, and revised in 1999, called for "cooperation in situations in areas surrounding Japan that will have an important influence on Japan's peace and security." Hence, the guidelines provided for JMSDF operational cooperation with U.S. forces to include enhanced Japanese surveillance and minesweeping support.

A number of nations observed that China's actions unnecessarily threatened the peace, stability, and economic prosperity of Asia. Leaders in Seoul expressed the fear that Kim Jong-il's North Korean regime, following China's example, might see military force as a means for solving its conflict with South Korea. The government of the Philippines, similarly concerned about China's aggressive behavior, authorized the U.S. submarine *Bremerton*, destroyers *O'Brien* and *McClusky*, and combat stores ship *Niagara Falls* to refuel in the Philippines when those ships were en route from the Arabian Sea to waters off Taiwan during the crisis. Lee Kwan Yew, the iconic leader of Singapore, feared a U.S.-PRC conflict would badly hurt regional commerce and thwart "China's hopes of becoming an industrial nation in 25 years." Singapore's defense minister stressed the renewed importance of his country's security links to the United States, Great Britain, Australia, New Zealand, and Malaysia. Many other countries outside the region also reacted negatively to China's threatened use of force to resolve the Taiwan issue and pressure on the island nation's electoral process.

Finally, if the PRC's military leaders meant to scare the electorate on Taiwan to vote against Lee Tung-hui and other pro-independence candidates, they failed miserably. The people of Taiwan gave 74 percent of their vote to Lee and his pro-independence stance.

A Return to Normalcy in U.S.-PRC Relations

In many ways the 1995–1996 Taiwan Strait crisis was atypical of U.S.-PRC relations in the 1990s. Beijing and Washington wanted peace and stability to reign in the Western Pacific. In August 1997 the Seventh Fleet flagship, with Vice Admiral Robert J. Natter embarked, made the first visit to Hong Kong since the former British colony reverted to Chinese rule on 1 July. Commander Seventh Fleet hosted PLA Lieutenant General Liu Zhenwu and representatives of the Ministry of Foreign Affairs on board *Blue Ridge*, and the people ashore warmly received American Sailors.

Admiral Joseph W. Prueher, Commander in Chief, U.S. Pacific Command, worked especially hard with the Chinese during 1996 and 1997 to formalize an agreement that would help each party understand the rules of the road at sea and prevent unintended but destabilizing mishaps. On 19 January 1998 Secretary of Defense William H. Cohen and Defense Minister General Haotian Chi of the PRC signed the Military Maritime Consultative Agreement (MMCA), which established a mechanism for improving communication and other issues of mutual interest between the U.S. Navy and the PLAN. Misperceptions on both sides had much to do with the outbreak of the Taiwan Strait crisis. Indeed, General Chi observed that the MMCA related to maintaining "peace and stability in the Asia-Pacific region and the world at large." Prueher understood that the Incidents at Sea agreement with the Soviet navy had been instrumental in "deconflicting" ship and aircraft operations during the Cold War. A series of meetings took place in China and the United States in 1998 and early 1999 that dealt with relevant issues. In early summer, during President Clinton's second visit to China, he and President Zemin announced that they had established a direct "hot line," and shortly afterward, PLAN representatives attended Rim of the Pacific (RIMPAC) naval exercises for the first time.

In August 1998 *Blue Ridge*, with Vice Admiral Natter embarked, and the guided missile destroyer *John S. McCain* (DDG 56) made a four-day goodwill visit to Qingdao. The PLAN hosted a pierside gathering for American Sailors and hosted tours of Chinese destroyer *Qingdao* and frigates *Tongling* and *Xining*.

The accidental U.S. bombing of the Chinese embassy in Belgrade in May 1999 during the NATO-led war with Serbia briefly disrupted the goodwill between the two countries. The PRC cut military-to-military contacts and temporarily barred Seventh Fleet ship visits to Hong Kong. Angry Chinese demonstrators surrounded the U.S. Embassy in Beijing for days after the incident. But the crisis proved to be temporary.

Admiral Joseph W. Prueher, shown here as Commander in Chief, U.S. Pacific Command, became U.S. Ambassador to China after retiring from the Navy in 1999.

Rear Admiral Charles W. Moore Jr., commander of the Independence *battle group, discusses naval operations with Secretary of Defense William H. Cohen.*

SAFEGUARDING THE PEACE

China's top priority at the turn of the 21st century was to enhance the domestic prosperity of the developing country and to enter the ranks of the world's economic powerhouses. Leaders in Beijing also recognized that America's military dominance in Asia discouraged North Korean aggression and helped restrain Japanese political and military ambitions. As before the crisis, the United States wanted to nurture democratic governance and free market enterprise among its Asian allies and encourage China's development as a "responsible stakeholder" in the international system.

Deterring North Korea

Washington remained concerned over the threat posed by North Korea's heavily armed, well-trained, and highly motivated military forces. The Communist regime of Kim Il-sung and his son Kim Jong-il fielded over one million fighting men (including a large contingent of elite special forces troops), 14,000 tanks, 10,000 artillery pieces, multiple rocket launchers, 1,000 aircraft, and 25 submarines during the 1990s. North Korean leaders deployed the bulk of these forces along the Demilitarized Zone near the 38th parallel and within striking distance of the South Korean capital, Seoul.

More alarming to U.S. and allied leaders was North Korea's arsenal of weapons of mass destruction (WMD). During the Cold War the Soviet Union and other countries had provided the North Koreans with ballistic missiles capable of delivering nuclear or conventional warheads and chemical weapons that included Sarin, Phosgene, and other deadly substances.

Seventh Fleet and other U.S. armed forces deployed to the Western Pacific displayed their military strength and combat readiness in visible exercises meant to discourage North Korean aggression. In keeping with U.S. treaties of alliance with Japan and Republic of Korea the Seventh Fleet presence left no doubt that the United States would defend these countries.

Concern had increased in March 1993 when the North Korean government put the country in a "state of readiness for war," declared its intention to withdraw from the Nuclear Non-Proliferation Treaty, and barred international inspectors from its nuclear processing sites. The international community suspected that North Korea was developing its own nuclear weapon capability. Tension heightened when North Korea fired a Nodong-1 missile and antiship missiles into the Sea of Japan/East Sea. With a range of 400 or more miles, the Nodong-1 could have hit targets in all of South Korea and parts of western Japan.

To stiffen allied defenses, in April 1994 the Defense Department deployed Patriot surface-to-air missile batteries, attack helicopters, armored fighting vehicles, and 1,000 troops to South Korea. The National Command Authority dispatched the Seventh Fleet's forward-deployed *Independence* battle group, and later the *Kitty Hawk* battle group, to waters off the Korean peninsula. CINCPAC assigned Commander Seventh Fleet additional responsibility as Commander, Combined Naval Component Command for the defense of South Korea.

As the likelihood of a destructive war seemed to increase, the Clinton administration opened negotiations with North Korea to end the confrontation. On 21 October 1994 the United States and North Korea signed an Agreed Framework in which the United States pledged to replace North Korea's plutonium-processing facility with light water reactor power plants and heating oil supplies.

Only a few months later, amid contentions that the United States was not living up to the provisions of the Agreed Framework, North Korea resumed its plutonium-processing and ballistic missile programs and made threatening remarks aimed at Japan and South Korea. In response, the Clinton administration placed the *Enterprise* and *Abraham Lincoln* battle groups on heightened readiness. In addition, during the summer and early fall of 1995, Seventh Fleet and Republic of Korea Navy (ROKN) forces carried out staff talks and naval exercises to ensure readiness for combat. In the annual Exercise Ulchi Focus Lens 95 and Exercise Freedom Banner 95, U.S. Navy,

U.S. Marine, and ROKN forces practiced operations ashore and afloat. In the former exercise, the Seventh Fleet leader, Vice Admiral Archie Clemins, served as the overall naval commander for the United Nations and Combined Forces commands.

In 1995 North Korea sent heavily armed troops into the Joint Security Area at Panmunjom and combat vessels across the Northern Limit Line into waters claimed by the Republic of Korea. In September 1996 South Korean military forces discovered a North Korean special operations midget submarine run aground on the east coast of South Korea. They killed all but one of the 24 crewmen and special operations troops who had come ashore earlier from the vessel. In July 1997 North Korean soldiers crossed into the Demilitarized Zone and got into a firefight with South Korean troops who killed or wounded several of the intruders.

On 31 August 1998 North Korea tested an advanced Taepo Dong missile, one section of which overflew Japan's main island of Honshu. In June 1999 things really heated up when, after repeated intrusions into South Korean fishing grounds, North Korean patrol boats, in the so-called "crab wars," opened fire on ROKN combatants off the west coast. The South Koreans returned fire and sank an enemy torpedo boat and damaged five other patrol boats, killing anywhere from 17 to 100 North Korean sailors. In the Battle of Yeonpyeong, the ROKN had only two vessels lightly damaged and nine of its sailors wounded. That same year Japan and the United States began joint work on the development of ship-based antimissile defenses similar to the U.S. Navy's Aegis battle management system.

Despite these periodic bellicose demonstrations, North Korea's leaders knew that resorting to hostilities ran the risk of full-scale combat with the military and naval power of the United States and its northeast Asian allies and the real risk of losing that war. Backed by this power, Washington used skillful diplomacy and international pressure to isolate the "rogue" North Korean regime and limit its nuclear and missile development ambitions.

Naval Diplomacy at Work

The Seventh Fleet presence reminded allies and potential foes alike that the United States meant to protect its interests in the region. The flagship *Blue Ridge* routinely visited Okinawa, Hong Kong, Brisbane, Sydney, Kuala Lumpur, Bali, Singapore, and numerous other ports in the Seventh Fleet area of responsibility where Commander Seventh Fleet could interact with foreign political and military leaders. Frequently, the ship hosted receptions and tours for thousands of people at each port. On the occasion of the 300th anniversary of the Russian navy in July 1996, *Blue Ridge* conducted a four-day visit to the port of Vladivostok and hosted a reception on board.

Reflecting the growing connection between the United States and Singapore, in 1993 the city state hosted the establishment there of the Commander, Logistics Group Western Pacific/CTF 73 headquarters. Shortly afterward the two nations agreed to bilateral relations between the U.S. Navy and Royal Singapore Navy. With the U.S. withdrawal from the Subic Bay naval base in the Philippines, this development gained importance as both nations stove to maintain maritime security in the South China Sea and the Strait of Malacca.

Ensuring that the U.S. alliance treaties with Japan, the Republic of Korea, the Philippines, Australia, and New Zealand were not seen by friend or potential foe as mere pieces of paper, in any given year Seventh Fleet units participated in 90 to 100 multinational (combined) and multi-U.S. service (joint) exercises. In 1997, a typical year of the decade, the Seventh Fleet organized or participated in 91 sea, air, ground, special operations, and command post exercises with military forces from Japan, South Korea, Thailand, Mauritius, Bangladesh, Indonesia, Malaysia, and the Philippines.

One such event, Exercise Tandem Thrust 97, involved more than 28,000 personnel, 43 ships, and 250 aircraft from the U.S. and Australian armed forces. Major combatants included the flagship *Blue Ridge*, carrier *Independence*, amphibious ships *Essex* (LHD 2) and *New Orleans* (LPH 11), guided missile cruiser *Mobile Bay* (CG 53), and attack submarine

Salt Lake City (SSN 716). Veteran warships *Perth*, *Brisbane*, *Torrens*, *Sydney*, and *Melbourne* represented the Royal Australian Navy. Throughout March, the two allies worked at the Shoalwater Bay Training Area in Queensland, Australia, to hone their skills in combined amphibious, airborne assault, and logistic operations. The primary goal of the exercise was to enhance the two nations' use of electronic command and control technologies in conducting Pacific-region contingency operations. From the U.S. perspective, the exercise reaffirmed the benefits of the longtime American-Australian connection. In that regard, Seventh Fleet ships made 31 port visits to cities around the country and pumped over $10 million into local economies.

The Seventh Fleet was vital not only to the defense of Asian allies from direct attack, as provided for in bilateral treaties, but to the peaceful resolution of disputes over contested maritime territories. Both Japan and Russia claim sovereignty over the Japanese Northern Territories/southern Kurile Islands of the North Pacific; Japan and South Korea lay claim to Takeshima/Dok-do in the Sea of Japan/East Sea; and Japan and China assert ownership of the potentially oil-rich Senkaku/Diaoyutai islands in the East China Sea. At least five maritime nations, including the People's Republic of China, claim all or part of the Spratly chain in the South China Sea. The United States, concerned with maintaining peace and stability in the region, helped persuade the countries involved that it would not be beneficial to press their claims by force.

Supporting UN Peacemaking in East Timor

The Seventh Fleet's forward deployment and readiness for action proved of inestimable value in 1999, when the United Nations worked to limit fighting in East Timor in the Indonesian Archipelago. Fighting began when armed East Timorese and rogue members of the Indonesian military reacted angrily to a vote by a sizable majority of East Timor's citizens in favor of independence from Indonesia. On 15 September 1999 UN Security Council Resolution 1264 called on member nations to deploy ground, air, and naval forces to East Timor to restore peace and security. With Australia in the lead of International Forces in East Timor, or INTERFET, soldiers, sailors, airmen, and police from 20 nations deployed to the troubled country in Operation Stabilize. These forces oversaw and encouraged the departure from East Timor of all Indonesian military forces and anti-independence militias. As part of the stabilization process, they also provided food and medical care to the tens of thousands of East Timorese refugees displaced by the inter-communal fighting.

The Seventh Fleet guided missile cruiser *Mobile Bay*, already participating in combined exercises off Australia with the Royal Australian Navy, became immediately available. Australian commanders of Stabilize recognized that the ship's advanced Aegis battle management system would serve as an especially valuable asset to the operation. The cruiser's Link-16 communications suite could provide other warships and ground force headquarters with real-time information on potential air and surface threats captured on the ship's electronic display systems. *Mobile Bay* and the Military Sealift Command's *Kilauea* (T-AE 26), a 20,000-ton ammunition ship equipped with two CH-46 Sea Knight logistic support helicopters, constituted the initial element of U.S. Joint Task Force, Timor Sea Operations.

East Timor (Timor Leste).

Ammunition ship Kilauea *(T-AE 26) supported Operation Stabilize off East Timor in 1999.*

Commander Seventh Fleet also dispatched to East Timor the Sasebo-based amphibious assault ship *Belleau Wood* carrying the Marines and helicopters of the 31st Marine Expeditionary Unit, which arrived off Dili, the capital, on 1 October. CH-46 and CH-53 Sea Stallion helicopters of Marine Medium Helicopter Squadron 265 immediately began transporting critical supplies of food directly from logistic ships to refugee camps and isolated villages. These naval forces enabled the United States to limit the American "footprint" ashore, a key U.S. foreign policy requirement. Washington wanted to highlight the fact that the UN oversaw the operation and that Australia, not the United States, directed the military effort. The helicopters operating from *Belleau Wood* and *Kilauea* also provided critical logistical support to the military forces from other nations ashore and afloat.

By early November, relieved by the amphibious assault ship *Peleliu* and the Military Sealift Command support ship *San Jose* (T-AFS 7), *Belleau Wood* and *Mobile Bay* headed home to Japan and praise for a job well done. The U.S. naval commitment to Operation Stabilize ended in February 2000 when INTERFET transferred operational authority to an international police force ashore and wrapped up its peacekeeping responsibilities in East Timor. The government and people of East Timor, free from the threat of politically inspired violence, could now pay attention to building their new nation.

The Hainan Incident

Even in peacetime, American Sailors in the Western Pacific routinely carry out duties that put their lives in jeopardy. Their heavy responsibilities demand a consistent demonstration of courage, professionalism, and dedication to the mission. One such test occurred on April Fools' Day, 2001—and it was no joke.

Before dawn that day, an EP-3E Aries II intelligence-collection plane of Fleet Air Reconnaissance Squadron (VQ) 1 took off from the airfield at Kadena on Okinawa for a planned and routine patrol along the coast of China. The Navy had conducted operations like this for years. The EP-3E, piloted by Lieutenant Shane Osborn, and another 23 men and women of VQ-1, the "World Watchers," had almost completed the patrol by 0915 when two J-8II "Finback" fighter interceptors of the Chinese PLAN approached the American plane over international waters about 70 miles southeast of Hainan Island in the South China Sea. The PRC did not like foreign ships or aircraft operating in this area near its military installations on Hainan or further south in the Paracel Islands claimed by Beijing. Chinese Lieutenant Commander Wang Wei twice flew his fighter dangerously close to the EP-3E and on his third pass collided with an engine propeller of the American plane. The propeller cut the jet in two. The Chinese pilot did not survive when his plane crashed into the EP-3E and plummeted in two parts into the sea from 22,500 feet. The other Chinese pilot asked headquarters for permission to shoot down the unarmed American plane, but his superiors denied the request.

The collision severely damaged the EP-3E's left outboard propeller, radar dome, and left aileron, forcing the plane into a steep, upside-down 14,000-foot dive. Lieutenant Osborn thought they would all be killed. But demonstrating superb airmanship, for which the Navy later awarded him the Distinguished Flying Cross, Osborn brought the aircraft under control, readied his crew for an emergency bail-out, and prepared to land the crippled plane on Hainan.

In the meantime the well-trained crew went into action to destroy the plane's intelligence collection equipment and highly classified data. As the pilot wrestled the plane toward a landing field on the island, the crew smashed onboard gear and obliterated sensitive documents. Despite making repeated radio calls for permission to make an emergency landing on Hainan, Shane's communications went unanswered. But determined to save his crew and the plane, the lieutenant pressed on and safely landed the EP-3E. For another 15 minutes, as armed Chinese guards closed in around the plane, the crew continued to destroy sensitive materials.

Lieutenant Shane Osborn, with Admiral Thomas Fargo, Commander in Chief, U.S. Pacific Fleet, answers questions about the crash of a Chinese jet fighter into his unarmed patrol plane over international waters near Hainan Island on 1 April 2001.

For the next ten days the Chinese detained the crew on the island and tried to get them to "admit their guilt." Despite sometimes unpleasant interrogation methods, the Chinese fed, housed, and treated the Americans decently. On 11 April U.S. Ambassador to China Joseph Prueher (former Commander in Chief, Pacific Command and retired four-star admiral) presented Foreign Minister Tang Jiaxuan with a "letter of two sorries." The document related that the United States was "very sorry" for the death

Marine Flagship

Belleau Wood (LHA 3), commissioned in 1978 and a veteran of service in the Western Pacific during the 1980s, became the Navy's only forward-deployed amphibious assault ship when she made her home at the Sasebo naval base in September 1992. Her Sailors and Marines hardly had time to enjoy their new surroundings in Japan when duty called. That November Belleau *Wood* and other Seventh Fleet ships evacuated American military and civilian personnel from the Subic Bay naval base, which ceased operations. For the remainder of the 1990s, the 40,000-ton amphibious assault ship with 30 helicopters, several landing craft, and 3,000 Sailors and Marines took part in numerous combined exercises with Japanese, Australian, Thai, and South Korean naval forces and visited ports throughout the operational area. The ship also helped evacuate U.S. and other forces from Somalia, monitored the UN no-fly zone over Iraq in Operation Southern Watch, and participated in the UN peacekeeping mission in East Timor.

Amphibious assault ship Belleau Wood *(LHA 3).*

In 2000 *Belleau Wood* and the amphibious assault ship *Essex* (LHD 2) figured in an ingenious measure to minimize family separations. *Essex* relieved *Belleau Wood* in Sasebo so the latter ship could undergo overhaul and maintenance in San Diego; the ships simply swapped crews so the Sailors and their families could stay where they were in Sasebo and San Diego.

Several years later *Belleau Wood* served as the flagship for the commander of the Sasebo-based Expeditionary Strike Group 3, Brigadier General Joseph V. Medina, the first Marine general officer to command a force of naval warships.

After the 11 September 2001 attacks, *Belleau Wood* and the other ships of the expeditionary strike group deployed to the Western Pacific, Indian Ocean, and North Arabian Sea to support President George W. Bush's Global War on Terrorism and combat operations in Afghanistan. The amphibious assault ship's aircraft then flew close air support strikes in Iraq during Operation Iraqi Freedom. Following 27 years of active service, *Belleau Wood* was decommissioned on 28 October 2005.

Amphibious assault ship Essex *(LHD 2), foreground, and* Belleau Wood *steaming together.*

of the Chinese pilot and for the EP-3E making the unauthorized landing on Hainan. The Chinese authorities then released the American crew and three months later their plane.

The incident left U.S. naval leaders questioning the benefit of the previous years of military-to-military engagement. Indeed, only two weeks before the Hainan incident, Commander Seventh Fleet, Vice Admiral James W. Metzger, had met in Shanghai with Vice Admiral Zhao Guojun, commander of the PLAN's East Sea Fleet. Such meetings normally went well, but they were not able to prevent periodic military-to-military clashes.

Shortly after the Hainan incident, President George W. Bush approved a request from Taiwan to purchase diesel-electric submarines, P-3 Orion antisubmarine aircraft, and four *Kidd*-class destroyers. He also allowed Defense Department officials to brief Taiwan's military on the Patriot PAC-3 missile defense system. On 25 April 2001 Bush said the United States would do "whatever it took to help Taiwan defend herself."

From 1995 to 2001 the Seventh Fleet successfully carried out its mission of ensuring peace and stability in the Asia-Pacific region through deterrence and readiness honed in multinational exercises. The fleet accomplished positive actions such as military-to-military exchanges, port visits, multinational exercises, and the East Timor support operation. The successful performance of the mission enabled peaceful resolution of the confrontations with China over Taiwan in 1995–1996 and the EP-3E collision near Hainan Island in 2001. Frequent and visible U.S. shows of force almost always occurred when North Korea initiated belligerent actions in Northeast Asia. Without firing a shot, the Seventh Fleet helped deflate hostile confrontations and helped convince America's allies that they could count on the U.S. commitment to their defense in times of peril.

Chairman of the Joint Chiefs of Staff General Henry H. Shelton presents awards to the crew members of the Navy EP-3E Aries patrol plane involved in the Hainan incident.

Chapter 9

TERRORISTS, PIRATES, AND WEAPONS PROLIFERATORS

In line with national and theater objectives of the 21st century, the U.S. Seventh Fleet engaged primarily in activities that enhanced multinational partnerships and ensured peace and security in the Western Pacific's maritime domain. The fleet joined with navies, coast guards, and national security agencies from many Pacific Rim nations in the successful effort to defeat threats from nonstate terrorists, pirates, and weapons-proliferating governments.

The U.S. and Allied Response to 9/11

International terrorism emerged as a major threat to Asia's peace, stability, and maritime trade in the new century. One of the most horrific events in modern history marked the year 2001. On 11 September terrorists espousing a radical interpretation of Islam crashed civilian airliners into the World Trade Center towers in New York City, the Pentagon in northern Virginia, and a field in central Pennsylvania. The combined attacks killed close to 3,000 Americans and hundreds of people from other nations. Osama Bin Laden's al-Qaeda terrorist group promised to kill more American citizens in the United States and abroad. Al-Qaeda, hosted and protected by the Taliban government in Afghanistan, made common cause with like-minded Islamist terrorist groups in Europe, Africa, and Asia. These groups targeted not only Americans but governments and peoples around the world dedicated to religious tolerance, the rule of law, and basic human rights.

A New York City firefighter looks up at what remains of the World Trade Center destroyed by Islamist terrorists on 11 September 2001.

The United States responded immediately and robustly. In Operation Enduring Freedom, U.S. Special Forces units deployed to Afghanistan and teamed up with the anti-Taliban, anti-al-Qaeda forces of the Northern Alliance to drive the terrorists out of the capital, Kabul, by the end of October 2001. Only days after 9/11, the Seventh Fleet dispatched the *Kitty Hawk* carrier battle group from Yokosuka to the North Arabian Sea, joining with other U.S. and allied naval, air, and ground forces to push the terrorists out of the population centers and into the mountains along the Afghan-Pakistan border. As a reflection of the Navy's versatility and flexibility, *Kitty Hawk* served as a launch platform for embarked U.S. Special Forces helicopters rather than the usual combat air wing of fixed-wing aircraft, which had been offloaded in Japan.

127

Admiral Dennis Blair, head of the Pacific Command, speaks in early 2002 with a U.S. Special Forces officer whose men are helping train Philippines units going after Abu Sayyaf terrorists.

Asian Terrorism and Piracy on the Rise

The terrorist threat to Southeast Asia posed by Abu Sayyaf, Jemaah Islamiyah, and other al-Qaeda-affiliated groups demanded the Seventh Fleet's close attention. While separatist Muslims on Mindanao and other southern Philippine islands had been battling the government of the Philippines for decades, the Abu Sayyaf group tied their efforts to the global jihadist movement. The group's founder, Abdurajak Janjalani, born on the Philippine island of Basilan, fought alongside Osama Bin Laden against the Soviets in Afghanistan in the 1980s and returned to his home imbued with religious zeal and fanatical determination.

Abu Sayyaf had a long history of violence. In August 1991 its guerrillas attacked the missionary ship MV *Doulous* in the port of Zamboanga City, killing two Christian missionaries. U.S. intelligence analysts directly tied Abu Sayyaf to the ambitious 1995 plot, Operation Plan Bojinka, to kill President Clinton and the Pope, bomb U.S. embassies in Bangkok and Manila, and destroy American passenger planes over the Pacific. The plot was foiled only when explosives stored in the Manila apartment of the chief plotter, Ramzi Yousef, ignited a fire, which alerted the authorities. That same year Abu Sayyaf guerrillas landed by boat near Ipil in the Philippines, killed close to 100 people, cleaned out seven banks, and burned the town to the ground. Philippine military forces killed Abdurajak in December 1998, but the group lived on under his brother Kadaffy and increasingly resorted to piracy and kidnapping for ransom. The terrorists kidnapped 21 tourists at a resort on an island off Malaysia in April 2000. In May 2001 the group abducted 20 tourists, including Americans Martin and Gracia Burnham and Guillermo Sobero at the Dos Palmas resort on the Philippine island of Palawan. The terrorists released most of the abductees but beheaded Sobero. They held the Burnhams until the following year when a Philippine army raid resulted in the death of Martin but rescue of Gracia.

Witness to History

Kitty Hawk (CV 63) figured prominently during much of the Seventh Fleet's history. Commissioned in April 1961, the carrier entered Yokosuka, Japan, in October 1962. *Kitty Hawk* served as the temporary Seventh Fleet flagship when Vice Admiral Thomas H. Moorer relieved Vice Admiral William A. Schoech that same month. Following a visit to the ship in June 1963, President John F. Kennedy observed that *Kitty Hawk* "gives real meaning to the phrase 'our first line of defense'."

The ship's wartime experience began in June 1964 when Communist gunners in Laos shot down the RF-8A Crusader flown by Lieutenant Charles F. Klusmann of Light Photographic Squadron 63. After a harrowing 86 days in captivity, the young pilot escaped; a search and rescue helicopter plucked him from the jungle. In November 1965 the ship's air wing flew strikes against Viet Cong forces in South Vietnam.

Kitty Hawk completed five more combat deployments to Southeast Asia, during which her fighter squadrons downed six North Vietnamese MiGs and her attack squadrons hit hundreds of bridges, supply depots, rail yards, petroleum storage sites, and troop concentrations in North Vietnam, South Vietnam, and Laos.

During the late 1970s and 1980s *Kitty Hawk* asserted the Seventh Fleet's presence in Asian waters but especially in the North Pacific and Indian Ocean where the Soviet Pacific Fleet mounted a challenge. On numerous occasions Soviet bombers and reconnaissance planes flew menacingly close to the carrier, and naval vessels shadowed her passage. In March 1984 the Soviets got too close; a Victor I attack submarine unexpectedly surfaced under the carrier then involved in an exercise with the Republic of Korea Navy. Despite the potential for catastrophe, the crash did not seriously damage either vessel.

The Seventh Fleet's Kitty Hawk *(CV 63) deployed to waters off Pakistan and hosted U.S. Special Forces units for Enduring Freedom operations in Afghanistan, February 2001.*

After a stint in U.S. ports, *Kitty Hawk* operated off Somalia in support of the United Nations humanitarian mission and in the Arabian Gulf during the 1990s. Flying in support of Operation Southern Watch over Iraq to enforce a no-fly mandate, the carrier's air wing dodged antiaircraft fire and launched retaliatory strikes.

Kitty Hawk relieved *Independence* (CV 62) as America's only forward-deployed carrier when she steamed into Yokosuka in August 1998. During the next four years the ship took part in combined and joint exercises in the Western Pacific. In the wake of the 11 September 2001 al-Qaeda terrorist attacks on America, however, *Kitty Hawk* deployed to the North Arabian Sea in Operation Enduring Freedom. After another deployment in the Far East, the ship returned to war in March 2003, when Carrier Air Wing 5 carried out numerous strikes against Saddam Hussein's armed forces in Operation Iraqi Freedom. *Kitty Hawk*'s squadrons paid particular attention to the Medina Republican Guard armored division, which they bombed repeatedly with deadly precision guided munitions. The old Seventh Fleet warrior finally turned over her Western Pacific duties to *George Washington* (CVN 73) in August 2008 and headed home. The Navy decommissioned *Kitty Hawk* in 2009 after 48 years of memorable service.

Jemaah Islamiyah and other violent terrorist groups targeted foreigners and Western commercial interests in Indonesia and Malaysia. Jemaah Islamiyah operatives would have attacked Seventh Fleet warships anchored off Singapore in late 2001 if not for swift action by local authorities that thwarted the plan. Regional security forces frustrated other radical Islamist plans to attack Seventh Fleet vessels offshore or in area ports. A video captured in Afghanistan showed that terrorists had staked out a bus stop in Singapore frequented by American Sailors. Co-religionists in southern Thailand launched police station and schoolhouse bombings to register their displeasure with the Bangkok government. Radical Islamists bombed the Indonesian ferry *Kalifornia* in late 2001, killing or injuring 56 Christians. In October 2002 al-Qaeda operatives loaded a rubber Zodiac boat with explosives, steered it toward the French tanker *Limburg* in the Gulf of Aden, and exploded the package against the hull. That same month Islamist terrorists exploded bombs at several locations on the island of Bali, Indonesia, killing 202 Indonesians and foreigners, including 88 Australians. This loss to Australia, with a much smaller population than the United States, resembled the 9/11 attacks on America. Bombing attacks that killed or wounded hundreds of mostly Indonesian people also occurred in 2003, 2004, and 2005. The success of al-Qaeda-inspired terrorist attacks in the United States, and later Spain and Great Britain, energized radicals to attack Americans throughout Southeast Asia and posed a real threat to peace and stability in the region.

The fact that piracy had existed in Asian waters for at least a thousand years did not lessen concern for the safety of maritime traffic that moved between the Arabian Gulf, Indian Ocean, South China Sea, and East China Sea. Maritime chokepoints, especially the narrow Strait of Malacca between Singapore, Malaysia, and Indonesia, through which 50,000 ships passed each year, appeared particularly vulnerable to armed pirates operating from fast boats. Global authorities counted 2,463 pirate attacks or attempts from 2000 to 2006, with 25 percent of them taking place in Indonesian waters. In 22 instances during 2005, armed pirates came alongside vessels underway in Southeast Asian waters, used grappling hooks to board, and made away with thousands of dollars worth of goods.

In the first decade of the 21st century it was hard to distinguish pirates from terrorists. The former traditionally acted for financial gain while the latter sought to achieve religious and political goals. But pirates sometimes used religion as a cover for their greed, and terrorists needed money to finance their attacks. In one incident during 2003, guerrillas operating from the Indonesian province of Aceh seized control of a fully loaded oil tanker en route from Singapore to Penang in Malaysia and ransomed the ship's officers for $52,000. In March 2005, 35 pirates armed with machine guns and rocket-propelled grenade launchers seized an Indonesian tanker in the Strait of Malacca and extorted a ransom for release of their hostages. The following month, armed pirates stormed a ship filled with tin in a Malaysian port, unloaded the cargo, took the ship to sea, and made good their escape in a fast boat.

These armed takeovers sometimes not only resulted in the deaths of crewmen and passengers but also forced the shipping companies to pay ransom, which drove up insurance rates. In the volatile year of 2005, the Joint War Committee of Lloyd's Market Association declared the Strait of Malacca a "war-risk" zone, which significantly raised insurance rates for the ships transiting those waters. Counterterrorism experts worried that terrorists would sink a huge oil tanker in the vital strait to stop traffic, detonate a liquefied natural gas carrier in port, or use a captured vessel as a platform to launch missiles, drop mines, or deploy fast attack boats.

Multinational Action to Combat Terrorism and Piracy

The Seventh Fleet had shouldered much of the burden for protecting the sea lines of communication and oceangoing commerce in the Western Pacific during the Cold War. U.S. naval leaders then saw the major threat to maritime intercourse as emanating from the conventional naval forces of the USSR, China, and other Communist nations.

The early 21st century threat to oceanic trade proved much more diverse, complex, and resistant to decisive counteraction by the Seventh Fleet acting alone. In addition to international terrorism, the transfer of illegal arms and explosives, drug smuggling, territorial disputes, piracy, and other factors clearly mandated a new, more comprehensive multinational approach to maritime security. Even before 11 September 2001, Admiral Dennis Blair, commander in chief of the Pacific Command, had promoted the concept of "security communities." He called for collective efforts to resolve "regional points of friction; contribute armed forces and other aid to peacekeeping and humanitarian operations to support diplomatic solutions; and plan, train, and exercise . . . armed forces together for these operations."

In this new era, the United Nations and regional groupings often took the lead in fostering multinational antiterrorism and antipiracy efforts. As called for in the UN Convention on the Law of the Sea, member nations worked to bring the force of international law to issues relating to territorial waters, seabed minerals, and fisheries. In the aftermath of 9/11, the Asia Pacific Economic Cooperation (APEC) organization developed a counterterrorism plan that detailed measures for combating port and shipboard security and piracy. The Philippines, Indonesia, Malaysia, and Thailand formed an antiterrorism coalition in 2002 and their navies frequently exercised together.

The following year the Association of Southeast Asian Nations (ASEAN) promulgated Bali Accord II that called on member states—the United States was not a member but supported its goals—to fight cooperatively against maritime terrorism, piracy, and smuggling. In July 2004 the navies of Indonesia, Malaysia, and Singapore combined forces in Operation Malsindo, which protected maritime commerce against terrorists and pirates in the Strait of Malacca. In November 2004, 16 countries, led by Japan and including the ASEAN members plus China, South Korea, Bangladesh, India, and Sri Lanka, signed the Regional Cooperation Agreement on Combating Piracy and Armed Robbery against Ships. The parties to the agreement concurred in the establishment of an Information Sharing Center in Singapore that maintained databases, conducted analyses, and shared information on piracy in the region.

Singapore even considered the stationing there of several Seventh Fleet combatants to operate against pirates. The following year the UN's International Maritime Organization sponsored the signing of a Cooperative Mechanism to improve security management by 25 nations whose ships transited the Strait of Malacca. In 2006, at their annual meeting, ASEAN members signed a Convention on Terrorism with provisions for tracking the region's terrorist networks, training camps, and finances.

Japan Steps Up to the Plate

Conscious of the vulnerability of its sea lines of communication to maritime law-breakers, Japan vigorously advocated multinational antiterrorism and antipiracy efforts. Tokyo directed its efforts toward multinational antipiracy action after pirates seized the Japanese-owned merchant ship *Alondra Rainbow* en route from Indonesia to Japan in 1999. The Indian Navy and Coast Guard recaptured the ship and turned her over to Japan. Shortly afterward, Japan sponsored an international conference to address the piracy issue. Japan's coast guard joined with like forces from six Southeast Asian countries to conduct antipiracy exercises. In 2000 the Japan Maritime Self-Defense Force, aptly characterized by naval analyst Bernard Cole as "East Asia's most capable naval force on any given day," took part in several combined exercises concerning antipiracy with Seventh Fleet, South Korean, and other naval forces.

The Japanese valued the U.S. connection. "The United States, especially its navy, is indispensable" and "a major contributor to regional stability," observed Japanese naval officer Hiroshi Ito, adding, "only the U.S. military can provide common tactical procedures in possible conflicts based on the doctrines it created with its partners."

Soon after the 11 September attacks on America, the JMSDF dispatched a naval tanker and escorting destroyers to the Indian Ocean in support of Operation Enduring Freedom. From 2002 on, this contingent included an Aegis destroyer. The Japanese force in the Indian Ocean eventually provided 30 percent of the fuel needed by ships of the ten-nation naval coalition. By September 2005 the JMSDF had provided 410 million liters of fuel worth $140 million—free of charge. These JMSDF support operations continued to the end of 2009.

The JMSDF favored exercising with other navies. As emphasized by Admiral Toru Ishikawa, at the time chief of staff of the JMSDF, "there are no borders at sea; the navies of the world share the high seas as a common domain. Multilateral naval cooperation builds a common foundation to cope with maritime-related problems by developing relationships that foster stability."

The U.S.-Japan connection had become so well established and accepted by the Japanese people that in December 2004 both governments agreed to the replacement in 2008 of the conventionally powered carrier *Kitty Hawk* with nuclear-powered carrier *George Washington* (CVN 73). The issue of nuclear-powered ships operating in Japanese ports had been a hot issue before, but it caused relatively little stir in this new era. Indeed, the fact that U.S. nuclear-powered warships had visited Japanese ports more than 1,200 times without incident between 1964 and 2010 helped ease local concerns.

Not only Japan but other Pacific maritime nations paid close attention to the piracy threat in Southeast Asia. In April 2004 the United States and ASEAN jointly sponsored a workshop on "Enhancing Maritime Anti-Piracy and Counter Terrorism Cooperation in the ASEAN Region." In September 2005 the United States and 33 other nations signed the "Jakarta Statement" that pledged increased efforts to assure maritime security in the Malacca area.

By 2010 there was a decided drop-off in pirate attacks in the Strait of Malacca. Indeed, observers credited multinational efforts during the decade with "reducing the incidence of piracy throughout the Asia-Pacific, and such cooperation has knit the nations together in a regional counterpiracy community." Vice Admiral John M. Bird determined that the decrease in piracy incidents in Southeast Asia resulted directly from the cooperative efforts by regional navies and his Seventh Fleet.

Partnering with the Indian Navy

Strong support for comprehensive policing of the sea lanes throughout Asia came from another, unexpected quarter—India. The Indian Navy took action to foster maritime security in the Indian Ocean, through which pass half of the world's container ships and two-thirds of the world's oil tankers. In the words of one Indian government document, "since trade is the lifeblood of India, keeping our SLOCs [sea lines of communication] open in times of peace, tension or hostilities is a primary national maritime interest." The Indian Navy sponsored exercises with naval forces from Singapore, Britain, France, Bangladesh, China, South Korea, Japan, and the United States. As the Indian Navy's retired Vice Admiral P. S. Das observed, joint naval programs with the navies of the developed nations "facilitate our overall interfaces with other major powers and establish the legitimacy of India's maritime power in this part of the world."

Rear Admiral Terry Blake, commander of Carrier Strike Group 11, with Indian Navy Rear Admiral Robin K. Dhowan on the bridge of the Indian Navy carrier Viraat *during Exercise Malabar 07 in the Bay of Bengal.*

Concerns over a growing Chinese naval presence in the South China Sea and the Bay of Bengal, territorial disputes in the Himalayas, and China's transfer of nuclear weapons technology to Pakistan fostered a closer U.S.-India connection. Another aspect of the connection was the widespread belief in India—which U.S. foreign policy supported—that the nation should take its rightful place as a great power, and its navy—the world's fourth largest—to establish an international presence.

During Operation Enduring Freedom in Afghanistan in 2002, the Indian Navy protected U.S. shipping moving through the Strait of Malacca, allowed over-flight of the country, and opened its ports for refueling of Seventh Fleet warships fighting terrorism. The navies of India and Indonesia began joint patrols of Six Degree Channel west of the Strait of Malacca in September 2004. In November the Seventh Fleet commander, Vice Admiral Jonathan Greenert, met with officers of the Indian Navy on board *Blue Ridge* off Guam to improve the interoperability of the two navies. The officers paid particular attention to planning for Exercise Malabar 2004, an annual exercise held off and on since 1992.

In June 2005 the two countries signed a ten-year agreement. The New Framework for the U.S.-India Defense Relationship provided for the sharing of weapons technology and joint protection of critical sea lanes. Indian naval officers recognized that "India shares many U.S. concerns, including the fight against terrorism, operations against piracy, and safety of sea lanes." In the words of one study, "cleansing Asian waters of these universal scourges has become a matter of real and growing concern" to India. Much like the 2001 al-Qaeda attack on the United States, in November 2008 members of an Islamist terrorist organization launched attacks across the city of Mumbai, a major port on the Indian Ocean, killing 165 people.

Attack submarine Santa Fe *took part in the 2005 Exercise Malabar with the Indian Navy.*

The U.S.-India relationship blossomed in the early 21st century. Both countries faced a deadly threat from radical Islamists. Muslim separatists in Kashmir, Mumbai, and elsewhere have targeted the Indian state for decades. The United States and India—the latter the most populace democracy on earth—share a strong belief in representative government and the rule of law. India's embrace of free market enterprise and globalization after the Cold War produced an economy almost as powerful as China's and dependent on oceangoing commerce and overseas energy sources to supply better than 90 percent of its needs.

In the fall of 2005 Seventh Fleet and Indian Navy units carried out Malabar 05. The event marked India's largest naval exercise in history with another navy. Carriers *Nimitz* and *Viraat*, cruisers, destroyers, submarines, and naval aircraft based afloat and ashore took part. The two navies practiced maritime interdiction; visit, board, search, and seizure drills; search and rescue; and antisubmarine warfare. With attack submarine *Santa Fe* (SSN 763) playing the role of the aggressor, the combined U.S. and Indian naval forces engaged in realistic antisubmarine warfare maneuvers.

Much the same occurred in 2007 when Malabar became multilateral. Indian, Japanese, Australian, Singaporean, and Seventh Fleet naval forces then exercised in the Bay of Bengal. In the words of analyst Michael J. Green, the event sent a signal that "the major maritime democracies had the capacity to work together to maintain open sea-lanes of communication and welcomed others willing and able to do the same." Malabar 09, which took place in the Pacific—far from the Indian Ocean—involved warships from the Seventh Fleet as well as the Indian Navy destroyer *Ranvir* and the JMSDF destroyer *Kurama*.

U.S. Initiatives to Secure the Sea Lanes

The United States and its Seventh Fleet gladly joined with other regional navies to maintain peace and stability in the Western Pacific and launched several new programs. The Regional Maritime Security Initiative, or RMSI, called for a partnership of willing nations to share information to identify and keep track of maritime threats. Normally, national law enforcement, coast guard, and military forces of the associated nations dealt with threats in their own waters, but American leaders envisioned greater success through a multinational approach. Although several Southeast Asian nations raised concern over sovereignty issues, the U.S. initiative spurred action. Singapore and Malaysia, for instance, shared intelligence and cooperated in the patrol of the busy Strait of Malacca.

A December 2002 incident in the Indian Ocean motivated Washington to initiate another measure. U.S. intelligence suspected that North Korean merchant vessel *So San* planned to deliver Scud ballistic missiles to Yemen, site of the 2000 suicide bombing attack on guided missile destroyer *Cole* (DDG 67) and home to al-Qaeda terrorist groups. A Spanish ship involved in the maritime interdiction patrol off Afghanistan with U.S. naval forces intercepted the merchantman. When special operations forces rappelled on board, they discovered 15 Scud ballistic missiles, not the cement itemized in its cargo manifest. The Spanish, however, lacked the legal power to seize the contraband cargo, so they allowed the ship to proceed into port.

To address this deficiency in the law, in May 2003 President Bush announced the Proliferation Security Initiative (PSI), which stressed intercepting weapons of mass destruction, especially those being transported by sea. Intelligence made clear that North Korea and other countries were either selling or giving nuclear weapon materials,

The guided missile destroyer Cole *(DDG 67), heavily damaged by a terrorist attack on 29 October 2000 in the harbor of Aden, Yemen, is towed to safety by a Military Sealift Command ship.*

ballistic missiles, and other dangerous munitions to terrorist groups and rogue nations. The PSI detailed diplomatic and law enforcement measures, supported by intelligence information, for identifying, tracking, and intercepting vessels carrying contraband cargoes.

The JMSDF hosted a PSI exercise in October 2004. In August 2005 Singapore sponsored a PSI intercept exercise called Deep Sabre in the South China Sea that involved naval forces from the United States, Australia, New Zealand, the United Kingdom, and Japan. Within four years of the inauguration of the PSI, naval forces, coast guards, customs offices, and other government agencies from 80 countries were sharing information on the suspected seaborne transportation of illicit materials and frustrating that trade. In 2009 the United States suspected that the Burmese military junta intended to acquire nuclear materials to develop its own arsenal of weapons. In June of that year U.S. intelligence discovered the North Korean-owned merchant ship *Kang Nam* heading for Burma (Myanmar) and determined that the ship carried illicit cargo. The United States referenced UN Security Council Resolution 1874, established to sanction North Korean behavior, and dispatched Seventh Fleet units to track the ship. In response to Chinese pressure on Burma and U.S. monitoring of the ship's passage, Pyongyang ordered the merchantman back to North Korea without completing her mission. In August India held and searched another North Korean vessel supposedly destined for the Middle East that steamed close to Burma. Indeed, by the end of 2009 international observers credited the employment of UNSCR 1874 with frustrating a number of North Korean attempts to ship weapons and other suspicious cargoes overseas.

A Sailor from guided missile cruiser Lake Champlain *(CG 57) practices his visit, board, search, and seizure skills.*

Multinational Exercises at Sea

The Pacific Command's Cooperation Afloat Readiness and Training (CARAT) program, begun in the mid-1990s, involved bilateral naval exercises with a number of Southeast Asian nations. After 2001 these annual exercises practiced the maritime interdiction of terrorists and pirates and by the end of the decade involved the navies of the United States, Singapore, Indonesia, Malaysia, Brunei, Philippines, Thailand, Cambodia, and Bangladesh. The Seventh Fleet's Commander, Logistics Group Western Pacific/Task Force 73 handled the overall coordination of CARAT from its office in Singapore. These multinational actions at sea worked on maritime surveillance, interdiction, and visit, board, search and seizure procedures, training designed to combat terrorism and other illegal activity.

The 2007 exercise typified the CARAT program. Commander Destroyer Squadron 1 served as the CARAT task group commander reporting to Commander Task Force 73, Rear Admiral Kevin M. Quinn. Units taking part included the dock landing ship *Fort McHenry* (LSD 43), guided missile destroyer *Paul Hamilton* (DDG 60), guided missile frigate *Rodney M. Davis*, and rescue and salvage ship *Safeguard* (ARS 50). In addition, Seventh Fleet P-3C Orions, SH-60 Seahawk helicopters, Seabees, a Coast Guard training team, and Army veterinarians participated.

The spring 2009 CARAT program occurred in the Philippines. In April and May combat vessels of the Seventh Fleet and Philippine Navy, including *John S. McCain*, *Chafee* (DDG 90), *Harpers Ferry* (LSD 49), *Bienvenido Salting* and *Rajah Humabon*, operated in the Philippine Sea. American Seabees and Filipino military construction units built a technology and education center in Lapu Lapu City. Navy dentists carried out a medical civic action program (MEDCAP) in Cordova. Seventh Fleet, U.S. Coast Guard, and Philippine units practiced visit, board, search, and seizure measures in the Cebu Strait.

In June, Seventh Fleet units teamed up with military forces from Malaysia and Singapore for CARAT exercises. As part of the effort, Rear Admiral Nora W. Tyson, Commander, Logistics Group Western Pacific, officiated at the opening of a primary school in Kuantan, Malaysia, built by American and Malaysian sailors. Seventh Fleet ships *Harpers Ferry*, *Chafee*, *Chancellorsville* (CG

American and Filipino sailors involved in a 2007 joint Cooperation Afloat Readiness and Training (CARAT) program, load supplies destined for an orphanage in Zamboanga on the Philippine island of Mindanao.

62), and *Chung-Hoon* (DDG 93) joined Singapore Navy ships *Stalwart*, *Interpid*, and tank landing ship *Endeavor* for at-sea maneuvers. From the deck of *Harpers Ferry*, Rear Admiral Do Viet Cuong of the Vietnam People's Navy observed the maneuvers in anticipation of his navy's participation in forthcoming CARAT exercises.

In July the action moved to Indonesia and Thailand. Seabees of Naval Mobile Construction Battalion 40 laid a concrete foundation at a primary school in Bekasi, Indonesia, while at sea Sailors and Marines carried out visit, board, search, and seizure and small arms exercises with their Indonesian counterparts. U.S. and Thai sailors practiced air and surface operations in the Gulf of Thailand.

Similar exercises under the name Southeast Asia Cooperation against Terrorism (SEACAT) honed naval skills in boarding team tactics and techniques and small boat skills. For instance, naval units from the Seventh Fleet, Philippines, Thailand, and Singapore worked on maritime intercept operations during a week-long SEACAT in August 2009.

Rear Admiral Nora W. Tyson, Commander, Logistics Group Western Pacific, left, and officers of the Royal Brunei Navy observe a joint training CARAT exercise, May 2010.

The Seventh Fleet also built on the longstanding Cobra Gold exercises with Thailand to include naval forces from Japan, Singapore, and Indonesia and to concentrate on peacekeeping and contingency responses. In February 2009 *Essex* and the other ships of the Expeditionary Strike Group (Task Force 76), based at White Beach on Okinawa, joined naval forces from Thailand and Singapore for Cobra

Warships of the United States and the Philippines conduct a CARAT exercise in May 2009.

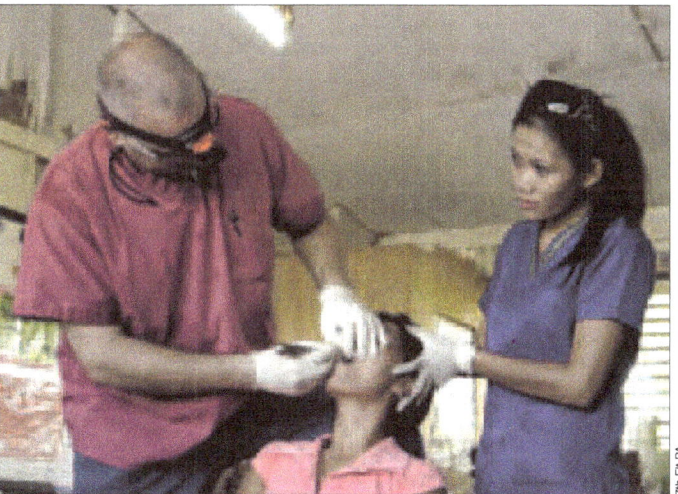

With a Filipina nursing student assisting, a Seventh Fleet dentist removes a patient's tooth during a MEDCAP mission in the Philippines.

Seabees from Naval Mobile Construction Battalion 40 and Indonesian marine engineers work together building a school during July 2009 in the CARAT Indonesia program.

Gold exercises in the Gulf of Thailand. That same month Sailors and Marines from *Boxer* (LHD 4) and the 13th Marine Expeditionary Unit visited the Republic of Maldives in the Indian Ocean to take part with local military forces in Exercise Coconut Grove, a series of humanitarian assistance projects.

To better prepare Sailors and Marines for antiterrorism measures at sea, the Seventh Fleet ramped up specialized training. In May 2009, for example, Seahawk aircrews from Helicopter Anti-Submarine Squadron (HS) 14, Marines from the Fleet Antiterrorism Security Team Pacific (FASTPAC), and crewmembers from *George Washington* conducted small-arms live-fire and "fast-rope" drills on the carrier's deck.

In the apt words of analyst John F. Bradford, by the end of the 21st century's first decade "all extra-regional powers involved in Southeast Asian maritime affairs had aligned their interests toward maritime security cooperation, especially protecting navigation in strategic sea lanes from transnational threats." Most important among these powers were the United States, Japan, Australia, and India, which had demonstrated commitment to maritime security cooperation in Southeast Asia.

Winning the Fight against Terrorists, Pirates, and Weapons Proliferators

By 2010 international, regional, and U.S. actions had significantly reduced pirate attacks, instances of suspected WMD transported by sea, and other illegal activities in Asia's maritime domain. Multinational and bilateral patrols had dramatically increased the presence of maritime forces in dangerous waters. Ashore, the counterterrorism forces of Indonesia, Malaysia,

Thailand, and Singapore had broken up one terrorist cell after another through the use of improved intelligence-gathering measures and the death or swift prosecution and imprisonment of terrorists. Reportedly, government forces in Indonesia, Malaysia, and Singapore had arrested nearly 500 Jemaah Islamiyah members by late 2008. Many people in these countries were horrified that the bombings carried out by al-Qaeda and Jemaah Islamiyah terrorists killed mostly fellow Muslims, debased the religion, and destroyed tourist industries on which so many people depended for their livelihood. At the same time the governments of these countries increased their efforts to win "hearts and minds" in affected regions through enhanced economic development and the negotiated settlement of grievances with inhabitants.

Australia's May 2009 white paper laying out the country's future security policies and the buildup of its military forces echoed the general sentiment among regional nations that they and their American partners were successfully coping with the terrorist threat to Southeast Asia. Australian analysts Jack McCaffrie and Chris Rahman summarized the document's thrust when they observed that while the terrorist threat would "remain extant, the spread of regional extremist networks will be constrained by ongoing counterterrorism efforts."

The counterterrorism campaign mounted by the Philippines and the United States proved especially fruitful. Only weeks after the 9/11 attacks on America, the two governments signed an agreement allowing U.S. forces to store military weapons and supplies in the Philippines, establish temporary counterterrorism camps there, and overfly the country. The United States provided the Philippines with a ten-fold increase in military aid to a total of $19 million in 2002. The funds bought counterterrorism training and C-130B Hercules transport aircraft, HU-1H "Huey" helicopters, M-16 rifles, grenade launchers, mortars, sniper rifles, night vision goggles, and a 360-ton *Cyclone*-class coastal patrol boat.

In 2002 the government and armed forces of the Philippines initiated Operation Balikatan (Shoulder to

Left: *A U.S. Marine takes part in the annual U.S.-Thai Cobra Gold exercise during February 2010.*

Shoulder), employing the longstanding name of U.S.-Philippine exercises, on the southern island of Basilan, an Abu Sayyaf stronghold. The U.S. Pacific Command deployed 4,000 troops to Luzon and an additional 1,300 U.S. Special Forces, Seventh Fleet Seabees, and conventional troops to Basilan to support the Filipinos by providing military advice, counterinsurgency training, transportation, intelligence, and essential equipment. American service members, however, were authorized to fight only in self-defense. Labeled Operation Enduring Freedom–Philippines, the U.S. effort also included medical support, road-building, well-digging, and school construction, with the aim of impressing on Philippine military leaders the importance of a "soft-power" approach in winning the support of the island people.

Within months the operation produced positive results. Supported by U.S. military resources, in early June Philippine naval forces equipped with U.S.-supplied intelligence information and night-vision goggles, located, intercepted, and killed a top Abu Sayyaf leader moving by boat from Basilan to the large island of Mindanao. Other Abu Sayyaf guerrillas fled Basilan.

The U.S-Philippine campaign measurably improved security and economic development on Basilan and earned praise and support from the population. The Philippine armed forces set up the National Development Support Command specifically to win "hearts and minds." In the apt words of a Rand Corporation study, the Filipinos increasingly understood that "the best way to defeat a terrorist insurgency is to provide people with what the rebels cannot: roads, bridges, businesses, houses, schools, electricity, medical centers, and medicines—in short better governance." The United States followed up this success by providing $4.6 billion more in economic and military assistance. In 2003, during the visit to Washington of Philippines President Gloria Macapagal-Arroyo, President Bush designated the Philippines a "Major Non-NATO Ally."

By the end of 2003 Filipino forces supported by U.S. military resources had killed or captured several hundred Abu Sayyaf members. But the snake still had fangs. In its most daring and bloody exploit, in February 2004 Abu Sayyaf saboteurs set off a crude improvised explosive device—16 sticks of dynamite stuffed into a hollowed out television set—on board the 10,000-ton *Superferry 14*, loaded with 900 passengers. One hundred sixteen people died from the blast or from drowning.

During the next three years U.S. and Philippine forces carried out many more training, humanitarian assistance, and information-sharing missions throughout the islands. As Commander Joint Task Force 515, Commander Seventh Fleet provided maritime support to Operation Enduring Freedom–Philippines. Seventh Fleet SEALs instructed Filipino

Marines and Sailors operating from Seventh Fleet amphibious dock landing ship Harpers Ferry (LSD 49) *pose in March 2006 with villagers on the Philippine island of Jolo. A team of over 500 American and Filipino military personnel provided local people with medical, dental, and construction assistance.*

units in jungle survival, marksmanship, maritime surveillance, boat handling, and special warfare.

In the especially successful 2006 Operation Plan Ultimatum, a 7,000-man, ten-battalion Philippine task force, supported by 200 U.S. military personnel and intelligence, training, and funding, targeted the remaining 500 Abu Sayyaf guerrillas on the southern islands of Jolo and Tawi Tawi. During the nine-month campaign, Filipino special forces killed Abu Sayyaf's leader, Khaddafy Janjalani; his second-in-command, Abu Solaiman; and Jundam Jamalul, aka "Black Killer"; and killed or captured another 107 guerrillas. The rest fled in "penny packets" deep into the hills or to other islands. By 2009 they counted no more than 100 hard-core fighters. As the guerrillas moved out, the army of the Philippines moved in to establish a permanent presence. And as the number of terrorist bombings and ambushes declined, businesses and markets sprang up in island towns, and the people ventured out at night once again.

In Exercise Balikatan 06, 2,800 Philippine and 5,500 U.S. military personnel took part. The American units accomplished seven medical civic action programs, four engineering civic action projects (ENCAPs), counterterrorism training, and humanitarian assistance on the islands of Luzon, Cebu, and Sulu. During the MEDCAPs, the Americans gave free medical care to 11,000 Filipinos and veterinary care to many of their animals and built four new schools. The medical staff of the hospital ship *Mercy* (T-AH 19) brought care to the people on Basilan, Sulu, and Tawi Tawi. When a Southeast Asian storm caused a mudslide that destroyed the town of Guinsagon on Leyte

A Seventh Fleet utility landing craft puts Marines ashore in the Philippines to take part in the 2009 Balikitan "Shoulder to Shoulder" exercise.

TERRORISTS, PIRATES, AND WEAPONS PROLIFERATORS

Island, 2,500 American forces immediately deployed to the area to aid the survivors. Assistance from the U.S. Agency for International Development enabled 115 banks and rural cooperatives on the southern islands to loan money to farmers and reportedly helped turn thousands of guerrillas into corn, rice, and seaweed farmers. In September 2007 the U.S. and Philippine governments signed an agreement that provided $190 million over a five-year period for the reintegration of guerrillas into civilian society, school construction, and civic action programs on Mindanao. In Balikatan 09, American and Filipino sailors and marines carried out amphibious exercises on Luzon. The combat vessels involved were Seventh Fleet warships *Essex* and *Tortuga* (LSD 46).

While the United States extended much less counterterrorism support to Indonesia, it still made a difference. From 2001 to 2004 Washington provided Jakarta with $47.5 million to train Indonesian police in counterterrorism tactics. Recognizing newly elected President Susilo Bambang Yudhoyono's strong support for democratization of the political process, the United States resumed military assistance to Indonesia in 2005 and encouraged military-to-military contacts. Washington also enabled Indonesian officers to study at the National Defense University, the Naval War College, and other U.S. military institutions of higher learning.

Some military aid improved the communications and coastal surveillance capability of Indonesia's navy in the critical Strait of Malacca and in waters between Indonesia, Malaysia, and the southern Philippines. American leaders were especially keen on increasing maritime domain awareness in the latter region, the so-called southern back door to the Philippines. Washington expressed interest in an Australian proposal, "Coast Watch South," to set up a number of Filipino-staffed stations on shore with both radar surveillance and interdiction capabilities. Jakarta created an especially effective counterterrorism unit—Special Detachment 88—that killed or captured 450 militants between 2005 and 2009. The Indonesian government's dedicated and sustained effort to neutralize the threat of terrorism through public education and "de-radicalization" programs proved even more effective at reducing the terrorist threat.

Fear and foreboding marked the first years of the 21st century in the Asia-Pacific region. Islamist terrorists traumatized citizens in the Philippines, Indonesia, and Thailand with deadly suicide bombings and other violence. Pirates seized merchant ships in Southeast Asian waters with seeming impunity. And North Korea sold and transported missiles and other banned munitions to unsavory governments and terrorist groups worldwide. But by 2010 the United States and other members of the Asia-Pacific community had put in place concrete and coordinated programs to fight terrorism, piracy, and weapons proliferation. The number and severity of terrorist attacks had declined dramatically in the Philippines and Indonesia. Pirates rarely risked confrontation with the international naval and coastal forces guarding the sea lanes of Southeast Asia. And regional powers had cooperated to thwart North Korea's attempts to smuggle missiles and other banned munitions to the Middle East. The Seventh Fleet, the most capable, flexible, and ubiquitous naval force in the Western Pacific, formed the core of this successful multinational effort to rid the region of terrorists and secure the maritime commons.

CHAPTER 10

PARTNERS AND ADVERSARIES

AS THE SEVENTH FLEET TOOK THE LEAD in the effort to fight terrorists, pirates, and weapons proliferators, it honed its ability to deal with potential conventional threats from Asia-Pacific nation states. North Korean belligerence posed a special concern. Differences with the People's Republic of China also demanded the fleet's continued vigilance and readiness in the 21st century.

In 2001 Admiral Dennis Blair, who headed the Pacific Command, suggested using the nation's long-time and successful bilateral relationships with regional navies as a foundation on which to build a multilateral Asia-Pacific security structure. Admiral Gary Roughead—deputy commander of the Pacific Command in 2004, commander of the Pacific Fleet from July 2005 to April 2006, and Chief of Naval Operations at the end of the decade—detailed the reasons why he thought the 21st century would be the "Pacific Century." The Pacific region, home to 40 nations and 60 percent of the world's population, covered more than half of the globe, was defended by the six largest military forces in the world, and boasted four of America's top trading partners. The admiral presciently observed that stability in the Asia-Pacific region depended on access to the "free and unrestricted flow of trade and commerce" and central to that condition was U.S. seapower; that is powerful combat-ready U.S. naval forces forward-deployed for quick, decisive action. Yet, he added, "[W]hile the Pacific Fleet's most important role is to fight and win our nation's wars, it is not all about combat power. Sea power, particularly in today's security environment, is about access . . . that allows the United States to project its message of peace and freedom from the sea."

He and other naval leaders from Asia-Pacific nations understood that the U.S. Seventh Fleet's stabilizing influence in the region helped balance the other powers and kept potential belligerents in check. The fleet's forward deployment in the Western Pacific enabled countries in the region to maintain lower defense budgets and to concentrate on political, economic, and social development. Put succinctly by a Naval War College analyst, "our presence is a moneymaker on two fronts: they [Asian nations] spend less on defense and more on development."

The United States and its Seventh Fleet were the principal actors in the multinational effort to maintain economic prosperity and political stability in East Asia. Historic animosities dating to World War II and before prevented China, Japan, South Korea, or the nations of Southeast Asia from serving as the prime facilitator for coordinated security action. Only the United States had the economic, political, and military power—and the experience of a half-century of leadership in the Far East—to play that role. As former National Security Council official Evan S. Medeiros observed, the United States has long been "the security partner of choice."

Maritime dominance depended on the readiness of and interoperability with the other U.S. armed services and with America's naval allies. Admiral Roughead saw transnational criminal activities such as piracy, WMD proliferation, Islamist terrorism, and human and narco-trafficking as the most immediate threats to Asia-Pacific's security and stability. His antidote to those ills was not only to strengthen the existing network of maritime nations—the United States, Japan, Singapore, Thailand, Australia, and South Korea—but to encourage inclusion of the naval forces of India, Indonesia, and especially the People's Republic of China. The unifying thread would be mutual respect for national sovereignty, common interests, and increased maritime domain awareness through information sharing.

An MH-60S Knighthawk of Helicopter Combat Support Squadron 11 assigned to carrier Abraham Lincoln *(CVN 72) transfers supplies as part of the international effort to aid the survivors of the December 2004 Indian Ocean tsunami.*

The Pacific Fleet led the way to increase maritime domain awareness, establishing a Cooperative Maritime Forces Pacific connection with more than a dozen regional navies. The object of this cooperative effort: share real-time information on security in the maritime sphere. Admiral Roughead concluded that an emphasis on search and rescue, humanitarian assistance, and disaster relief in their combined exercises would enhance interoperability and trust among naval forces.

Indian Ocean Tsunami Relief

One example showed the way. The Seventh Fleet and the navies of Australia, Japan, India, and other nations responded swiftly to the December 2004 Indian Ocean tsunami disaster. Caused by a 9.1 to 9.3 earthquake, the massive tsunami devastated coastal communities in 11 countries across the Indian Ocean and killed almost 200,000 people.

At the direction of the Pacific Command, Marine Lieutenant General Robert R. Blackman Jr. established Joint Task Force 536 on 28 December to manage the U.S. response to the natural disaster. He chose as the site for his headquarters Utapao, Thailand, because U.S., Thai, and other naval forces had often operated from the base in the annual Cobra Gold exercises.

Commander Pacific Command Admiral Thomas Fargo and Commander Pacific Fleet Admiral Walter F. Doran, immediately recognizing the gravity of the crisis in the Indian Ocean, announced Operation Unified Assistance and ordered all available ships to head to the disaster zone. On 28 December the Seventh Fleet commander, Vice Admiral Greenert, ordered the *Abraham Lincoln* strike group, under Rear Admiral Douglas Crowder, to depart Hong Kong and head for Indonesia. Before the amphibious assault ship *Bonhomme Richard* (LHD 6) and other

Indonesians and American Sailors and Marines of amphibious assault ship Essex (LHD 2) unload bags of rice to feed needy refugees in Indonesia's hard-hit Aceh Province, January 2005.

ships of an expeditionary strike group sortied from Guam, supply personnel from *Bonhomme Richard* used an authorized credit card to buy $50,000 worth of timber, plastic sheeting, and other building materials from the local Ace Hardware store.

Fort McHenry quickly deployed from Sasebo, Japan, and arrived in waters off Indonesia's Aceh Province at the same time as Seabees from Naval Mobile Construction Battalion 40 arrived by air from their base in Okinawa. Soon afterward, *Essex* steamed from her station in the Arabian Gulf to the disaster area. Operating from Utapao, the P-3 Orions of Patrol Squadron 8 searched the Indian Ocean for survivors of the tsunami.

By 5 January, a mere ten days after the tsunami struck, more than 25 U.S. ships, 45 fixed-wing aircraft, and 58 helicopters were supporting Operation Unified Assistance and had already delivered to affected areas more than 600,000 pounds of water, food, and other essential items. Every hour, *Abraham Lincoln*'s onboard distilling equipment filled nearly 800 five-gallon jugs of fresh water that were helicoptered to shore.

Chief of Naval Operations Vern Clark suggested to John Howe, the director of Project Hope, an international humanitarian organization, that the Navy and Project Hope join forces in the tsunami relief effort. Howe agreed and put out a call for volunteer doctors and nurses to supplement the medical staff of hospital ship *Mercy*, slated to head to Southeast Asia. More than 4,000 people applied for the 210 billets! When the hospital ship departed San Diego on 8 January, she had a full Project Hope and Navy complement on board.

Key logistics commands ensured that critical relief supplies continued to flow into the affected areas around the Indian Ocean. The Logistics Group Western Pacific and the Naval Regional Contracting

Center, both located in Singapore, were responsible for the loading of Military Sealift Command vessels with bottled water, food, and medicine, which were delivered to ships off Indonesia for the transfer ashore via helicopter. The fleet and industrial supply centers located in Guam and Yokosuka supported the mammoth logistical effort.

Recognizing the multinational dimensions of the tsunami relief effort, the Pacific Command redesignated Joint Task Force 536 as Combined Support Force 536 on 3 January. The Seventh Fleet units worked especially well with the other naval forces deployed off Indonesia for relief work. The fact that Admiral Doran and Admiral Arun Prakash, Chief of Staff of the Indian Navy, had been classmates at the Indian Defense Services Staff College certainly facilitated their interaction. And Australian Army Lieutenant Colonel Michael Prictor remarked that "we arrived in Indonesia at about the same time as the Americans and we could work together almost immediately because we work together so often." He added that "there were no cultural barriers, no misunderstandings . . . so we were able to get in there and start delivering that aid straight away."

Support facilities in Japan provided considerable assistance. American and Japanese employees at the Yokosuka Fleet Industrial Supply Center facilitated the delivery to Aceh of 10,000 pounds of water, 600,000 pounds of food, 23,000 pounds of medical supplies, and 39,000 tons of general supplies.

In late February–March 2005 *Blue Ridge* deployed to Phuket, Thailand, a resort town badly damaged by the tsunami. Marines from the 2nd FAST and *Blue Ridge* Sailors pitched in to clear the rubble of a destroyed police station and distributed to displaced people in the area 6,000 pounds of clothing, bottled water, and—no less important—baby diapers. Once off Indonesia, *Fort McHenry* hosted the visit of former Presidents George H.W. Bush and Bill Clinton to the disaster area, and her helicopters ferried relief supplies ashore and patients out to the hospital ship.

Admiral Roughead observed that such disaster relief operations "demonstrated the noteworthy effectiveness of international action by military forces, not in waging war, but in relieving human suffering and helping fellow human beings in need." Secretary of the Navy Donald C. Winter echoed those sentiments: "We have seen significantly positive impacts in Indonesia . . . as a direct result of our and other nations' humanitarian assistance and disaster relief."

The admiral also recognized that coordinated naval responses to natural disasters such as the 2004 tsunami could enhance regional cooperation. He enthusiastically supported *Mercy*'s five-month tour throughout Southeast Asia, and in the Pacific Partnership program he encouraged Seventh Fleet and other units to work with national and nongovernmental

Former President Bill Clinton thanks a Sailor and a Marine from dock landing ship Fort McHenry *(LSD 43) for their humanitarian efforts during Operation Unified Assistance, the U.S. program to help Indonesia recover from the Indian Ocean tsunami.*

Hospital ship Mercy *(T-AH 19) departs San Diego in May 2010 for humanitarian missions in the Far East.*

organizations to improve schools and medical facilities. In that regard, the *Essex* expeditionary strike group carried out civil-military projects in the Philippines while the Seabees did the same in Indonesia.

Securing the Maritime Domain

During a major address at the Naval War College in the fall of 2005, Admiral Michael G. Mullen, Chief of Naval Operations (and future Chairman of the Joint Chiefs of Staff), called for a "thousand-ship navy" from the world's maritime nations working together to ensure the freedom and security of the seas. While the U.S. Navy worked for that result with its global presence, he observed that combined action by all the maritime nations would be a force multiplier in thwarting threats at sea. Mullen broadened his initiative the following year at the Western Pacific Naval Symposium in Pearl Harbor, Hawaii, calling for a global maritime partnership that would facilitate multinational naval operations and information-sharing through the use of advanced technology.

In general, America's partners reacted positively to Mullen's proposal, although some were unsure they had the resources to support such an effort or wondered if the primary thrust of the concept was merely to secure U.S. interests. Japan and South Korea endorsed the global concept in

Chief of Naval Operations Admiral Michael Mullen championed international naval cooperation and efforts to ensure the security of the "maritime commons."

As Chief of Naval Operations, Admiral Gary Roughead redoubled efforts he made in his Pacific command billets to strengthen interaction with America's Asian allies.

principle. Admiral Eiji Yoshikawa, chief of staff of the Japan Maritime Self-Defense Force in 2007, commented that "no one nation should have to bear the burden of global security alone. Japan and other partners are ready to share this burden with their longtime friend, the United States." That said, the Japanese naval leader reminded Washington that "there are lingering international Cold War disputes that have yet to be resolved" and added with the usual Japanese understatement that "a regionally focused [U.S.] strategy is not without merit." He noted that bilateral security relationships—like the U.S.-Japan arrangement—had "proven quite successful, particularly at the regional level." Admiral Song Young Moo, Chief of Naval Operations of the Republic of Korea Navy, also highlighted the need for a regional approach to a strategy that dealt with terrorism at sea, weapons proliferation, piracy, and natural disasters.

To support his worldview, in June 2006 Admiral Mullen called for a 21st century U.S. maritime strategy to replace the document that had guided naval leaders in the last years of the Cold War. On 21 November 2007 Admiral Roughead, who succeeded Mullen as CNO; General James T. Conway, Commandant of the Marine Corps; and Admiral Thad Allen, Commandant of the U.S. Coast Guard, published *A Cooperative Strategy for 21st Century Seapower*. In addition to homeland protection, the strategy called for working with partners worldwide to prevent war and to secure the maritime domain, host to 90 percent of the world's trade and two-thirds of petroleum shipping. At any one time ships carrying 12 to 15 million cargo containers were at sea.

The authors stressed that "where tensions are high or where we wish to demonstrate to our friends and allies our commitment to security and stability, U.S. maritime forces will be characterized by regionally concentrated, forward-deployed task forces with the combat power to limit regional conflict, deter major power war, and should deterrence fail, win our Nation's wars as part of a joint or combined campaign." The two regions specified in the document—the Western Pacific and the Arabian Gulf/Indian Ocean—were both operational arenas for Seventh Fleet forces. The document also called for "expanded cooperative relationships with other nations [that would] contribute to the security and stability of the maritime domain for the benefit of all."

In support of this approach, Admiral Roughead visited Indonesia during August 2009 to take part there in the International Maritime Seminar during which he met with naval leaders from India, Australia, Singapore, Malaysia, and New Zealand to discuss ways to "ensure the safety, the security and the prosperity of the world's oceans." Alongside the president of Indonesia, Susilo Bambang Yudhoyono, Admiral Roughead also observed Indonesia's Presidential Sailing Pass in Review, with the Seventh Fleet carrier *George Washington*, guided

Seapower for the 21st Century

On 25 September 2008 *George Washington* (CVN 73) made history as she pulled into Yokosuka, Japan, to begin a tour of duty as the first forward-based nuclear-powered carrier. A few hundred people who opposed the presence of any nuclear-powered warships in Japanese ports demonstrated in front of Yokosuka's gate, but the event paled in comparison to similar protests during the late 1960s. The U.S. Navy's accident-free record in the years since then had persuaded most Japanese that the Seventh Fleet would continue to ensure the environmental safety of the ports from which its ships operated.

The 97,000-ton warship, propelled by two Westinghouse nuclear reactors enabling speeds in excess of 30 knots, was well prepared to maintain the peace in Northeast Asia. Her air wing boasted 80 combat aircraft, including advanced F/A-18E/F Super Hornet strike fighters. The combat veteran's aircraft had taken part in operations Southern Watch, Enduring Freedom, and Iraqi Freedom in the Arabian Gulf and North Arabian Sea.

The carrier represented an impressive workplace. Every day 6,250 crewmembers launched and recovered aircraft, handled four aircraft elevators, prepared 18,000 meals, distilled 400,000 gallons of water, and stood ready to operate the onboard defensive weapons that included Phalanx CIWS, Sea Sparrow surface-to-air missile launchers, and RIM-116 Rolling Airframe Missile launchers.

George Washington wasted no time establishing a presence in the Western Pacific. Soon after her arrival in the Far East the carrier took part in an international fleet review off South Korea. In the summer of 2009 the ship and her escorts visited Australia, Singapore, the Philippines, and Indonesia. To demonstrate the U.S. commitment to the defense of the Republic of Korea after the March 2010 sinking of the ROK Navy corvette *Cheonan* by North Korea, *George Washington* conducted exercises in the Sea of Japan/East Sea with South Korean air and naval forces. The pride of the Seventh Fleet capped off a memorable year in August with the first visit by a U.S. carrier since the Vietnam War to the port of Danang in the Socialist Republic of Vietnam. *George Washington* would continue to serve as a strong symbol of the U.S. commitment to peace and stability in the Seventh Fleet area of responsibility.

Nuclear-powered carrier George Washington *(CVN 73) departs Yokosuka in June 2009 for operations in the Western Pacific.*

Enthusiastic Japanese citizens tour George Washington, *the Navy's only forward-deployed carrier, in December 2009. Seventh Fleet commanders consider it vital that the people of Japan understand and appreciate the value to their security of the U.S. Navy's presence in Japan and close cooperation with the country's defense forces.*

Ordnancemen handle a George Washington *F/A-18 Hornet's missiles. The carrier's combat aircraft provide the fleet with real hitting power.*

missile cruiser *Cowpens* (CG 63), and guided missile destroyers *McCampbell* (DDG 85), *Fitzgerald* (DDG 62), and *Mustin* (DDG 89) representing the U.S. Navy.

America's Ambassador in Far Eastern Waters

An important responsibility of Commander Seventh Fleet is to maintain frequent and positive contact with the civilian and military leaders of the nations in the operational area and to demonstrate America's concern for the well-being of their people. In any given year *Blue Ridge*, with Commander Seventh Fleet embarked, visits ports all over the Western Pacific and Indian Ocean. In 2000, for instance, the flagship's itinerary included Townsville and Darwin, Australia; Dili, East Timor; Singapore; Penang, Malasia; Phuket, Thailand; Kota Kinabalu, Malaysia; Cebu, Philippines; Kure, Japan; Chinhae, South Korea; Sasebo, Japan; Hong Kong, China; and her homeport, Yokosuka, Japan.

Commander Seventh Fleet and his subordinates not only met with their counterparts from the nations they visited, but took part in humanitarian projects. During a February 2004 visit to Kelang, Malaysia, 40 American Sailors made repairs at the Salvation Joy Haven Home for the Elderly. The Seventh Fleet Band entertained a large crowd of local folks with American pop and jazz music, and respectfully took a break when the call for prayer went out from a nearby mosque. That gesture reinforced the positive expressions from the audience. As one local man observed, "[A]s you can see, most of the crowd is Muslim, but these people aren't anti-American."

During a three-day visit to Subic Bay in the Philippines in April, Vice Admiral Robert F. Willard hosted a reception for Philippine Navy Chief of Naval Operations Vice Admiral Ernesto De Leon on board *Coronado* (AGF 11). Thirty-five Seventh Fleet Sailors used the time in port to repaint the Iram Elementary School in nearby Olongapo City. The guided missile cruiser *Cowpens* and dock landing ship *Harpers Ferry* made a port call on the Russian Far Eastern city of Vladivostok in July. The Russian Pacific Fleet hosted a Fourth of July event to honor America's Independence Day at a downtown memorial to the Russian naval dead of World War II. Russians toured the U.S. ships, and Seventh Fleet Sailors and Marines did the same on board the Russian antisubmarine warfare ship *Admiral Vinogradov*.

Several years later Vice Admiral Bird highlighted the irony of *Blue Ridge* making a port call on the Russian Pacific Fleet's

Russian sailors study a navigation chart during their tour of the Ticonderoga-*class guided missile cruiser* Cowpens *(CG 83), which visited Vladivostok in May 2009.*

Vice Admiral John M. Bird, Commander Seventh Fleet, third from left, joins other American and Russian naval officers and civilian officials in a parade in Vladivostok during May 2010 to mark the World War II victory over Nazi Germany.

main naval base: "When I entered the Navy 33 years ago, I could never have imagined the 7th Fleet flagship moored alongside a *Slava*-class cruiser in the closed city of Vladivostok."

In August 2009 Sailors from *Nimitz* volunteered to paint the hull of *Mikasa*, the flagship of Japanese Admiral Heihachiro Togo, the brilliant commander of Japan's decisive 1905 naval victory over Imperial Russia in the Battle of Tsushima. There was also a historical connection between the U.S. carrier and *Mikasa*: Admiral Chester W. Nimitz, the Pacific Fleet commander in World War II, had been instrumental after the war in preserving *Mikasa* as a historic visit ship near the Yokosuka naval base. That same month *George Washington* visited Manila, the first time in more than a decade a carrier had put in at the capital of the Philippines. This visit indicated that the Philippines increasingly valued the security connection to the United States.

In the fall of 2009 the guided missile destroyer *Lassen* (DDG 82) pulled into Vietnam's port of Danang. Historic irony accompanied the ship, named for Lieutenant Clyde E. Lassen, a Vietnam War Medal of Honor recipient. *Lassen*'s commanding officer, Commander Hung Ba Le, was born in Vietnam and his father, an officer in the South Vietnamese navy, once served at the Danang base, the U.S. Navy's largest logistic facility during the war.

During the visit of *Mustin* and *John S. McCain* to Donghae, South Korea, in May 2010, Sailors entertained residents of a retirement home and made repairs at the facility. But the fact that the latter's commanding officer, Commander Jeffrey Kim, was born in South Korea made headlines throughout the nation.

For 13 days during June 2010, several units reporting to Commander Seventh Fleet took part in Pacific Partnership 2010, a civic action program

Nimitz *(CVN 68) Sailors pose for a photo with Japanese citizens in January 2010 as a remembrance of their joint efforts to preserve battleship* Mikasa, *flagship of Admiral Heihachiro Togo during his decisive defeat of the Russian fleet in the Russo-Japanese War.*

Commander Hung Ba Le, commanding officer of guided missile destroyer Lassen *(DDG 82), speaks to the media during his ship's historic November 2009 visit to Danang in the Socialist Republic of Vietnam.*

in the environs of Qui Nhon hosted by the Socialist Republic of Vietnam's Ministry of Health. *Mercy*'s professional staff worked with Vietnamese and Australian medical personnel to deliver care to more than 19,000 patients in the port and surrounding province of Binh Dinh, once a hotbed of Communist guerrilla activity during the Vietnam War. Naval Mobile Construction Battalion 11 and Amphibious Construction Battalion 1 helped Vietnamese volunteers repair and modernize a local medical facility—appropriately named the Hope Center.

Preparing for Action

Seventh Fleet ships take part in more than one hundred exercises each year, some Navy-only or U.S. armed services-only, but most with America's Asia-Pacific allies. As one example, in the late spring of 2005, Seventh Fleet units joined Australian units in a Talisman Saber exercise, a biennial event that prepared the participants for combined contingency operations in the Asia-Pacific region. According to Vice Admiral Greenert,

Seventh Fleet Sailors share kindnesses and friendship with the residents of a nursing home in Busan, Republic of Korea.

the objectives of the exercise were to demonstrate each navy's ability "to operate multi-dimensional joint and combined forces" and "deliver responsive short-term readiness." The Seventh Fleet commander was looking at several levels of operability: "Can we surge quickly, integrate into a coalition, and win? If not, where are we falling short and how do we correct it?" The practice held in Shoalwater Bay in Queensland involved 11,000 U.S. and 6,000 Australian military personnel from their ground, air, and naval forces. The combined forces carried out amphibious landings, parachute drops, infantry maneuvers, and maritime operations in the Coral Sea.

U.S. and Australian amphibious forces exercise ashore in Shoalwater Bay, Australia, during the Talisman Saber exercise of July 2009.

Not only did the U.S.-Australian alliance prosper during the decade, but Australia strengthened its security relationships with Japan and South Korea. Australia's May 2009 defense white paper laid out an ambitious plan to bolster its armed forces with 12 new *Collins*-class conventional submarines and surface warships with advanced antiair and antisubmarine warfare systems. The buildup reflected Australia's concern over China's growing military capability and naval presence in the region.

Preparing for the most challenging assignment—a conflict in Northeast Asia—the Seventh Fleet maintained strong surface, air, and submarine units in the region and conducted frequent contingency exercises with other U.S. military forces and with South Korean naval forces. The most important combined exercises relating to the defense of South Korea were Ulchi Focus Lens, Foal Eagle, Ulchi Freedom Guardian, and Key Resolve. The annual exercises routinely involved tens of thousands of personnel from the United States and the Republic of Korea.

Royal Australian Navy replenishment tanker Success *proceeds on a parallel course with U.S. dock landing ship* Tortuga *(LSD 46) during the annual Talisman Saber exercise of 2009.*

No year passed during the decade without at-sea exercises for the Seventh Fleet and its longtime partner, the JMSDF. In February 2009, for example, the *John C. Stennis* (CVN 74) carrier strike group carried out antisubmarine warfare exercises in the Pacific Ocean with the Japanese destroyers *Amagiri* and *Oonami*. American naval leaders and Sailors frequently showed their appreciation for Japan's half-century of welcoming the forward-deployed warships of the Seventh Fleet. In May 2009, for instance, Vice Admiral Bird hosted the visit of two of Japan's top naval officers to U.S. naval vessels forward deployed at Yokosuka. He led the tour of the fast attack submarine *Seawolf* (SSN 21) for Vice Admiral Tohru Izumi, commander in chief of the JMSDF Self-Defense Fleet, and Vice Admiral Mikio Nagata, commander of the Fleet Submarine Force. That same month, the Seventh Fleet Band performed at the 70th annual Shimoda Black Ships Festival, marking Commodore Matthew C. Perry's 1854 visit to Japan and the seminal trade agreement between the United States and Japan.

The U.S.-Japan connection also prospered in the development of defensive weapon systems meant to discourage or defeat ballistic missiles launched from North Korea or China. The United States and Japan established a five-year program to develop a JMSDF antiballistic missile capability or "sea-based midcourse defense (SMD) system." It bore fruit in December 2007 when Japanese Aegis destroyer *Kongo* shot down a dummy missile with a U.S. Standard Missile 3 at the Navy's Pacific Missile Range Facility in Hawaii. After the successful test Tokyo, with Washington's assistance, equipped over the next three years four of its destroyers with the proven antimissile system.

Commander Republic of Korea Fleet Vice Admiral Jung-hwa Park and Commander U.S. Seventh Fleet Vice Admiral John M. Bird reach an agreement in March 2010 on the transition of wartime operational control of naval forces in Korean waters from the U.S. Navy to the ROK Navy.

Carrier John C. Stennis *(CVN 74), attack submarine* Seawolf *(SSN 21), and Japanese destroyer* Oonami *during a 2009 undersea warfare exercise in the Pacific Ocean.*

Japanese and American sailors take part in a January 2010 ceremony marking the 50th anniversary of the U.S.-Japan Mutual Security Treaty.

The Seventh Fleet band marches through the streets of Shimoda in the 2009 Black Ships Festival commemorating Commodore Matthew C. Perry's 1854 visit that established economic and political ties between the United States and Japan.

Guided missile destroyer Curtis Wilbur *(DDG 54) fires an SM-2 air defense missile during readiness training in September 2009.*

In a larger sense the connection between the Seventh Fleet and the JMSDF was, in the words of Vice Admiral Bird, "arguably the most critical Navy-to-Navy partnership in the world." On the occasion of the 50th anniversary of the U.S.-Japan Treaty of Mutual Cooperation and Security in January 2010, Bird noted that "not a day goes by that our two fleets are not somehow working together—whether training or participating in an exercise, sharing information, coordinating operations, or planning for contingencies."

Looking back on the U.S.-Japan alliance, Bird observed that "working together, we kept the forces of darkness in check, and allowed Japan and the nations of this region to grow strong economies and vibrant democracies. . . . We have promoted democracy, respect for human rights, and free markets."

The U.S.–PRC Connection

One big question for U.S. naval leaders of the 21st century was the role China would play. Only the People's Republic of China possessed the military forces and resources to challenge America's presence in Asia and its interaction with regional nations and their navies.

In the first years of the decade, China did not mount an outright challenge to that presence. Beijing hoped its top priority—the rapid and sustained growth of China's domestic economy—would foster national unity and the continued political control of the Chinese Communist Party. The PRC government also recognized that this economic growth helped limit dissent from disaffected members of the majority Han Chinese population and from Tibetans, Muslim Uighurs, and Falun Gong religious adherents. In 2004 alone, there were thousands of mass protests in China involving almost four million people.

Beijing's leaders were also intent on convincing the Chinese residents of Taiwan and the former British colony of Hong Kong that their economic prosperity would not be jeopardized by an aggressive PRC foreign policy. Strong sentiment existed among China's political class that the country should look to domestic concerns and retain its continental, defensive focus.

The health of China's economy depended on two major factors—exports and access to foreign sources of energy. By 2009 more than 90 percent of China's foreign trade moved by sea, and seaborne oil imports constituted more than 80 percent of oil imports. China, the third largest shipbuilding nation in the world, managed a fleet of 300,000 oceangoing merchantmen, coastal vessels, and smaller craft. China was already the world's fifth largest investor in seabed development in 2004, and by 2006 the maritime industry accounted for nearly 10 percent of China's gross national product. One of Beijing's major trading partners, the United States consumed 21 percent of China's global exports in 2007 and kept millions of Chinese employed. By July 2010 China had surpassed Japan to become the world's second most powerful economy after that of the United States.

China depended on oil that arrived via the South China Sea and Indian Ocean from the Arabian Gulf and Africa. By 2010 China was the second greatest consumer of oil in the world after the United States. Many pragmatic Chinese analysts concluded that "cooperation with other oil-consuming great powers, including the United States, [was vital] in order to secure stability of the oil and gas supply." Analysts Andrew Ericson and Lyle Goldstein have contended that "without adequate oil supplies, China's economy would grind to a halt as fuel shortages shut down trucks, ships, aircraft, and much of the rail system." Naval War College scholars Toshi Yoshihara and James R. Holmes aptly concluded that "assuring safe passage for merchantmen bearing energy supplies from the Indian Ocean has come to obsess Beijing."

In one of China's most prestigious military journals, PLAN Senior Captain Xu Qi wrote that China's "long period of prosperity [as well as] the Chinese nation's existence, development, and great resurgence [all] increasingly rely on the sea. . . . Sea lines of communication [are becoming] lifelines of national existence [and] development." Moreover, given China's contiguous borders with Pakistan and Burma, access by sea to the ports and naval bases of these Beijing-friendly nations became increasingly important in the 21st century.

A Chinese confrontation with India, Japan, South Korea, or the nations of Southeast Asia—many having military alliances with the United States—over control of the oil routes would be fraught with risk for Beijing. The navies of Japan, Taiwan, the ASEAN nations, and India would pose considerable problems for the PLAN. Chinese leaders understood that the PRC's aggressive behavior over Taiwan in 1995 and 1996 had sparked a military confrontation with the United States and sent negative shock waves throughout Asia.

Beijing also recognized that China could not match the post–Cold War power of the U.S. armed forces in general and the Seventh Fleet in particular. As a U.S. Defense Department document concluded, China "is neither capable of using military power to secure its foreign energy investments nor of defending critical sea lanes against disruption." Indeed, according to Ericson and Gabriel B. Collins, "a wide variety of influential Chinese experts, including scholars, policy analysts, and members of the military, believe that the [U.S. Navy] can sever China's seaborne energy supplies at will and in a crisis might well choose to do so." This action would clearly torpedo China's continued economic progress.

Cooperation with the United States and the maritime nations of Asia stood the best chance of ensuring the security of oceangoing commerce and China's access to overseas energy resources. U.S. foreign policy encouraged China's evolution as a proponent of the global economic system and a trusted member of the international community.

With respect to China, in 2006 Admiral Roughead, as commander of the Pacific Fleet, alluded to discussions underway as part of the Military Maritime Consultative Agreement to

Senator John McCain visits the guided missile destroyer John S. McCain *(DDG 56), named for his father and grandfather, both distinguished U.S. Navy flag officers, April 2009.*

"increase transparency and decrease uncertainty and risk of miscalculation between the navies of the United States and China." He believed such interaction would encourage China's "peaceful rise in the region and will show it to be a responsible stakeholder in the maritime domain." Another prescient American, Senator John McCain, recognized that despite significant differences with the PRC over its domestic governance and human rights, "the U.S. shares common interests with China that can form the basis of a strong partnership on issues of global concern, including climate change, trade, and proliferation" of nuclear weapons. In 2009 President Barak Obama noted that the United States and China "can work together constructively bilaterally and with others to reduce tensions" if China "agrees to play by the rules and act as a positive force for balanced world growth."

If the United States tried to ostracize China, it simply would not work. As Australian analyst Paul Dibb noted, U.S. policy should not "demonize China as the next 'evil empire.' Neither Japan, South Korea, nor Australia would be willing parties to such an ill considered approach." Evan Medeiros echoed the statement: "[N]one of these nations want to choose between the United States and China, and all reject having to make such a choice." He added, "none want China to dominate the region. . . [but] all want China to play a major role in managing regional challenges." Green suggested that India too would be unlikely to join a "contain China" coalition. Pursuing a strategy to contain China as during the Cold War, as viewers made clear, would be a nonstarter; the "danger in pushing too hard for an American-led [anti-China] bloc is that the United States may end up being the only member."

There were indications that the PRC would act as a force for stability. Beijing's 1997 incorporation of Hong Kong into the PRC had not been heavy-handed, and the island city's residents were accorded some freedoms unavailable to Chinese on the mainland. And there were other examples of Chinese accommodations. In late 2000 China and Vietnam signed an agreement establishing maritime boundaries and fishing areas in the Gulf of Tonkin. In 2003 China and India signed a declaration of friendship and cooperation, and the navies of the two countries held joint exercises for the first time. That same year China expressed its intention to avoid conflict with other claimants to the Spratly Islands in the South China Sea and formally joined ASEAN's Treaty of Amity and Cooperation in Southeast Asia. China's pivotal role in the Six-Party Talks (involving the PRC, U.S., Russia, Japan, South Korea, and North Korea) with North Korea's Kim Jong-il over his nation's development of a nuclear arsenal highlighted how important China could be in assuring regional peace and stability.

In December 2004 Chinese Premier Hu Jintao's government published a document relating to the PLA that charged the military with playing "an important role in maintaining world peace and promoting common development." Bejing's reaction to Japanese testing of a U.S. antiballistic missile system in December 2007 seemed relatively mild. The prevailing view in Beijing, according to Ericson and Goldstein, was that "as long as China's navy continuously engages with the outside world, developing opportunities to partner with other countries, the world will come to accept, and even welcome, a strong Chinese navy."

The PRC endeavored to work with the U.S. in the maritime domain, as shown in its membership, along with the United States, Canada, Japan, South Korea, and Russia, in the North Pacific Heads of Coast Guards Association, which dealt with maritime security issues. Chinese and U.S. Coast Guard units also conducted annual search and rescue exercises. From 2002 to 2007 the U.S. Coast Guard worked successfully with many Chinese government agencies on maritime safety and other issues. In May 2006 USCGC *Sequoia* (WLB 215) made the first visit by a Coast Guard vessel to China when she tied up at Shanghai. A month later USCGC *Rush* (WHEC 723) visited Qingdao. Chinese fisheries patrol boats annually

U.S. Coast Guard high endurance cutter Rush *(WHEC 723) works with Chinese People's Liberation Army Navy ships during maritime safety exercises in July 2010.*

Commander U.S. Pacific Fleet Admiral Gary Roughead converses with the commander of China's South Sea Fleet Vice Admiral Gu Wengen in November 2006 when a Seventh Fleet contingent visited Zhanjiang.

joined with coast guard vessels and patrol aircraft from the United States, Japan, and Russia to take action against illegal fishing in the North Pacific. In the spring of 2007 the PLAN chief of staff, Admiral Wu Shengli, visited the United States. In December 2008 Beijing deployed two destroyers and an auxiliary to the Gulf of Aden to take part in international antipiracy patrols.

The United States made other moves to further U.S.-China maritime cooperation. In November 2002 the Seventh Fleet destroyer *Paul F. Foster* (DD 964) visited Qingdao, and the next month U.S. naval representatives attended a meeting there on maritime and air safety. In September 2004 for the first time Seventh Fleet warships visited Zhanjiang, homeport of the PLAN's South Sea Fleet, when the guided missile cruiser *Cowpens* and guided missile frigate *Vandegrift* (FFG 48) made a port call. In October the PLAN destroyer *Shenzhen* and supply ship *Qinghai* visited Guam. In 2004 *Blue Ridge* made a port call on Shanghai, China, where the Seventh Fleet commander, Vice Admiral Willard, met with Vice Mayor Feng Guoqing and Vice Admiral Zhao Guojun, commander of the East Sea Fleet, one of China's three main combat formations. While in port Seventh Fleet Sailors and Marines toured the PLAN guided missile frigate *Lian Yun Gang*.

In November 2006 Admiral Roughead, then Pacific Fleet commander, visited Beijing, Shanghai, and Zhanjiang to oversee a bilateral search and rescue exercise involving the guided missile destroyer *Fitzgerald*, amphibious transport dock *Juneau* (LPD 10), and PLAN units.

U.S. naval vessels regularly visited Hong Kong, a favorite Seventh Fleet liberty port.

To commemorate the 60th anniversary of the founding of the People's Republic of China, in April 2009 *Fitzgerald* took part in an International Fleet Review in the port of Qingdao. On hand for the occasion were Admiral Roughead, then-Chief of Naval Operations, and Vice Admiral Bird, Commander Seventh Fleet. As an indication of how far U.S.-Chinese relations had come, probably few Chinese or Americans present understood the irony of the Seventh Fleet Rock Band entertaining citizens of the port city that was the fleet's homeport during the early years of the red-hot Cold War.

Deterrence of and Readiness for War

While the fleet worked to enhance collective security and multinational cooperation in the maritime domain of the Western Pacific, deterrence of war and readiness for war remained core responsibilities. Indeed, Vice Admiral Bird put special emphasis on warfighting readiness during his tenure as Commander Seventh Fleet. The events of 9/11 compelled naval leaders to counter terrorism but, in the words of retired Rear Admiral Michael McDevitt, "the 'old' concerns remain—Korea, China's stance toward Taiwan, China's across the board military modernization."

Moreover, the erratic, confrontational, and nuclear-armed regime of North Korean leader Kim Jong-il frequently threatened the United States, South Korea, and Japan with war and defied UN resolutions and Six-Party diplomatic efforts with regard to its nuclear capability. In June 2002, apparently to retaliate for its defeat in the sea Battle of Yeonpyeoung of June 1999, the North Korean navy attacked and sank an ROKN patrol boat, killing eight South Korean sailors. In February 2003 Pyongyang sent a MiG-19 over the Northern Limit Line and fired an antiship missile into the Sea of Japan/East Sea. The following month four North Korean MiGs closed on a U.S. Air Force RC-135S intelligence-gathering plane over the same waters, one jet coming within 50 feet of the American plane. Soon afterward, Kim's regime launched another antiship missile into the sea. Then, North Korean guards on the DMZ fired on and damaged a South Korean guard post. On 5 July 2006 (4 July, Independence Day in the U.S.) North Korea launched multiple Scud, No Dong, and Taepodong II missiles into the Sea of Japan/East Sea. Pyongyang's above-ground nuclear tests in October erased all doubt about the existence of a nuclear weapon capability in North Korea. In April 2009 North Korea again successfully launched an advanced Taepodong II ballistic missile.

In the face of aggressive acts by Kim's government and continued intransigence in the Six-Party Talks over North Korea's development of nuclear-weapons, the United States and the Republic of Korea reaffirmed the importance of their defensive alliance. In March 2009 Vice Admiral Bird met with Vice Admiral Jung-hwa Park, Commander in Chief, Republic of Korea Fleet, in Busan, South Korea.

Minehunter Avenger *(MCM 1) at the pier in Sasebo and decked out in honor of the 50th anniversary of the U.S.-Japan Mutual Security Treaty, January 2010.*

The two men signed an operational plan, largely developed through the hard work during previous years of Rear Admiral James P. "Phil" Wisecup, then Commander, Naval Forces Korea. The plan saw the ROKN taking the operational lead during wartime and the Seventh Fleet taking a supporting role.

ROKN guided missile destroyer Sejong the Great *and Seventh Fleet carrier* George Washington *underway in 2009.*

Park observed that "our signatures [on the plan] here serve as a reminder to all that the U.S. and the Republic of Korea stand side by side to defend this free nation." They anticipated the turnover of operational control in 2015.

Several months later Secretary of the Navy Ray Mabus met with top officials in Busan to highlight once more the strength of the U.S.-ROK alliance. Bird worked closely with his South Korean counterpart to improve interoperability and information sharing between the Seventh Fleet and the ROKN. U.S. and South Korean naval leaders also worked to strengthen their mine countermeasures capability. In 2010 mine clearance vessels *Avenger* (MCM 1) and *Defender* (MCM 2) began operating from the naval base at Sasebo, Japan, and MH-53 Sea Dragon mine-hunting helicopters moved forward to Pohang, South Korea.

In September Bird, his task force commanders, and their South Korean counterparts gathered in Busan and Seoul to streamline Seventh Fleet–ROKN command-and-control procedures. To reinforce the importance of the U.S. commitment to South Korea, the admiral and his task force commanders used the occasion to travel to the armistice site at Panmunjom, where they stood on South Korea's forward defense line, only a few feet from North Korea.

In October 2009 Seventh Fleet and ROKN units conducted a bilateral exercise to highlight the importance of security and stability in Northeast Asia. For the first time in 12 years, the U.S. Navy's forward-deployed carrier *George Washington* steamed into the Yellow Sea/West Sea. The nuclear-powered *Nimitz*-class warship, part of Rear Admiral Kevin M. Donegan's Battle Force Seventh Fleet (TF 70), operated in company with the guided missile cruisers *Cowpens* and *Shiloh* (CG 67) and guided missile destroyer *Fitzgerald*. A pair of ROKN ships—guided missile destroyer *Sejong the Great* and destroyer *Kan Jan Chan*—exercised with the American carrier task force.

In March 2010 a North Korean submarine torpedoed the ROKN corvette *Cheonan*, sinking the ship and killing 46 South Korean sailors. In addressing new ensigns of the JMSDF in May 2010, Vice Admiral Bird emphasized that "we are concerned about North Korea, a dangerous and unpredictable regime . . . with its provocations,

Military Sealift Command salvage ship Salvor *(T-ARS 52) supports the ROK Navy's recovery of* Cheonan *sunk by a North Korean submarine in March 2010.*

Commander Seventh Fleet Vice Admiral John M. Bird speaks to new ensigns of the Japan Maritime Self-Defense Force during his May 2010 visit to the training ship Kashima *in Yokosuka.*

proliferation concerns and efforts to further develop weapons of mass destruction." In July Secretary of State Hilary Clinton remarked that "an isolated and belligerent North Korea has embarked on a campaign of provocative, dangerous behavior." During the summer of 2010 Seventh Fleet and ROKN units carried out antisubmarine exercises in the Sea of Japan/East Sea to highlight allied solidarity. This exercise occurred despite Pyongyang's threat to "counter [the exercise] with their powerful nuclear deterrent." In July all five members of the UN Security Council, including China, passed a resolution condemning the torpedoing of *Cheonan* but, at Beijing's insistence, made no reference to North Korea as the culprit.

China: A Regional Partner or a Regional Threat?

During the first decade of the 21st century China usually acted responsibly on the international stage and refrained from provocative actions. But there were exceptions. In November 2004 a JMSDF P-3C patrol plane discovered an unidentified undersea vessel in Japan's territorial waters near Sakishima. Tokyo concluded that the intruder, which eventually withdrew to international waters, was a Chinese nuclear-powered submarine. The Ministry of Defense issued National Defense Program Guidelines that reaffirmed Japan's intention to prevent future violations of its surrounding seas. In the fall a flotilla of PLAN Russian-made *Sovremenny*-class guided missile destroyers operated menacingly around islands in the East China Sea claimed by Beijing and Tokyo. The Chinese reportedly trained antiaircraft weapons on a Japanese P-3C that flew near the PLAN ships.

In January 2007 the Chinese destroyed one of their old weather satellites orbiting 537 miles above the earth with an antisatellite missile. With this capability, the PRC had the potential to neutralize America's fleet of navigation, communication, intelligence, and targeting satellites.

In November 2007 the PRC took actions that introduced a chill to U.S.-Chinese relations. First, Beijing refused to allow Seventh Fleet minesweepers *Patriot* (MCM 7) and *Guardian* (MCM 5), low on fuel and facing an approaching storm, to refuel in Hong Kong. Then the PRC denied the *Kitty Hawk* battle group a long-planned visit to the former British colony. Washington ordered the carrier group north to Japan—via the Taiwan Strait. Soon afterward, Admiral Timothy J. Keating, commander of the U.S.

A crewman of a Chinese vessel attempts to snag the towed array cable of Impeccable *in the South China Sea 75 miles south of Hainan Island in March 2009.*

The Military Sealift Command's ocean surveillance ship Impeccable *(T-AGOS 23) supports the Navy by using both passive and active sonar arrays to detect and track undersea threats.*

Pacific Command, told Chinese leaders in Beijing that their permission was not required for U.S. naval vessels to transit the international waters of the strait.

By 2008 China had positioned over 1,000 ballistic and cruise missiles in the region opposite Taiwan, increasing that number by 100 every year.

To dissuade the PRC from applying any military pressure on Taiwan during the March 2008 national elections, Washington deployed the *Kitty Hawk* and *John C. Stennis* strike groups just to the east of the island.

In March 2009, in a coordinated action, five Chinese ships harassed *Impeccable* (T-AGOS 23), an unarmed Military Sealift Command surveillance ship operating in waters 75 miles south of China's Hainan Island. Two of the Chinese ships approached perilously close to the U.S. vessel, forced her to come to an all-stop to avoid a collision, and attempted to snag her towed acoustic array with a grappling hook. U.S. leaders considered the Chinese actions a dangerous breach of the UN Convention on the Law of the Sea and universally accepted maritime safety procedures.

In following months Chinese naval officers used provocative language in communications with Seventh Fleet commanders, and PLAN vessels interfered with the safe passage of U.S. ships to

A Marine AH-1W Super Cobra operates from amphibious assault ship Peleliu *(LHA 5) in June 2010.*

People's Liberation Army Navy marines stand at attention during the visit of Seventh Fleet units to Zhanjiang, People's Republic of China, in November 2006.

signal Beijing's widely disputed contention that the South China Sea belonged to China.

During 2010 Beijing repeatedly called the South China Sea a "core interest" and implied the use of force to back up that claim. At ASEAN's Asian Regional Forum meeting in the summer, the United States, Vietnam, and ten other nations with interests in the region called for a multilateral approach to the issue. Secretary of State Clinton observed that the United States opposed "the use or threat of force by any claimant" to the South China Sea.

U.S. leaders grew increasingly concerned about Beijing's long-term intentions. Chinese displeasure over the January 2010 announcement that the United States would provide Taiwan with $6.4 billion in defensive arms prompted Beijing to suspend military-to-military contacts. In May, Vice Admiral Bird gave voice to his views: "We . . . are concerned about China. Let me say right up front that we don't consider China an enemy. But we are troubled by their lack of transparency as they build up their military in such a rapid fashion." He added, "just consider what happened last month, when ten ships and submarines of the PLA Navy's East Sea Fleet crossed the Ryuku island chain,

Guided missile cruiser Lake Erie *(CG 70), foreground, steams alongside Chinese guided missile destroyer* Shijiazhuang *and tanker* Hongzehu *in a January 2010 chance encounter in the Pacific Ocean east of the Philippines.*

conducted exercises around [a Japanese island] and flew helicopters very close to Japanese ships. The government and the people of Japan were troubled by this, justifiably so."

The increasing dedication of resources to the PLAN by the end of the decade brought on line advanced warships, amphibious vessels, aircraft, cruise missiles, and submarines. One of Beijing's primary goals, frequently voiced by government spokesmen, continued to be incorporation of Taiwan and its citizens into the People's Republic of China.

An amphibious assault vehicle enters the sea from the well deck of dock landing ship Harpers Ferry (LSD 49) *in a 2010 exercise off Okinawa's White Beach.*

Aviation Boatswain's Mate (Fuel) 2nd Class Ranulfo C. Gonzalez handles a JP-5 fuel hose on board amphibious assault ship Essex.

One of Washington's top foreign policy responsibilities was to prevent that transition if it negated the wishes of the people on Taiwan or involved the use of military force. The Seventh Fleet, the primary instrument of U.S. policy in the Western Pacific, conducted numerous joint and combined exercises designed to discourage Chinese plans to establish sea control around Taiwan, deny those waters to U.S. naval units, or launch an amphibious/airborne invasion of the island.

Preparing for Future Threats

To deal with regional contingencies, especially a major theater conflict, the Pacific Fleet had established Joint Task Force 519 in 1999. The intent then was to re-energize the Pacific Fleet as a warfighter rather than a mere force-provider. Commander Seventh Fleet was and is the Maritime Component Commander of

The Venerable One

No U.S. naval vessel has seen, and indeed made, as much modern history as the Seventh Fleet command ship *Blue Ridge* (LCC 19). Commissioned in November 1970, *Blue Ridge* made her Western Pacific debut in January 1972 when she became the flagship of the Seventh Fleet's amphibious force at Subic Bay. That same year the ship took part in amphibious landings on the northern coast of South Vietnam and dodged fire from North Vietnamese shore batteries near the Demilitarized Zone. *Blue Ridge* assisted in Operation End Sweep, the clearance of mines from Haiphong harbor during 1973 and returned to waters off Vietnam in April 1975 for the last act in the long Vietnam drama. Along with a large flotilla of other Seventh Fleet ships, she helped evacuate tens of thousands of Vietnamese and Americans in Operation Frequent Wind.

Command ship Blue Ridge *(LCC 19) at Yokosuka in September 2009.*

In October 1979 the Navy made *Blue Ridge* the flagship of Commander Seventh Fleet forward-based at Yokosuka, Japan. From that point on, she took part in missions that would be her forte—visiting ports throughout the Western Pacific, hosting shipboard tours by foreign dignitaries, and serving as the command post for naval exercises with the Japan Maritime Self-Defense Force, the Royal Australian Navy, and other allied navies.

Captain J. Stephen Maynard, commanding officer of Blue Ridge, *thanks Captain Wen Rulang of the Chinese People's Liberation Army Navy for a scrapbook of the command ship's two-day visit to the South Sea Fleet port of Zhanjiang in March 2005.*

Blue Ridge and other Seventh Fleet units operated in the waters of Northeast Asia on the eastern fringes of the USSR at the height of the Cold War. On one occasion, Soviet warships challenged the passage of the flagship between the Soviet occupied Kurile Islands and Japan's Hokkaido Island. A Soviet guided missile cruiser communicated to *Blue Ridge* that the U.S. ship had violated Soviet territorial waters. *Blue Ridge* replied that she was "exercising [the] right to transit the strait connecting two international waters" and continued steaming through without further interference.

Blue Ridge went to war again in the fall of 1990 when she put in at Bahrain in the Arabian Gulf to serve as the flagship of Vice Admiral Henry H. Mauz Jr. (and later Vice Admiral Stanley R. Arthur), dual-hatted as Commander, U.S. Seventh Fleet/Commander, U.S. Naval Forces Central Command. At sea in the Northern Arabian Gulf, *Blue Ridge* steamed alongside the warships of Battle Force Zulu when allied forces liberated Kuwait and defeated Saddam Hussein's forces in Operation Desert Storm.

After the Gulf War, *Blue Ridge* continued to represent the United States during port calls and other official functions. The flagship made frequent visits to Vladivostok, Shanghai, and other naval bases of former Cold War adversaries. In March 2005, for instance, *Blue Ridge* made a port call at Zhanjiang, China, home of the People's Liberation Army Navy's South Sea Fleet. For the remainder of the decade *Blue Ridge* continued to serve as a floating headquarters for Commander Seventh Fleet, made port visits for officers and enlisted personnel to meet with Asian counterparts, and participated in humanitarian works throughout the Seventh Fleet's area of responsibility.

Landing craft tied up in the well deck of Essex *during the 2010 Cobra Gold exercise off Thailand.*

JTF 519. In a crisis, as many as 400 naval personnel would deploy from their duty stations worldwide to Japan and embark in *Blue Ridge* to strengthen the joint task force staff. Since the flagship could steam to any location in the Seventh Fleet's area of responsibility, the joint force commander had the ability to direct operations in proximity to a crisis and not have to worry about acquiring a headquarters ashore. As observed by Admiral Doran, commander of the Pacific Fleet in 2003, JTF 519 "has the distinct advantage of operational independence in theaters where access is problematic either politically or because of significant force protection requirements." The first exercises to test this use of the flagship, named Terminal Fury, occurred in October and December 2002 and affirmed the utility of the floating task force headquarters.

The Navy took other steps strengthening its ability to manage potential conflicts in the Far East. The Bush-era Defense Department's Quadrennial Defense Review established that 60 percent of the Navy's warships would be deployed to the Pacific, a move endorsed by the Obama administration.

Task Force 74, the submarine arm, constitutes one of the fleet's most powerful warfighting components. As a submariner, Bird certainly had a warm spot in his heart for the undersea vessels, but the Seventh Fleet commander hit the mark when he noted that "in the Pacific you rely on submarines more than anything else; they are the killer arrow in our warfighting quiver giving me options and capabilities that don't exist anywhere else."

In 2010 the nuclear-powered attack submarines *Buffalo* (SSN 715), *City of Corpus Christi* (SSN 705), and *Houston* (SSN 713), supported by submarine tender *Frank Cable* (AS 40), presented a formidable threat to all would-be aggressors in the operational area. The forward deployment of two of the Navy's four nuclear-powered ballistic missile submarines,

Attack submarine Tucson *(SSN 770) during a Seventh Fleet-ROK Navy exercise in July 2010.*

Ohio (SSGN 726) and *Michigan* (SSGN 727), between 2007 and 2010 significantly strengthened the Guam-based task force. In addition, *Florida* (SSGN 728) operated from Diego Garcia. The converted ships are capable of launching a combined total of 462 Tomahawk cruise missiles.

The combat power of these submarines enabled Commander Seventh Fleet to present a real conventional deterrent to potential aggressors. The stealth, speed, and flexibility of these warships also helped the fleet commander gather intelligence on the open-sea and littoral activities of potential adversaries and provide advance warning of any pending attacks. If deterrence failed, the submarines could launch strike operations with Tomahawk cruise missiles and initiate special operations with unmanned aerial and undersea vehicles and Navy SEALs. To publicize the combat power of the Seventh Fleet, on 28 June 2010 *Michigan* visited Busan, South Korea; *Ohio* put in at Subic Bay in the Philippines, and *Florida* made port at Diego Garcia in the Indian Ocean—simultaneously.

In the first years of the momentous 21st century, the U.S. Navy in general and the Seventh Fleet in particular redoubled efforts to foster partnerships with the naval forces of the Asia-Pacific region to secure the maritime domain for the benefit of all. Recognizing that "smart power" could be a powerful tool for the United States, the Seventh Fleet devoted considerable attention to winning friends afloat and ashore. At the same time, in keeping with its vital readiness and warfighting responsibilities, the Seventh Fleet operated to discourage aggressive behavior by North Korea, China, and other potential belligerents and honed the professional skills of its commanders and Sailors. The Seventh Fleet continued to provide the United States and its allies with "Ready Power for Peace."

APPENDIX

Commanders, U.S. Seventh Fleet

Vice Admiral Arthur S. Carpender	19 Feb 1943–26 Nov 1943
Vice Admiral Thomas C. Kinkaid	26 Nov 1943–19 Nov 1945
Vice Admiral Daniel E. Barbey	19 Nov 1945–08 Jan 1946
Admiral Charles M. Cooke Jr.*	08 Jan 1946–24 Feb 1948
Vice Admiral Oscar C. Badger**	24 Feb 1948–28 Aug 1949
Vice Admiral Russell S. Berkey**	28 Aug 1949–04 Apr 1950
Rear Admiral Walter F. Boone, Acting	04 Apr 1950–19 May 1950
Vice Admiral Arthur D. Struble	19 May 1950–28 Mar 1951
Vice Admiral Harold M. Martin	28 Mar 1951–03 Mar 1952
Vice Admiral Robert P. Briscoe	03 Mar 1952–20 May 1952
Vice Admiral Joseph J. Clark	20 May 1952–01 Dec 1953
Vice Admiral Alfred M. Pride	01 Dec 1953–19 Dec 1955
Vice Admiral Stuart H. Ingersoll	19 Dec 1955–28 Jan 1957
Vice Admiral Wallace M. Beakley	28 Jan 1957–30 Sep 1958
Vice Admiral Frederick N. Kivette	30 Sep 1958–07 Mar 1960
Vice Admiral Charles D. Griffin	07 Mar 1960–28 Oct 1961
Vice Admiral William A. Schoech	28 Oct 1961–13 Oct 1962
Vice Admiral Thomas H. Moorer	13 Oct 1962–11 Jun 1964
Vice Admiral Roy L. Johnson	11 Jun 1964–01 Mar 1965
Vice Admiral Paul P. Blackburn Jr.	01 Mar 1965–07 Oct 1965
Rear Admiral Joseph W. Williams, Acting	07 Oct 1965–13 Dec 1965
Vice Admiral John J. Hyland	13 Dec 1965–06 Nov 1967
Vice Admiral William F. Bringle	06 Nov 1967–10 Mar 1970
Vice Admiral Maurice F. Weisner	10 Mar 1970–18 Jun 1971
Vice Admiral William P. Mack	18 Jun 1971–23 May 1972
Vice Admiral James L. Holloway III	23 May 1972–28 Jul 1973
Vice Admiral George P. Steele	28 Jul 1973–14 Jun 1975
Vice Admiral Thomas B. Hayward	14 Jun 1975–24 Jul 1976
Vice Admiral Robert B. Baldwin	24 Jul 1976–31 May 1978
Vice Admiral Sylvester R. Foley Jr.	31 May 1978–14 Feb 1980
Vice Admiral Carlisle A.H. Trost	14 Feb 1980–16 Sep 1981
Vice Admiral M. Straser Holcomb	16 Sep 1981–09 May 1983
Vice Admiral James R. Hogg	09 May 1983–04 Mar 1985
Vice Admiral Paul F. McCarthy Jr.	04 Mar 1985–09 Dec 1986
Vice Admiral Paul D. Miller	09 Dec 1986–21 Oct 1988
Vice Admiral Henry H. Mauz Jr.	21 Oct 1988–01 Dec 1990
Vice Admiral Stanley R. Arthur	01 Dec 1990–03 Jul 1992
Vice Admiral Timothy W. Wright	03 Jul 1992–28 Jul 1994
Vice Admiral Archie R. Clemins	28 Jul 1994–13 Sep 1996
Vice Admiral Robert J. Natter	13 Sep 1996–12 Aug 1998

Vice Admiral Walter F. Doran	12 Aug 1998–12 Jul 2000
Vice Admiral James W. Metzger	12 Jul 2000–18 Jul 2002
Vice Admiral Robert F. Willard	18 Jul 2002–06 Aug 2004
Vice Admiral Jonathan W. Greenert	06 Aug 2004–12 Sep 2006
Vice Admiral Douglas Crowder	12 Sep 2006–12 Jul 2008
Vice Admiral John M. Bird	12 Jul 2008–10 Sep 2010
Vice Admiral Scott R. Van Buskirk	10 Sep 2010–07 Sep 2011
Vice Admiral Scott H. Swift	07 Sep 2011–

* Commander, U.S. Seventh Fleet changed to Commander, U.S. Naval Forces Western Pacific, 1 January 1947.

** Commander, U.S. Naval Forces Western Pacific, with additional duty as Commander, U.S. Seventh Fleet from 1 August 1949 to 11 February 1950 when the entity became solely U.S. Seventh Fleet.

Commander Seventh Fleet Vice Admiral Jonathan Greenert, on board the amphibious assault ship Essex *(LHD 2) in Sasebo, Japan, praises the work of the ship's Sailors and Marines during Exercise Balikatan in the Philippines, April 2006.*

ABBREVIATIONS

AAWC	Antiair Warfare Commander
AD	Destroyer Tender
AE	Ammunition Ship
AF	Stores Ship
AFS	Combat Stores Ship
AGC	Amphibious Force Flagship
AGER	Environmental Research Ship
AGF	Auxiliary Command Ship
AGI	Auxiliary, General, Intelligence
AH	Hospital Ship
ANZUS	Australia, New Zealand, United States
AO	Oiler
APA	Attack Transport
APEC	Asia Pacific Economic Cooperation
ARS	Repair Ship
AS	Submarine Tender
ASEAN	Association of Southeast Asian Nations
ASW	Antisubmarine Warfare
ATS	Salvage Ship
AV	Seaplane Tender
BB	Battleship
CA	Heavy Cruiser
CARAT	Cooperation Afloat Readiness and Training
CG	Guided Missile Cruiser
CIA	Central Intelligence Agency
CIC	Combat Information Center
CINCPAC	Commander in Chief, U.S. Pacific Command
CIWS	Close-in Weapon System
CJTF	Commander Joint Task Force
CLG	Guided Missile Light Cruiser
CNO	Chief of Naval Operations
COMUSNAVCENT	Commander, U.S. Naval Forces Central Command
CGN	Guided Missile Cruiser (nuclear-powered)
CTF	Commander Task Force
CV	Aircraft Carrier
CVA	Attack Aircraft Carrier
CVAN	Attack Aircraft Carrier (nuclear-powered)
CVE	Escort Aircraft Carrier
CVN	Aircraft Carrier (nuclear-powered)
CVS	Antisubmarine Warfare Aircraft Carrier
DAO	Defense Attaché Office
DD	Destroyer
DDG	Guided Missile Destroyer
DE	Destroyer Escort
DMS	Destroyer Minesweeper
DMZ	Demilitarized Zone
EMCON	Emissions Control
ENCAP	Engineering Civic Action Project
FAST	Fleet Antiterrorism Security Team
FF	Frigate
FFG	Guided Missile Frigate
FON	Freedom of Navigation
HARM	High-Speed Anti-Radiation Missile

HMH	Marine Heavy Lift Helicopter Squadron	NLL	Northern Limit Line
HMM	Marine Medium Helicopter Squadron	NMCB	Naval Mobile Construction Battalion
IFF	Identification Friend or Foe	OKEAN	Soviet Maritime Exercise
INTERFET	International Forces in East Timor	PAVN	People's Army of Vietnam
		PLA	People's Liberation Army
JCS	Joint Chiefs of Staff	PLAN	People's Liberation Army Navy
JMSDF	Japan Maritime Self-Defense Force	POW	Prisoner of War
		PRC	People's Republic of China
JTF	Joint Task Force	PSI	Proliferation Security Initiative
LAMPS	Light Airborne Multipurpose System	PT	Torpedo Boat
LCAC	Landing Craft Air Cushion	PTF	Fast Patrol Craft
LCC	Amphibious Command Ship	RHIB	Rigid-Hull Inflatable Boat
LED	Law Enforcement Detachment	RIMPAC	Rim of the Pacific (naval exercise)
LHA	Amphibious Assault Ship (general purpose)	RMSI	Regional Maritime Security Initiative
LHD	Amphibious Assault Ship (multipurpose)	ROC	Republic of China (Taiwan)
		ROK	Republic of Korea
LKA	Amphibious Cargo Ship	ROKN	Republic of Korea Navy
LPD	Amphibious Transport Dock	RRF	Ready Reserve Force
LSD	Dock Landing Ship	SAM	Surface-to-Air Missile
LSM	Medium Landing Ship	SEACAT	Southeast Asia Cooperation Against Terrorism
LST	Tank Landing Ship	SEAL	Sea Air Land (naval special forces)
LVT	Tracked Landing Vehicle		
MC	Medical Corps	SEATO	Southeast Asia Treaty Organization
MCM	Mine Countermeasures Ship		
MEB	Marine Expeditionary Brigade	SS	Steamship
MEDCAP	Medical Civic Action Program	SS	Submarine
		SSGN	Guided Missile Submarine
MiG	Soviet-made Fighter Aircraft	SSN	Attack Submarine (nuclear-powered)
MMCA	Military Maritime Consultative Agreement		
		T-AO	Fleet Replenishment Oiler
MSC	Military Sealift Command	T-AGOS	Ocean Surveillance Ship
NATO	North Atlantic Treaty Organization	TF	Task Force

George Washington *test-fires one of its Phalanx close-in weapon systems (CIWS) in May 2009 during a readiness drill.*

TG	Task Group
TLAM	Tomahawk Land Attack Missile
UN	United Nations
USCENTCOM	U.S. Central Command
USNAVCENT	U.S. Naval Forces Central Command
USSR	Union of Soviet Socialist Republics

VA	Attack Squadron
VBSS	Visit, Board, Search, Seizure
VF	Fighter Squadron
VFA	Strike Fighter Squadron
VP	Patrol Squadron
VQ	Fleet Air Reconnaissance Squadron
WHEC	High Endurance Cutter
WMD	Weapons of Mass Destruction

Guided missile destroyer Curtis Wilbur *(DDG 54) bucks heavy seas, a not uncommon occurrence for Seventh Fleet warships.*

ACKNOWLEDGMENTS

This illustrated history would not have been possible without the unstinting support and encouragement of Seventh Fleet commanders Vice Admirals John M. Bird, Scott R. Van Buskirk, and Scott H. Swift and Director of Naval History Rear Admiral Jay DeLoach. These leaders recognized the value of enlightening today's Sailors about the momentous history of this forward-deployed naval force and its vital contribution to American responsibilities in the Far East. Vice Admiral Bird and his equally supportive public affairs officer Commander Jeff Davis, hosted my visit to Japan and that of Commander James Reid of the NHHC's Naval Reserve Combat Documentation Detachment 206. We learned firsthand from conversations and recorded interviews with Commander Seventh Fleet, his principal task force commanders, staff officers, and naval personnel of all ranks about the fleet's current mission and responsibilities.

I would be remiss if I did not express my sincere thanks to past and current colleagues of mine at the Naval History and Heritage Command, including former Director of Naval History Rear Admiral Paul E. Tobin, USN (Ret.), Chief of the Histories and Archives Division Greg Martin, and Senior Historian Dr. Michael Crawford. I am also indebted to the staff members of the Operational Archives, Navy Department Library, and Curator Branch who did much to facilitate my research and writing. Pam Overmann of the Art Branch was especially helpful in the selection of appropriate visuals as was the Photo Section's Robert Hanshew and Ed Finney. Tim Frank, my colleague on the Cold War Gallery project, provided me with a wealth of illustrative material. My fellow historians Dr. John Sherwood, Dr. Jeffrey Barlow, Dr. David Winkler, Dr. Timothy Francis, and especially Dr. Robert J. Schneller encouraged my work and shared their considerable insight on the Navy's modern operational history. Indeed, Dr. Schneller's *Anchor of Resolve: A History of U.S. Naval Forces Central Command/Fifth Fleet* in many ways served as a model for this history of the Seventh Fleet.

I am truly grateful to Sandy Doyle and Wendy Sauvageot of the Publications Branch for professionally converting my draft narrative and rough illustrative materials into a worthy finished publication.

Jan Herman and André Sobchinski of the Bureau of Medicine and Surgery's historical office provided me with several striking visuals. Captain Todd Creekman, executive director of the Naval Historical Foundation as always encouraged and facilitated my historical endeavors.

I would especially like to thank the following individuals, distinguished scholars of the U.S. Navy's modern involvement in Asian affairs, each of whom read all or parts of my draft manuscript and offered their sage advice: Captain Peter Swartz, Center for Naval Analyses; Captain Bernard D. "Bud" Cole, USN (Ret.), National Defense University; Dr. Roger Dingman, Professor Emeritus, University of Southern California; widely published naval analyst Norman Polmar; David F. Winkler, Naval Historical Foundation; Bruce A. Elleman, Naval War College; and respected authorities on Asia Paul Giarra and James Auer.

As always, I am indebted to my wife, Beverly, and sons Jeffrey, Brian, and Michael for their unwavering support and patient understanding of my obsession with our Navy's consequential history.

Lastly, I dedicate this work to the men and women who have served and are serving in the U.S. Seventh Fleet, America's guardian in Asia.

Amphibious assault ship Essex *(LHD 2) launches a RIM-7P Sea Sparrow surface-to-air missile during a live-fire session in joint exercise Valiant Shield in September 2010.*

SUGGESTED READING

Given the broad span of time covered and the momentous events involving the Seventh Fleet, there are literally thousands of good books that discuss some aspect of its defense of U.S. security interests in the Western Pacific, Indian Ocean, and Asia. One of the primary reasons for the illustrated work presented here, however, is to provide a one-volume treatment of the Seventh Fleet's history that relates to its current mission. The purpose of this bibliographical essay is to identify a few of the most comprehensive, balanced, readable, and useful works on the most important chapters within the overall Seventh Fleet story.

Any investigation of the Navy's role in World War II must start with the 15-volume series *History of United States Naval Operations in World War II* (Boston, MA: Little Brown) produced by the dean of naval historians, Samuel Eliot Morison. The books that deal with individual Seventh Fleet campaigns and battles are *Breaking the Bismarcks Barrier*, *New Guinea and the Marianas*, *Leyte*, and *Liberation of the Philippines*. His shorter summary history, *The Two-Ocean War: A Short History of the United States Navy in the Second World War* (New York: Galahad Books, 1963), covers the fleet's operations under MacArthur from the Solomons through the Philippines. How the Navy interacted with MacArthur and his Army and Army Air Forces generals during the hard slog on the road to Tokyo can be found in Gerald Wheeler's well-done treatment *Kinkaid of the Seventh Fleet: A Biography of Admiral Thomas C. Kinkaid, U.S. Navy* (Washington: Naval Historical Center/Naval Institute Press, 1996). The biography entitled *MacArthur's Amphibious Navy: Seventh Amphibious Force Operations, 1943–1945* (Annapolis, MD: Naval Institute Press, 1969) by Kinkaid's most prominent amphibious commander, Vice Admiral Daniel E. Barbey, provides a wealth of operational detail. *Eagle Against the Sun: The American War with Japan* (New York: Vintage Books, 1985) by Ronald H. Spector, a former Director of Naval History, provides a good analysis of how the Seventh Fleet fit into the overall Allied scheme in the South and Southwest Pacific. Other good works that cover the campaigns in New Guinea and the Philippines are William M. Leary's *We Shall Return! MacArthur's Commanders and the Defeat of Japan, 1942–1945* (Lexington: University Press of Kentucky, 1988) and Stanley L. Falk's *Liberation of the Philippines* (New York: Ballantine Books, 1971). The pivotal battle of Leyte Gulf is well treated by Thomas Cutler in his *The Battle of Leyte Gulf, 23–26 October, 1944* (New York: Harper Collins, 1994). There is no more riveting account of the battle and the role in it of Commander Ernest Evans and "Taffy 3" than James D. Hornfischer's award-winning *The Last Stand of the Tin Can Sailors: The Extraordinary World War II Story of the US Navy's Finest Hour* (New York: Bantam Dell, 2005).

The activities of the Navy and Marine Corps in the postwar occupation of southern Korea and northern China are featured in Spector's *In the Ruin's of Empire: The Japanese Surrender and the Battle for Postwar Asia* (New York: Random House, 2007). The Seventh Fleet's movement of Chiang Kai-shek's armies is detailed in Edwin B. Hooper, Dean C. Allard, and Oscar P. Fitzgerald's *The Setting of the Stage to 1959*, Volume I in the series *The United States Navy and the Vietnam Conflict* (Washington: Naval Historical Center, 1976).

There are numerous books on the experiences in the Korean War of Seventh Fleet warships, aircraft squadrons, and Sailors, but the three most comprehensive are *United States Naval Operations: Korea* (Washington: Naval History Division, 1962) by James A. Field; *The Sea War in Korea* (Annapolis, MD: Naval Institute Press, 1957) by Malcolm W. Cagle and Frank A. Manson; and *The U.S. Navy in the Korean War* (Annapolis, MD: Naval Institute Press, 2007) by Edward J. Marolda, ed. A good overview of military operations in the war, including those of the Navy and Marine Corps is provided by Allan Millett in his *The War for Korea, 1950–1951: They Came from the North* (Lawrence: University of Kansas Press, 2010). Amphibious operations are covered in Robert D. Heinl's classic *Victory at High Tide: The Inchon-Seoul Campaign* (Philadelphia: J.B. Lippincott, 1968) and Merrill L. Bartlett's *Assault from the Sea* (Annapolis, MD: Naval Institute Press, 1983). Richard P. Hallion's *The Naval Air War in Korea* (Baltimore, MD: Nautical & Aviation Publishing Co. of America, 1986) presents detailed information on the role of carrier and shore-based aviation units. The role of naval leaders in the war can be found in C. Turner Joy's classic *How Communists Negotiate* (New York: Macmillan, 1955) and Clark Reynolds' colorful biography of one-time Commander Seventh Fleet Vice Admiral Joseph Clark entitled *On the Warpath in the Pacific: Admiral Jocko Clark and the Fast Carriers* (Annapolis, MD: Naval Institute Press, 2005).

The Seventh Fleet's involvement in the Taiwan Strait crises of the 1950s, the French Indochina War, and the early years of the Vietnam conflict are discussed in broad terms in *From Pearl Harbor to Vietnam: The Memoirs of Admiral Arthur W. Radford* (Stanford, CA: Hoover Institution Press, 1980) by Radford and Stephen Jurika; *The Approaching Storm: Conflict in Asia, 1945–1965* (Washington: Naval History & Heritage Command) by Marolda; and *High Seas Buffer: The Taiwan Patrol Force, 1950–1979* (Newport, RI: Naval War College Press, 2012) by Bruce A. Elleman. Hooper's *The Setting of the Stage to 1959* and Marolda and Oscar P. Fitzgerald's *From Military Assistance to Combat*, Volume II in the series *The United States Navy and the Vietnam Conflict* (Washington: Naval Historical Center, 1986), cover the same subjects in more detail. The best treatment of the 1958 Taiwan Strait Crisis is included in Joseph F. Bouchard's *Command in Crisis: Four Case Studies* (New York: Columbia University Press, 1991). The Seventh Fleet's close relationship with the Japan Maritime Self-Defense Force is insightfully chronicled in James E. Auer's *The Postwar Rearmament of Japanese Maritime Forces, 1945–1971* (New York: Praeger Publishers, 1973). The entries on the Yokosuka and Sasebo bases, especially those by Roger Dingman, and on the Philippines bases in Paolo E. Colletta's *United States Navy and Marine Corps Bases, Overseas* (Westport, CT: Greenwood Press, 1985), are especially useful.

Many good works provide overall context and operational detail on the fleet's role in the long Vietnam War. Richard L. Shreadley in *From the Rivers to the Sea: The U.S. Navy in Vietnam* (Annapolis, MD: Naval Institute Press, 1992) and Marolda in *By Sea, Air, and Land: An Illustrated History of the U.S. Navy and the War in Southeast Asia* (Washington: Naval Historical Center, 1994) provide overviews of the major naval operations in North and South Vietnam, Laos, and Cambodia. Edwin E. Moise's *Tonkin Gulf and the Escalation of the Vietnam War* (Chapel Hill: University of North Carolina Press, 1996) is an authoritative source on that pivotal episode. Task Force 77's contribution is comprehensively covered in *On Yankee Station: The Naval Air War over Vietnam* (Annapolis, MD: Naval Institute Press, 1987) by John B. Nichols and Barrett Tillman; *Aircraft Carriers at War: A Personal Retrospective of Korea, Vietnam, and the Soviet Confrontation* (Annapolis, MD: Naval Institute Press, 2007) by James L. Holloway III; *The Naval Air War in Vietnam, 1965–1975* (Annapolis, MD: Nautical and Aviation Publishing Co. of America, 1981) by Peter Mersky and Norman Polmar; *Launch the Intruders: A Naval Attack Squadron in the Vietnam War, 1972* (Lawrence: University of Kansas Press, 2005), by Carol Reardon; and *Afterburner: Naval Aviators and the Vietnam War* (New York: New York University Press, 2004), and *Nixon's Trident: Naval Air Power in Southeast Asia, 1968–1972* (Washington: Naval History & Heritage Command, 2009) by John Darrell Sherwood.

Operations involving naval amphibious forces are featured in *Sea Soldiers in the Cold War: Amphibious Warfare, 1945–1991* (Annapolis, MD: Naval Institute Press, 1995) by Joseph H. Alexander and the Marine Corps' eight-volume *U.S. Marines in Vietnam* (Washington: History and Museums Division, HQ USMC, 1977–1997). The role of Seventh Fleet and U.S. Coast Guard coastal patrol forces is well covered in Alex Larzelere's *The Coast Guard at War: Vietnam 1965–1975*

(Annapolis, MD: Naval Institute Press, 1997). Jeffrey Grey's *Up Top: The Royal Australian Navy and Southeast Asian Conflicts, 1955–1972* (St. Leonards, Australia: Allen & Unwin, 1998) discusses the interaction of Australian and Seventh Fleet units conducting bombardment operations off the coast of Vietnam.

The ordeal of America's prisoners of war is comprehensively treated in Stuart Rochester's *The Battle Behind Bars: Navy and Marine Corps POWs in the Vietnam War* (Washington: Naval History Heritage Command, 2010) and (with Frederick Kiley) *Honor Bound: American Prisoners of War in Southeast Asia, 1961–1973* (Annapolis, MD: Naval Institute Press, 2007). An authoritative source on the *Mayaguez* action is John Guilmartin's *A Very Short War: The Mayaguez and the Battle of Koh Tang* (College Station: Texas A&M University Press, 1995).

The Seventh Fleet's response to the Vietnam era's Soviet and North Korean provocations is well covered in David F. Winkler's *Cold War at Sea: High-Seas Confrontation between the United States and the Soviet Union* (Annapolis, MD: Naval Institute Press, 2000), Richard A. Mobley's *Flash Point North Korea: The Pueblo and EC-121 Crises* (Annapolis, MD: Naval Institute Press, 2003), Mitchell B. Lerner's *The Pueblo Incident: A Spy Ship and the Failure of American Foreign Policy* (Lawrence: University of Kansas Press, 2002), and Narushige Michishita's *North Korea's Military-Diplomatic Campaigns, 1966–2008* (London and New York: Routledge, 2010).

Crewmen of Greeneville *(SSN 772) stand by during the attack submarine's approach to the ROK Navy base at Chinhae in September 2010.*

The confrontation between the Seventh Fleet and the Soviet Pacific Fleet, development of the Maritime Strategy, and buildup of the 600-ship Navy are described in general terms in John F. Lehman's *Command of the Seas* (New York: Scribner's, 1988); Elmo R. Zumwalt Jr.'s *On Watch: A Memoir* (New York: Quadrangle/NY Times Book Co., 1977); John Hattendorf's *The Evolution of the U.S. Navy's Maritime Strategy, 1977–1986* (Newport, RI: Naval

War College Press, 2004); and Peter M. Swartz's *U.S. Navy Forward Deployment, 1801–2001* (Alexandria, VA: Center For Naval Analyses, 2001).

The Seventh Fleet's central role in operations Desert Shield and Desert Storm is comprehensively covered in Marolda and Robert J. Schneller's *Shield and Sword: The United States Navy and the Persian Gulf War* (Annapolis, MD: Naval Institute Press, 2001) and Marvin Pokrant's two volumes: *Desert Shield at Sea: What the Navy Really Did*, and *Desert Storm at Sea: What the Navy Really Did* (Westport, CT: Greenwood, 1999).

The best one-volume treatment of the Taiwan Strait crisis of 1995–1996 is John Garver's *Face Off: China, the United States, and Taiwan's Democr*atization (Seattle: University of Washington Press, 1997), while Bernard D. Cole's *The Great Wall at Sea: China's Navy Enters the Twenty-First Century* (Annapolis, MD: Naval Institute Press, 2010) provides great detail and analysis on the actions of the People's Liberation Army Navy and the Seventh Fleet from the mid-1990s to the present.

No single book covers the Seventh Fleet's operations to counter the actions of confrontational nations, terrorists, and pirates in the first decade of the 21st century. Indeed, the best coverage is provided in the comprehensive articles published in the *Naval War College Review* and to a lesser extent the U.S. Naval Institute *Proceedings*. That being said, a number of books do provide valuable relevant information, including *Sea Lanes and Pipelines: Energy Security in Asia* (New York: Praeger Security International, 2008) by Bernard D. Cole; *Small Boats, Weak States, Dirty Money: Piracy & Maritime Terrorism in the Modern World* (London: Hearst and Co., 2010) by Martin N. Murphy; and *Red Star over the Pacific: China's Rise and the Challenge to U.S. Maritime Strategy* (Annapolis, MD: Naval Institute Press, 2010) by Toshi Yoshihara and James R. Holmes. Bruce A. Elleman's *Waves of Hope: The U.S. Navy's Response to the Tsunami in Northern Indonesia* (Newport, RI: Naval War College Press, 2007) provides great detail on the fleet's involvement in the 2004 disaster.

INDEX

Unless otherwise noted in parentheses, ships and units are United States forces. Page numbers in *italics* at the end of an entry refer to photo captions.

A-1 Skyraider, 59
A-4 Skyhawk, vi, 59–60
A-6 Intruder, 59–61, 92,106; *61*
A-7 Corsair II, 59, 65, 72; *65, 72*
Abraham Lincoln (CVN 72), 110–11, 120, 144–45; *144*
Abu Sayyaf, 128, 139, 140–41
Aceh Province, Indonesia, 130, 145–46; *145*
Acheson, Dean, viii, 18, 20
AD Skyraider, 29, 41
Adelaide (Australian), 103
Aden, Gulf of, 130, 160
Admiralty Islands, vii, 2
Admiral Vinogradov (Russian), 150
Aegis battle management system, 95, 107, 113, 121–22, 132, 154
Afghanistan, xi, xii, 83, 125, 127–30, 133–34
Agency for International Development, 142
AGI (auxiliary general intelligence ship [Soviet]), 75, 77
Agreed Framework, xii, 120
Agreement on Cessation of Hostilities in Indochina, 39
AH-1W Super Cobra (Marine), 165, 166; *165*
Air Cathay passenger plane, attack on, 40
Ajax (AR 6), *47*
Akula-class nuclear-powered attack submarine (Soviet), 89
Alaska, Gulf of, Soviet Pacific Fleet in, 79
Aleutian Islands, 3, 96, 98
Allen, Thad, 148
Allied Naval Forces Southwest Pacific Area, commander of, 1
Alondra Rainbow (Japanese), 131
Alpha strikes, 59–60
Amagiri (Japanese), 153
Amchitka Island, Alaska, 96
American Corsair (merchantman), *64*
"America's Gibraltar of the Pacific," 48
Amphibious Construction Battalion 1, 152
Amphibious Evacuation Force, 42
Amphibious Force Seventh Fleet, 1, 2, 10, 13, 45, 48, 167
Amphibious Force Western Pacific, commander of, 39
Amphibious Ready Group Alpha, 66–67
Amphibious Ready Group/Special Landing Force, 63
Anderson (DD 786), 20
Anemometr (Soviet AGI), 75
Antietam (CV 36), 18, 21
ANZUS Security Treaty, viii, 84
Aquino, Corazon, 100, 111
Arabian Gulf, operations in, 115, 130, 145, 148, 157; during Desert Storm 101–7, 111–12, 167; after Gulf War, 129, 149. *See also* Northern Arabian Gulf
Arabian Peninsula, 104, 108
Arab-Israeli conflict, 108

Arizona (BB 39), *2*
Arkansas (CGN 41), 110
Arthur, Stanley R., 104–8, 167, 171; *104*
ASEAN Asian Regional Forum, 165
ASEAN Convention on Terrorism, 131
Asia Pacific Economic Cooperation, 131
Asia-Pacific region, U.S. Navy and stability in, 96–100, 118, 126, 132, 142–43, 152, 170
Association of Southeast Asian Nations, 131
Atlanta (CL 104), 19
Atsugi airfield, Japan, 47
Attack Carrier Striking Force, 42, 59
Attack Squadron 94; *65*
Attack Squadron 153, 60
Attack Squadron 155, 60
Australia, xiv, 100, 118, 139, 142–44, 146, 148–50, 152–53, 158; in East Timor, 123; in Gulf War, 102–3, 105; and maritime exercises, 121–23, 133–34, 135; in Korean War, 24; and SEATO, ix, 44–45, 52; and terrorist bombing in Bali, 130; in Vietnam War, 58, 62; in World War II, 1, 4, 9–10
Australian 7th Infantry Division, 10
Australian White Paper of 2009, 139, 153
Avenger (MCM 1), 162; *161*
Axe Murder incident, xi, 77

B-52 bombers, 78
Bach Long Vi (Nightingale Island), 60
Backfire bombers (Soviet), 87, 92
Badger, Oscar, 20–21, 171
Bahrain, 102, 108, 167
Bali Accord II, 131
Bali, Indonesia, 121, 130
Balikpapan, Borneo, 10
Bandung Conference, 42
Bangkok, Thailand, 40, 44–45, 128, 130
Bangladesh, xii, 80–81, 101, 112, 121, 131–32, 135
Banner (AGER 1), 75
Barbey, Daniel E., 1, 9–10, 14, 16–17, 21, 171
Barbour County (LST 1195), 68
Barnett, J. T., 8
Barrett, Mark, 77
Basilan Island, Philippines, 128, 139–41
Bataan Peninsula, 10
Batson, Jack E., 60
Battle Force Seventh Fleet, 162
Battle Force Sixth Fleet, 102
Battle Force Zulu, 85, 104–6, 167
battles: Leyte Gulf, vii, 3–8, 10; *3, 5, 7*; Midway, vii; Surigao Strait, 4–6; *6*; Tsushima, 151; Yeonpyeong, xii, 121

183

Battleaxe (British), 103
Bay of Bengal, U.S. Navy in, 81, 133, 134; *132*
Beakley, Wallace M., 49–50, 171
Beaufort (ATS 2), 107–8
"Bedcheck Charlies," 29
Begor (APD 127), *29*
Bekasi, Indonesia, 137
Belgrade, Serbia, xiv, 119
Belleau Wood (LHA 3), 112, 115, 123, 125; *112, 125*
Benner (DD 807), 21
Bennion (DD 662), 4, 6; *5*
Berbera, Serbia, Soviet base at, 83
Bering Sea, 96, 98
Berkey, Russell S., viii, 20, 171
Besslednyy (Soviet), 75
Biak Island, 4
Bien Hoa airfield, South Vietnam, 58
Bienvenido Salting (Philippines), 136
Bin Laden, Osama, 127–28
Bird, John M., 132, 150–51, 154–56, 160–65, 168, 172; *vi, 150, 154*
Black Killer, 141
Black Swan (British), 23
Blackman, Robert R., 144
Black Ships Festival (Shimoda, Japan), 154; *156*
Blair, Dennis, 131, 143; *128*
Blake, Terry, *132*
Blakley, John H., 8
Blue (DD 744), 102
Blue House Raid, 76
Blue Ridge (LCC 19), 85, 121, 133, 146, 150, 160, 167–68; *vi, 86, 167, back cover*; and China, 115, 118–19; in Gulf War, 85, 102, 107; *107*; in Vietnam War, 68; *65*
Boise (CL 47), 4
Bombay, India. *See* Mumbai
Bon Homme Richard (CVA 31), 73
Bonhomme Richard (LHD 6), 144–45
Boniface, Arthur, 77
Bordelon, Guy P., 29
Boxer (CV 21), 18, 20, 35, 38
Boxer (LHD 4), 138
Bradford, John F., 138
Bremerton (SSN 698), 116, 118
Brewton (FF 1086), 87
Brisbane (Australian), 62, 122
Briscoe, Robert P., 36, 171
British Commonwealth, 54
Brooklyn (CL 40), 3
Brown, Eldon W., 24
Bucher, Lloyd, 76
Buffalo (SSN 715), 168
Bull, Lyle F., 60
Bunker Hill (CG 52), 102, 105, 113, 115
Burke, Arleigh, 49–50; *43, 49*
Burma, 135, 157
Burnham, Gracia, 128
Burnham, Martin, 128

Burns, John J., 70
Busan, South Korea, 26, 160–62, 170; *152*
Bush, George H.W., xi, 146
Bush, George W., xiii, 125–26, 134, 140, 168

C-130B Hercules, 139
Cabezon (SS 334), 20
California (BB 44), 4, 9
Callaghan (DD 994), 116
Cam Ranh Bay, 59, 71, 84
Cambodia, xiii, 39, 44, 64–67, 70–72, 98, 135; *70*
Cape Cod (AD 43), 110
Carl Vinson (CVN 70), 96
Carlson, Harold G., 29
Carney, Robert B., 38
Carpender, Arthur S., 1, 171
Carrier Air Group 5, 41
Carrier Air Wing 2, 85
Carrier Air Wing 5, 129
carrier battle groups, xiv, 89, 96, 102, 113–17, 127
carrier task forces, 33, 38, 45, 53, 77–78, 96, 162
carrier task groups, 46, 50, 75
Carter, Jimmy, 89, 91
Catamount (LSD 17), 51; *51*
Catfish (SS 339), 20, 33
cease-fires, ix, 51, 100; in French Indochina War, xi; in Gulf War, 108; in Indo-Pakistan War, 80–81; in Korean War, x, 55; after Laos crisis, 53; in Vietnam War, 66
Cebu Island, Philippines, xii, 110–11, 141
CH-46 Sea Knight, 122–23
CH-53 Sea Stallion, 123
Chafee (DDG 90), 136–37
Chancellorsville (CG 62), 137
Chandler, Theodore E., vi, 9
Changi Naval Base, Singapore, 112
Cheonan (South Korean), xv, 149, 162–63
Chiang Kai-shek, ix, 12, 15, 18, 20–21, 33, 49, 114; *49*; in Taiwan Strait crises, 40, 42, 44, 48–51; *41*; in World War II, 16–17
Chiang Kai-shek, Madame, 15
Chiang Ching-kuo, 114
Chicago (CG 11), 62
Chief of Naval Operations (U.S.), xiii; Burke, Arleigh, 43, 49; Carney, Robert B., 38; Clark, Vern, 145; Fechteler, William M., 2, 35; Hayward, Thomas B., *91*; Holloway, James L., III, 77; King, Ernest J., 1; Mullen, Michael G., 147–49; *147*; Roughead, Gary, 143, 148, 150, 160; *148*; Sherman, Forrest P., 19; Watkins, James B., 99; *92*; Zumwalt, Elmo R., Jr.,13, 81, 89; *81*. *See also individual names*
Chilean Navy, 3
China Aid Act, 20
China Theater. *See* Wedemeyer, Albert C.
Chinese Communist Party, 12, 84, 114, 117, 156
Chinese Ministry of Foreign Affairs, 118
Chinese Nationalist 52nd Army, 18
Chinese Nationalist navy, 99

Chinese Naval Training Center, Qingdao, 20–21
Christie, Ralph W., 4
Christopher, Warren, 116
Chung-Hoon (DDG 93), 137
City of Corpus Christi (SSN 705), 168
civic action, 136, 141–42, 151
Clark, Eugene F., 26–27
Clark, Joseph J., 171; *36*
Clark, Mark, *36*
Clark, Vern, 145
Clark Air Base, 71, 100, 109–10
Clemins, Archie R., 115, 121, 171
Clinton, Bill, 114–20, 128, 146; *146*
Clinton, Hilary, 163, 165
Coast Watch South, 142
Cockade (British), 24
Cohen, William H., 118–19; *119*
Cole, Bernard D., 131
Cole (DDG 67), xii, 134; *134*
Collins, Gabriel B., 157
Collins-class submarines (Australian), xvi, 153
Columbia (CL 56), 9
Columbus (SSN 762), 116
Combined Naval Component Command, commander of, 120
Combined Support Force 536, 146
command and control, 71, 115, 122, 126, 162
Constellation (CVA 64), 58, 60–61, 65, 98; *61*
Conway, James T., 148
Cooke, Charles M., 17–19, 21, 171; *17*
Coontz (DLG 8), 61
Cooper, Joshua, 5; *5*
Cooperation Afloat Readiness and Training, 135–36; *136*
Cooperative Maritime Forces Pacific, 144
Cooperative Mechanism, 131
A Cooperative Strategy for 21st Century Seapower, 148
Coral Sea (CVA 43), vi, x, 59–60, 68, 96; *60, 65*
Cornell University, 114
Coronado (AGF 11), 150
counterterrorism, 130–31, 139, 141–42
Cowpens (CG 63), 150, 160, 162; *150*
"crab wars," 121
Crawford, Ernie L., 30
Crowder, Douglas, 144, 172
Crowe, William J., 98
Cunningham, Randy, 61–62
Curtis Wilbur (DDG 54), *156, 176*
Curts (FFG 38), 106, 110; *106*
Cyclone-class coastal patrol boats, 139

Dachen Islands, ix, 41–42, 52
"Dambusters," 29
Damman, Saudi Arabia, 103
Dare, James A., 31
Das, P. S., *132*
Dean, John Gunter, 67
Defense Logistics Agency, 83
De Leon, Ernesto, 150

Deliver (ARS 23), 21; *21*
Demilitarized Zone, Korea, xi, 85, 120–21
Demilitarized Zone, Vietnam, 62, 167
Democratic People's Republic of Korea, 22
Department of Defense, 22, 120, 126, 157, 168
Deng Xiaoping, 84
Desoto Patrol, 56
Destroyer Division 111, 34
Destroyer Division 30, 37
Destroyer Squadron 1, commander of, 136
Destroyer Squadron 15, 83
Destroyer Squadron 56, 4
deterrence, 52, 71–74, 79, 92, 126, 148, 160, 170
Dhahran, Saudi Arabia, 103
Dhowan, Robin K., *132*
Diamond Head, Oahu, Hawaii, 79
Dibb, Paul, 158
Diego Garcia Island, 82–83, 102, 170; *82*
Dien Bien Phu, x, 38–39
Dingman, Roger, 73
diplomacy, naval, 18, 121–22
disaster relief, 101, 113, 144, 146
Dixie Station, 59
Donegan, Kevin M., 162
Donnelly, William N., 60
Doran, Walter F., 144, 146, 168, 172
Doremus, Robert B., 60
Dos Palmas resort, terrorist attack at, 128
Douglas H. Fox (DD 779), 31–32
Doulous (merchant ship, Philippines), 128
Doyle, James H., 25
Driscoll, Willie, 61–62
drug and alcohol abuse, Vietnam era, 71
drug smuggling, 131, 143
dry docks (U.S. Navy), 46, 71, 83
Duan Muang Airport, Thailand, 45
Dubuque (LPD 8), 102
Dulles, John Foster, 44, 51
Duncan, G. C., 41
Durbrow, Eldridge, 55

E-2 Hawkeye, 59, 93, 100
EA-6B Prowler, 92
earthquakes, responses to, 110, 144
East Indies, 1, 3–4, 12, 19
East Pakistan. *See* Bangladesh
East Sea Fleet, PLAN, 126, 160, 165
East Timor, xiv, 113, 122–26, 150; map of, *122*. *See also* Operations, Stabilize
Easter Offensive, x, 63, 85
EC-121 Warning Star, x, 77
Edson (DD 946), 66
Eisenhower, Dwight D., 37–39, 41, 43–44, 50
Endeavor (Singapore), 137
"Enhancing Maritime Anti-Piracy and Counter Terrorism Cooperation in the ASEAN Region," 132
Enterprise (CVAN 65), x, 59, 68, 73–75, 80–81, 96, 100

EP-3E Aries II, xii, 123–24, 126
Ericson, Andrew, 157, 159
Essex (CV 9), 35, 38, 41, 49; Essex-class aircraft carrier, 59
Essex (LHD 2), 121, 137, 142, 145–47, 166–68; *125, 145, 168, 172, 178*
Estes (AGC 12), 19, 21
Evans, Ernest E., 7
Exercises, combined (multinational), 83, 100, 131, 144, 166; Astra, 45; Balikatan, 141–42; *141, 172*; Cobra Gold, 98, 137–39, 144; *139, 168*; Coconut Grove, 138; Deep Sabre, 135; Firm Link, 45; Foal Eagle, 153; Freedom Banner, 120; Imminent Thunder, 104; Kernal Potlatch, 96; Key Resolve, 153; Malabar, 132–34; *132, 133*; Northern Wedding, 98; Ocean Link, 45; Phiblink, 45; Pony Express, *45*; Sea Link, 45; Talisman Saber, 152–53; *153*; Tandem Thrust, 121–22; Team Spirit, 96; Teamwork, 45; Terminal Fury, 168; Ulchi Focus Lens, 120, 153; Ulchi Freedom Guardian, 153; Valiant Shield, *178*
Expeditionary Strike Group 3, 125

F-1 Mirage, 106
F2H Banshee, 29
F-4 Phantom II, 59–60, 100
F4U Corsair, 29
F-8 Crusader, 59
F9F Panther, 23–24, 29
F-86F Sabre, 51
F/A-18 Hornet, 92
F/A-18E/F Super Hornet, 148; *149*
Falun Gong, 156
Far East Command, 18, 20, 34, 38, 48
Fargo, Thomas, 144; *124*
Fast Carrier Force, Seventh Fleet, 13
Faylaka Island, Kuwait, 108
Fechteler, William M., 2, 10, 35
Felt, Harry D., 41
Feng Guoqing, 160
Fife (DD 991), 102
5th Marine Expeditionary Brigade, 104
5th Marine Regiment, 27
Fighter Squadron 21, 60
Fighter Squadron 154, 60
First Indochina War, xi
1st Marine Division, 2, 13, 26–28
1st Viet Cong Regiment, 63
fishing, 31, 76, 86, 121, 159–60
Fitzgerald (DDG 62), 150, 160, 162
Fleet Air Reconnaissance Squadron 1, 124
Fleet Air Western Pacific, commander of, 47
Fleet Air Wing 1, 33
Fleet Aircraft Squadron 11, 47
Fleet Antiterrorism Security Team Pacific, 138, 146
Fleet Industrial Supply Center, Yokosuka, 146
FleetEx 83, 96
Fletcher-class destroyer, 4, 7
Florida (SSGN 728), 170
Foley, Sylvester R., 96, 171

Ford, Gerald R., 77, 84
Ford (FFG 54), 116
foreign policy, U.S.: post–World War II, 11, 16–17, 20; toward China, 52, 74, 117, 133, 157, 166; toward Japan 83; toward Soviets 79; in 21st century, 123
Formosa, 8, 14, 33
Formosa Patrol Force. *See* Taiwan Patrol Force
Formosa Resolution, ix, 41
Forrestal, James, 14
Forrestal (CVA 59), xii, 61, 71
Forrestal-class aircraft carriers, 59
Fort McHenry (LSD 43), 136, 145–46
4th Marine Expeditionary Brigade, 104
Fox, Mark I., 105
Fox (CG 33), 87
France, ix, 4, 22, 25, 37–40, 44, 132
Francis Hammond (FF 1067), 96
Frank Cable (AS 40), 168
free market enterprise, 120, 133
"freedom of navigation" cruises, 95, 96
French Foreign Legion, 38
French Indochina War, 38
French paratroopers, 38
Fujian Province, China, 52, 115
Fuso (Japanese), 4

Gary (FFG 51), 110
General Order Number 1, ix, 13
General W. M. Black (APB 5), 37
Geneva Agreements, ix, 39, 44, 53
George Washington (CVN 73), 129, 132, 138, 148–51, 162; *front cover, 149, 162, 175*
Gimpo airfield, South Korea, 27
Glenn, W. Lewis Jr., 97
Global War on Terrorism, 125
Glory (British), 24
Goldsborough (DDG 20), *103*
Goldstein, Lyle, 157, 159
Gonzalez, Ranulfo C., *166*
Gorshkov, Sergei, 79; *79*
Great Britain, ix, 20, 44, 74, 118, 130
Great Leap Forward, 48
Green, Michael J., 134
Greenert, Jonathan W., 133, 144, 152; *172*
Greeneville (SSN 772), *181*
Griffin, Charles D., 55, 171; *55*
Guadalcanal Island, Solomons, 1
Guam, 20, 70, 89–90, 94, 107–8, 111, 145–46, 160
Guardian (MCM 5), 163
Guidelines for Japan-U.S. Defense Cooperation, 118
Guinsagon, Philippines, destruction of, 141
Gulf War, 1990–1991, 101, 107, 167; air operations in, 104–7

Hainan incident, xii, 123, 124, 126
Hainan Island, China, 20, 35, 41, 83, 113
Haiphong, during the Vietnam War, x, 16, 64–65, 167
Halsey (DDG 23), 73

Halsey, William F., 1–3, 6, 8
Halsey-Doolittle Raid, 3
Han Chinese, 156
Han-class attack nuclear-powered attack submarine (Chinese), 113
Hancock (CVA 19), 49, 59–60, 66, 68
Hanoi, North Vietnam, x, 53, 56, 58–62, 83
HARM (high-speed anti-radiation missile), 92
Harold E. Holt (DE 1074), 70; *70*
Harpers Ferry (LSD 49), 136–37, 140, 150; *166*
Harpoon surface-to-surface missiles, 92, 94–95; *94*
Harrier vertical/short take-off and landing aircraft, 102
Harris, Jack, 60
Harry W. Hill (DD 986), 96
Hartman, Charles C., 34
Hashimoto, Ryutaro, 117
Hassayampa (AO 145), 71
Haven (AH 12), 40; *40*
Hawaii. *See* Pearl Harbor
Hawkins (DD 873), 21
Hayward, Thomas B., 90–92, 171
Heermann (DD 532), 7
Helena (CA 75), 34, 50
Helicopter Anti-Submarine Squadron 14, 138
Helicopter Combat Support Squadron 11, 144
Henry B. Wilson (DDG 7), 66, 70–71
Herrick, John J., 56–57; *57*
Hewitt (DD 966), 115
Higbee (DD 806), 62
Higgins, John M., *25*
"highway of death," 108
Hiroshima, Japan, 72
Hobart (Australian), 62
Ho Chi Minh, 20, 22, 37, 37, 39–40, 53, 56; *20*
Ho Chi Minh Trail, 56, 63
Hodge, John R., vii, 13–14; *14*
Hodges, Duane, 76
Hoel (DD 533), 7
Hokkaido Island, Japan, 96, 98, 167
Hollandia, New Guinea, vii, 2, 4
Holloway, James L. III, 4–6, 65, 75, 77, 171; *5, 65, 77*
Holmes, James R., 157
Honasan, Gregorio, 100
Hong Kong, Crown Colony of, 73, 121, 144, 150, 157; during Cold War, 74–75; relations with PRC, xii, 118–19, 158, 160, 163; and Korean War, 35; and Taiwan, 40; post–World War II, 19; during World War II, 8; 73, 74
Hongzehu (Chinese), *165*
Honshu Island, Japan, 98, 121
Hontz, Edward B., 108
Hope Center, Binh Dinh, Vietnam, 152
Hopewell (DD 681), 8, 50; *50*
Horner, Charles A., 105
Hornet (CV 8), 3
Hornet (CVS 12), 75
"hot line" to China,119
Houston (SSN 713), 168

Howard, Michael, 89
Howe, John, 145
HU-1H helicopter, 139
HU-16 amphibian aircraft, 60
Huaqing Liu, 84
Hu Yaobang, 84
human rights, 118, 127, 156, 158
human trafficking, 143
humanitarian assistance, xii, 78, 112, 138, 140–41, 144, 146
Hung Ba Le, 151; *152*
Hungnam, North Korea, x, 28–29, 55; *20*
Hunter, Charles B., 60
hunter-killer groups, 42, 45
Hurley, Patrick J., 15
Hussein, Saddam, xiii, 85, 101, 106, 117, 129, 167
Hwachon Reservoir dam, 29

Impeccable (T-AGOS 23), xiii, 164; *164*
Imperial Japanese Navy, vii, 4, 6–7, 10, 46–47
improvised explosive devices, 140
Incheon, South Korea, viii, 13–14, 25–27; *26, 27*
Incidents at Sea Treaty, 75, 118
Independence (CV 62), xii, 85 102, 104, 115–21, 129; *vi, 102, 117*
Independence Day, 150, 161
Indian Defense Services Staff College, 146
Indian Navy, 131–34, 146; *132, 133*
Indian Ocean: tsunami in, xiii, 144–47; U.S. operations in, 89–90, 98, 101, 111–12, 125, 129, 138, 148, 150
Indonesian Archipelago, 54, 122
Indo-Pakistan War, x, 80
Information Sharing Center, Singapore, 131
intelligence, 161, 163, 170; during Cold War, 37, 74–77; in Gulf War, 103; during Hainan incident, 123–24; in Korean War, 26–27, 33; on Soviets, 92; on terrorists, pirates, proliferators, 128, 134–35, 139, 141; in Vietnam War, 56–58, 71; in World War II, 4
international fleet reviews, 149, 160
International Forces in East Timor, 122
International Labor Day, 32
International Maritime Seminar, Indonesia, 148
Iowa (BB 61), 30
Iowa-class battleships, 92
Iram Elementary School, Olongapo City, Philippines, 150
Iran, 79, 82, 85, 105, 106, 108
Iraq, xi, xiii, 79, 85, 101–8, 117, 125, 129, 149, 167
Iron Hand, 59
Ishikawa, Toru, 132
Islamist terrorists, 127, 130, 142
Ivan Rogov (Soviet), 84, 87
Izumi, Tohru, iv, 154

J-8II Finback, 124
Jakarta, Indonesia, 139, 142
Jakarta Statement, 132
Jamaica (British), 23

Jamalul, Jundam, 141
Janjalani, Abdurajak, 128
Janjalani, Kadaffy, 128
Japan Maritime Self-Defense Force, 46, 83, 89–91, 131–32, 148, 163
Jemaah Islamiyah, 128, 130, 139
Jeremiah, David, 89
Jiang Zemin, 115, 117
Jinmen Island, China, ix, 41–42, 48–51
John A. Bole (DD 755), 102
John C. Stennis (CVN 74), 153–54, 164; *154*
John F. Kennedy (CV 67), ix, 102, 129
John Paul Jones, 7
John S. McCain (DDG 56), 119, 136, 151; *158*
Johnson, Lyndon B., ix, x, 56–58, 64–65, 76; *80*
Johnston (DD 557), 7–8; *7*
John Young (DD 973), 96
Joint Chiefs of Staff, 14, 25, 34, 48, 89, 101; chairman of, 14, 39, 77, 98, 126, 147; *38, 64, 77, 126*
joint exercises, 121, 129. *See also individual joint task forces*
Joint Security Area, DMZ of Korea, 77–78, 121
Joint Task Force Fiery Vigil, 109
Joint Task Force 519, 166
Joint Task Force 536, 144, 146
Joint Task Force Philippines, commander of, 100
Joint War Committee of Lloyd's Market Association, 130
Jolo Island, Philippines, 141; *140*
Joy, C. Turner, 3, 33
Jubail, Saudi Arabia, 103
Juneau (CL 119), 23, 34; *34*
Juneau (LPD 10), 160

Kabul, Afghanistan, 127
Kadena Naval Air Station, Okinawa, 48, 124
Kalifornia (Indonesia), 130
kamikaze attacks, vii, 3, 8–9; *9*
Kang Nam (North Korean), 135
Kan Jan Chan (South Korean), 162
Kashima (Japanese), *163*
Katz, Douglas, 108
Kearsarge (CVA 33), 41
Keating, Timothy J., 163
Keelung, Taiwan, 19, 34
Kelang, Malaysia, 150
Kennedy, John F., ix, 53–54, 56; *53*
Kenney, George C., 2
Khmer Rouge, xi, 66, 70
Khrushchev, Nikita, 79
Kidd-class guided missile destroyers, 126
Kiev (Soviet antisubmarine carrier), 89; *87*
Kilauea (T-AE 26), 122, 123; *123*
Kim Il-sung, 22, 75, 77–78
Kim Jong-il, 118, 120, 159, 160
King, Ernest J., 1
Kinkaid, Thomas C., vi, vii, 1–3, 6, 8–10, 13–16, 48, 171; *xvi, 10, 14*
Kirk (DE 1087), 66, 78, 96

Kirov (Soviet), 89
Kiska Island, Alaska, 3
Kissinger, Henry, 80
Kitty Hawk (CV 63), 65, 71, 113, 120, 127, 132, 163; *129*
Klintworth, Gary, 100
Klusmann, Charles F., 129
Knox (DE 1052), 66
Koh Tang Island, Cambodia, 70–71
Kojo, North Korea, 31
Kompong Som, Cambodia, 66
Kongo (Japanese), 154
Korean Air Lines 747 shootdown, xi, 87
Korean People's Army, 22, 27
Korean War, 6, 23, 29–37, 40, 45–48, 52, 84, 111, 113
Krupnyy-class destroyer (Soviet), 75
Kumano (Japanese), 7
Kurama (Japanese), 134
Kurile Islands, 87, 122, 167
Kurita, Takeo, 4, 7; *8*
Kuwait, xiii, 85, 101, 103–8, 167
Kyushu Island, Japan, 47, 83

LA-7 fighter aircraft (Chinese), 41
Lake Champlain (CG 57), 110; *135*
Lake Erie (CG 70), *165*
Laos, ix, 38–39, 44, 52–56, 59, 85, 129
LaPlante, John B., 104
Lapu Lapu City, Philippines, 136
Larson, Charles R., 109
LaSalle (AGF 3), 102, 107
Lassen, Clyde E., 151
Lassen (DDG 82), 151; *152*
Leahy, William D., 14
Lebanon crisis of 1958, 48
Lee Kwan Yew, 118
Lee Tung-hui, 114, 118
Lehman, John, 84, 92, 95
Lend-Lease vessels, 46
Leon, Strauss S., 16
Lexington (CVA 16), 49
Leyte (CV 32), 28
Leyte Island, Philippines, vii, 4, 8–9
Lian Yun Gang (Chinese), 160
Liberty Ships, 16
Libya. *See* Operations, El Dorado
Light Photographic Squadron 63, 129
light water reactor nuclear power plants, 120
Limburg (French), 130
limited war, 31–32, 36
Linebacker bombing, x, 59, 62, 66, 85
Lingayen Gulf, 8–9
Lingayen, Philippines, vii, 9
Link-16 communications suite, 122
Liu Huaqing, 99
Liu Zhenwu, 118
Lockwood (FF 1064), 78, 96
logistic support, 36, 39, 72, 91, 108, 112, 122

Logistics Group Western Pacific/Task Force 73, 39, 135–36, 145–46; commander of, 135–37. See also Tyson, Nora W.
Long, Robert L.J., 98
Long (DMS 12), 9
Long Beach (CGN 9), 97, 110
Lon Nol, 66
Los Angeles (SSN 688), 94; *Los Angeles*-class attack submarine, 95. See also *Columbus* (SSN 762)
Los Negros Island, Admiralty Islands, 2
Louisville (CA 28), 9
LST 472, 8
LST 738, 8; *9*
Luzon Attack Force, commander of, 9
Luzon Island, Philippines, vii, 8–10, 25, 109, 139–42; *108*
Lynde McCormick (DDG 8), 86
Lynx helicopters, 103
Lyons, James A., 86, 89, 92, 98–99; *99*

Mabus, Ray, 162
Macapagal-Arroyo, Gloria, 140
MacArthur, Douglas, vii, 13, 18–19, 48, 100; in Korean War, 20, 22, 25, 22, 26–28, 48; in World War II, 1–3, 4, 6, 10; *xvi, 3, 26*
McCaffrie, Jack, 139
McCain, John S. III, 158; *158*
McCampbell (DDG 85), 150
McClusky (FFG 41), 115, 118
McDermut (DD 677), 45
McDevitt, Michael, 160
McGinty (DE 365), 50
McNamara, Robert S., 56; *80*
Maddox (DD 731), ix, 56–57; *56, 57*
Maeda, Tetsuo, 89
Malacca, Strait of, 80–81, 86, 111, 121, 130–34, 142
Malaysia, 100, 128–31, 134–40
Manchuria, 14, 16, 20, 84
Manila, Philippines, 19, 48, 128, 151; Honasan coup in, xi, 100; Independence Day, vii, 18; and SEATO, ix, 44; during World War II, 10
Manila Bay (CVE 61), 9
Manila International Airport, 110
Manila Pact, 44
Mao Zedong (Mao Tse-tung), 37, 74, 84, 117; and establishment of PRC, viii; and Nixon visit, x; and civil war, 12, 16, 20–23; Taiwan Strait, policy toward, 40, 48, 53; *23*
March, Daniel, 105
Marfiak, Thomas, 105
Marine Heavy Lift Helicopter Squadron 463, 66
Marine Medium Helicopter Squadron 265, 123
Marine security detachments, 68
Maritime Component Commander, Joint Task Force 519, 166
maritime domain awareness, 142–44
maritime interception (interdiction) operations, 103, 134–35. See also Operations, Market Time
maritime prepositioning ships, 102–3

Maritime Prepositioning Squadron 2, 83
Maritime Strategy, 90–92, 95–96, 98, 100, 148
Mark, Chi-kwan, 74
Martin, Graham, 68
Martin, Harold M., 171
Maryland (BB 46), 4
Mason (DD 852), 19
Mauz, Henry H. Jr., 100–104, 167, 171; *101*
Mayaguez (merchantman), xi, 66, 70; *70*
Maynard, J. Stephen, 167
Mazu Island, China, xi, 42, 49
Medeiros, Evan S., 143, 159
medical civic action program, 136, 141; *137*
Medina, Joseph V., 125
Medina Republican Guard armored division, 129
Mekong Delta, 64, 69
Melbourne (Australian), 122
Mercy (T-AH 19), 141, 145–46, 152; *147*
Merrill (DD 976), 110
Metzger, James W., 126, 172
MH-53 Sea Dragon, 162
MH-60S Knighthawk, *144*
Michigan (SSGN 727), 170
Middle East, 101–2, 108, 111–12
MiG fighters, 76; MiG-17s, 51, 62, 85; MiG-21s, 60, 77, 105
Mikasa (Japanese), 151; *151*
Miles, Milton M., 14
military aid and assistance, 17, 20, 37–38, 54, 66, 139, 142
Military Maritime Consultative Agreement, xiv, 118, 157–58
Military Sealift Command, 64–66, 96, 103, 122–23, 134, 146, 163
Military Sea Transportation Service, 26, 39
military-to-military exchanges, xii, 113, 119, 126, 142, 165
Miller, Henry L., 58
Mindoro Island, Philippines, vii, 8, 25
Mine Countermeasures Force, xi
Mine Squadron 106, 16
Ministry of Defense, Japan, 163
Ministry of Health, Socialist Republic of Vietnam, 152
Minsk (Soviet), 80, 84, 87
Mispillion (T-AO 105), 78, 96
Mississippi (BB 41), 4
Missouri (BB 63), vii, 12, 28, 30, 55, 108; *12*
Mitcher, Marc, 2
Moale (DD 693), 8; *9*
Mobile Bay (CG 53), 121–23
Mongillo, Nick, 105
Montgomery, Glenn H., 106
Moo, Song Young, 148
Moore, Charles W. Jr., *119*
Moorer, Thomas H., 57–58, 129, 171; *64, 80*
Moscow (Soviet government reference), 13–14, 22, 34, 53, 65, 80, 83, 87, 91
Mountbatten, Louis, 9
Mount Pinatubo, xii, 108–12, 125; *108*
Mount Vernon (LSD 39), 68
Mullen, Michael G., 147–48; *147*

Mumbai, India, xiii, 133
Muraviev, Alexey, 79, 84, 89
Musashi (Japanese), 4
Mustin (DDG 89), 150–51
mutual defense treaties, viii, ix, 41–42, 49

Nagasaki, Japan, 72
Nagata, Mikio, 154
Nakasone, Yasuhiro, 84
Nashville (CL 43), 3, 4, 6; *3*
National Command Authority, 120
National Defense Program Guidelines, Japan, 163
National Defense University, 142
National Development Support Command, Philippines, 140
National Security Council, 22, 143; NSC-68, 22
Natter, Robert J., 118–19, 171
naval air stations, 111, 112; Cubi Point, Philippines, 48, 71, 110–12; *72*; Miramar, California, 61–62
Naval Force Presence Policy, 90
Naval Forces Far East, 20, 28, 32–33; commander of, 36, 46
Naval Forces Korea, commander of, 161
Naval Forces Vietnam, commander of, 64
Naval Group China, commander of. *See* Miles, Milton M.
naval infantry (Soviet), 83, 84, 87; *88*
Naval Mobile Construction Battalion 3, 48
Naval Mobile Construction Battalion 5, 48
Naval Mobile Construction Battalion 11, 152
Naval Mobile Construction Battalion 40, 137, 145; *138*
Naval Regional Contracting Center, Singapore, 146
naval supply depots, 71–72
Naval War College, 92, 142–43
Netherlands, vii, 1; and Netherlands East Indies, 1–4, 12, 19
New Britain, Solomon Islands, 1,
New Framework for the U.S.-India Defense Relationship, xiii, 133
New Guinea, vii, 1–4
New Jersey (BB 62), 30, 62, 97–98; *31*
New Mexico (BB 40), 9
New Orleans (LPH 11), 121
New Zealand, viii, ix, 1, 24, 44–45, 52, 118, 121, 135, 148
Ngo Dinh Diem, ix, 53–56, *55*
Niagara Falls (AFS 3), 108, 118
Nicholas (FFG 47), 106
night vision devices, 87, 139
Nimitz, Chester W., 1–2, 151
Nimitz (CVN 68), xii, 98, 115–16, 134, 151
Nimitz-class nuclear-powered aircraft carriers, 112, 162
9th Marine Amphibious Brigade, 68
Nishimura, Shoji, 4
Nitze, Paul, 22
Nixon, Richard M., x, 64–65, 80, 84, 89, 117
No Dong missiles, xiii, 162
Nootka (Canadian), *24*
North Arabian Sea, U.S. Navy operations in, 82, 85, 112, 125, 127, 129, 149
North Atlantic Treaty Organization, 44, 90, 98, 119, 140
North China, 13–14, 16–18, 21

North China Force, Seventh Fleet, 13
North Korean navy, 76, 161
North Pacific, U.S. operations in, 96–98, 129, 159–60
North Pacific Heads of Coast Guards Association, 159–60
Northeast Asia, 11, 77; during Korean War, 22, 38; during post–Cold War, 121, 126, 140, 153, 162, 167; and USSR, 74, 79, 89, 91–92, 95–100; during Vietnam War, 47–48, 53, 71–72
Northern Alliance, 127
Northern Arabian Gulf, 105, 107 166. *See also* Arabian Gulf
Northern Limit Line, 77, 121, 161
Northern Territories. *See* Kurile Islands
Northwest Pacific, 92
Novorossiysk (Soviet ship), 88
Nowell, Larry, 62
Nuclear Non-Proliferation Treaty, xii, 120

Obama, Barak, 158, 168
O'Brien (DD 725), 8, 115, 118
Office of the Chief of Naval Operations, 102
Ogier, Herbert L., 57
Ohio (SSGN 726), xiv, 170
OKEAN 75 (Soviet exercise), 79
Okinawa, 47–48, 89, 121, 145; exercises in, 96, 137; *166*; and China coast patrols, 23, 33–35, 124; relation to SEATO, 45; during World War II, 13
Okinawa (LPH 3), 66–67
Oklahoma City (CLG 5), 54, 68; *54*
Oldendorf, Jesse, 4–5, 9–10
Oldendorf (DD 972), 99, 102, 116
Oliver Hazard Perry-class guided missile frigate, 106
Ommaney Bay (CVE 79), 9
Oonami (Japanese), 153; *154*
Operations: Balikatan, 139; Chromite, 25; Decoy, 31; Desert Shield, xi, 101–2, 104; Desert Storm, 85, 104–5, 117, 167; *105* (map); Eagle Pull, xiii, 66; El Dorado Canyon, 102; End Sweep, 167; Enduring Freedom, xiv, 127, 129, 132–33; Enduring Freedom–Philippines, 139–40; Fiery Vigil, 109, 111; Frequent Wind, xiii, 68, 85, 167; Iraqi Freedom, xii, 125, 129; Lightning, 50; Magic Carpet, 3, 15; Malsindo, 131; Market Time, xii, 63–64, 71; Passage to Freedom, ix, 39, 52; *39*; Paul Bunyan, 77–78; Rolling Thunder, x, 59, 62, 85; Sea Angel, xiv; Sea Dragon, 62; Shooting Star, 98; Southern Watch, 125, 129, 149; Stabilize, xii, 122–23; Starlite, 63; 34A, 56; Unified Assistance, xiii, 144–46
Operation Plan Bojinka, 128
Operation Plan 13-45, 13
Operation Plan Ultimatum, 141
Oriskany (CVA 34), x, 61, 71, 74
Oryoku Maru (Japanese), 14; *14*
Osborn, Shane, 124; *124*
Ouellet (FF 1077), 87
Ozawa, Jisaburo, 6

P2V Neptune, 34–35, 40, 71
P-3 Orion, 71, 82, 126, 145, 163

P-4 motor torpedo boat (North Vietnamese), 57, 61
P4M Mercator, 37
P4Y Privateer, 33–34
Pacific Century, 143
Pacific Missile Range Facility, Hawaii, 154
Pacific Partnership programs, 146, 151
Page, Louis C., 160
Paracel Islands, 83, 124
Paris Agreement on Ending the War and Restoring Peace in Vietnam, x, 66
Park, Chung Hee, 76
Park, Jung-hwa, *154*
Passumpic (T-AO 107), 110
Pathet Lao, 53
Patriot (MCM 7), 163
Patriot missile, 120, 126
Patrol Squadron 8, 145
Patrol Squadron 28, 33
Patrol Squadron 46, 33
Paul F. Foster (DD 964), 160
Paul Hamilton (DDG 60), 136
PBM-5 Mariner, 34; *40*
PCE *851*, 8
Pearl Harbor, Hawaii, vi, 147; attack, vii, 1–2, 4–5, 25; *2*
Peleliu (LHA 5), 110, 123
Pennsylvania (BB 38), 4
Pentagon, attack on, xii, 127
People's Army of Vietnam, 56
People's Liberation Army, PRC, viii, xi, 20, 28, 40, 75, 113
People's Liberation Army Navy, PRC, 41, 99, 159, 163–65, 167; chief of staff of. *See* Liu Huaqing; Liu Zhenwu
People's Republic of China, xi, xii, 13–15, 37, 111, 119, 122; establishment of, x, 20; Hainan incident, 124; in Korean War, viii, 22, 28, 33–36; Taiwan Strait crises, reaction to, ix, xii, 41–42, 50–51, 114–18, 120; as "responsible stakeholder," 120, 158; in 21st century, xii, xiii, 143, 156–60, 163–64, 165; U.S.-PRC rapprochement, xi, xii, 79–80, 83–84, 99–100, 113; U.S. visits to, 99, 160; in Vietnam War, 53–54, 58–59, 65, 74
Permit (SSN 594), 72
Perry, William J., 108, 114–15
Perry, Matthew C., 154
Perth (Australian), 62, 122
Petropavlovsk, Russia, 91–92, 96, 98
Phalanx close-in weapons system, 95, 105, 149; *94*, *175*
Philippine Independence Day, ix; celebration of, *18*
Philippine Navy, 45, 136, 150
Philippine Sea, U.S. Navy operations in, 100, 136
Philippine Sea (CV 47), 28, 38, 41; *35*
Phillips, William K., 38
Phnom Penh, Cambodia, evacuation of, xi, 66–67
Phoenix (CL 46), xvi, 2, 4
Phuket, Thailand, 146, 150
Pickerel (SS 524), 33; *33*
pirates, 127, 130–31, 135, 138, 142
PIRAZ (positive identification radar advisory zone), 62
Plog, Leonard H., 24

Plunger (SSN 595), 72
port calls, 19, 54, 79, 167. *See also* ship visits
Port Royal (CG 73), 116
Prakash, Arun, 146
Presidential Sailing Pass in Review, Indonesia, 148
Prictor, Michael, 146
Pride, Alfred M., 41, 171; *41*
Princeton (CG 59), 107–8
Princeton (CV 37), 28–29, 45, 49
prisoners of war, 14, 66
Project Hope, 145
Proliferation Security Initiative, xiii, 134–35
Providence (CLG 6), *44*
Prueher, Joseph W., 118–19, 124; *119*
Pueblo (AGER 2), x, 76–77; *76*
Pyongyang, North Korea, viii, 24, 77–78; government actions of, 135, 161, 163

al-Qaeda, xiv, 127–30, 133–34, 139
Qaruh Island, Kuwait, 106
Qingdao, China, vii, xi, 14–21, 34, 99, 113, 119, 159
Qinghai (Chinese), 160
Qinhuangdao, China, 16
Quadrennial Defense Review, 168
Queensland, Australia, 122, 153
Qui Nhon, Vietnam, 58, 66, 152
Quinn, Kevin M., 136

RA-3B Skywarrior, 59
RA-5C Vigilante, 59
Rabaul, Solomon Islands, 1
Radford, Arthur W., 35, 39, 48; *38*
Rahman, Chris, 139
Rajah Humabon (Philippines), 136
Rand Corporation, 140
Ranger (CV 61), 96–98, 105; *58*, *97*
Ranvir (Indian), 134
RC-135S (U.S. Air Force), 161
Ready Reserve Force, 103
Reagan, Ronald, 84
Reasoner (FF 1063), 103
Red Crown, 62; ship, *62*
Red Sea, 83, 104
Reeves (CG 24), 99
Refugee Assistance Task Group, 66
Regional Cooperation Agreement on Combating Piracy and Armed Robbery against Ships, 131
Regional Maritime Security Initiative, 134
Rentz (FFG 46), 99
Renville (APA 227), vii, 19; *19*
Renville Agreement, vii, 19
Repose (AH 16), 21
Republic of China (Taiwan), ix, 12, 15, 20, 41–44, 49, 52, 113
Republic of Korea, viii, xiii, 120–21, 152, 161–62; chief of naval operations, 148; exercises, 121, 149, 153; during Cold War, 76, 78, 98; Fleet, commander in chief of, 162; and Korean War, 22, 29, 32

Republic of Korea Navy, xiii, 76, 120, 129, 154
Republic of Maldives, 138
Republican Guard of Iraq, 104, 129
RF-8A Crusader, 59, 129
Rhee, Syngman, 22
Richard S. Edwards (DDG 950), 96
Rim of the Pacific naval exercises, 119
RIM-116 Rolling Airframe Missile launchers, 149
River Squadron 5, 102
Rochester (CA 124), 28, 30, 33
Rockey, Keller E., 15–16; *16*
Rocky Mount (AGC 3), 14–15; *15*
Rodney M. Davis (FFG 60), 110, 136; *110*
Rogers (DD 876), 61
Roosevelt, Franklin D., 1, 4
Roughead, Gary, 143–46, 148, 157–60; *148*, *160*
Royal Australian Navy, 24, 62–63, 122, 153, 167
Royal Brunei Navy, 137
Royal Marines, 103
Royal Navy, viii, 15, 24, 82, 106
Royal Singapore Navy, 121
rule of law, 127, 133
Rupertus (DD 851), 19
Rush (WHEC 723), 159; *159*
Ryuku Islands, 165

S-3 Viking, 95
SA-2 Guideline surface-to-air missile, 61; *61*
Sabin, Lorenzo S., 39
Safeguard (ARS 50), 136
Safwan, Iraq, 108
Saigon, South Vietnam, 20, 37–40, 54–55, 58, 64, 66, 68–69, 85
St. Lo (CVE 63), vii, 8
Saint Paul (CA 73), 21, 28, 54–55; *55*
Sakhalin Island, Russia, xi, 87, 97
Salisbury Sound (AV 13), 45
Salt Lake City (SSN 716), 122
Salvation Joy Haven Home for the Elderly, 150
Salvor (T-ARS 52), 163
Samar Island, 7–8
Samuel B. Roberts (DE 413), 7
San Bernardino Strait, 4, 6–7
San Diego, California, 96, 125, 145; *97*, *147*
Sangley Point, 19, 48, 71–72, 111
San Jose (T-AFS 7), 123
Santa Fe (SSN 763), 134; *133*
Saratoga (CV 60), 102, 105
Sargo (SSN 583), 72
Sasebo, Japan, 111, 150; during Cold War, 47, 72–73, 83; during Korean War, 24, 47; ships based at, 102, 123, 125, 145, 162; *161*, *172*
Saudi Arabia, 101, 103–4, 107
Schoech, William A., 52, 129, 173
Schwarzkopf, Norman, 102, 105
Scud ballistic missiles, xiii, 134, 161
sea lines of communication, 65, 83, 130–32, 157

Sea of Japan/East Sea, xiii, 120, 122, 161; exercises in, 96, 149, 163; Korean War, operations in, 27, 34, 55; U.S. and Soviets in, 75–78, 87–89, 98
Sea of Okhotsk, 96–98
Sea Sparrow surface-to-air missile, 149; *178*
"sea-based midcourse defense (SMD) system," 154
Seabees, 9, 46–48, 72, 82, 110, 136–39, 145, 147; *138*
Seadragon (SSN 584), 72, *72*
SEALs, 106, 108, 140, 170
seapower, xiii, 35–36, 51–53, 56, 74, 143, 148
search and rescue, 129, 134, 144, 159
Seawolf (SSN 21), 154; *154*
2d Battalion, 4th Marines, 66, 68
Secretary of State, 18, 20, 44, 51, 80, 116, 163, 165
Segundo (SS 398), 20
Sejong the Great (South Korean), 162; *162*
Senkaku/Diaoyutai Island, 122
Seoul, South Korea, vii, 14, 27, 76, 98, 118, 120, 162
Sequoia (WLB 215), 159
Serbia, xii, 119
17th parallel of Vietnam, 39
Seventh Fleet Band, 150, 154; *156*
SH-3 Sea King, 59
SH-60H Seahawk, 95, 136, 138
Shanghai, China, 13–15, 55, 126, 160, 167
Shantou, China, 33, 35
Sharp, Ulysses S.G., 57
Shenzhen (Chinese), 160
Sherman, Forrest P., 19
Shijiazhuang (Chinese), 165
Shiloh (CG 67), 162
Shima, Kiyohide, 4
ship repair facilities, 45–46, 71–72, 109–11
ship visits, 72, 113, 119. *See also* port calls
Shoalwater Bay Training Area, Australia, 122; *153*
Short, Edwin T., 18
show of force, xi, 33–34, 81, 85
Shropshire (Australian), 4
Siam, Gulf of, 53, 63, 66–67. *See also* Thailand, Gulf of
Sidewinder missiles, 51, 59, 105
Sidorov, Vladimir, 98
Sihanoukville, Cambodia, 64, 66
Singapore, 111, 148; and exercises, 132, 134–37; during Cold War, 100, 118; post–World War II, 19; and SEATO, 45; ship visits at, 121, 130, 149–50; and terrorists, 131, 139, 143; and tsunami, 146
Sino-Soviet 30-year Treaty of Friendship, Alliance, and Mutual Assistance, viii, 20
Six Degree Channel, 133
"600-ship navy," 92, 95
Six-Party Talks, 159, 161
6th Marine Division, 13, 15, 21
Slava-class guided missile cruiser (Soviet), 151
"smart power," 170
Smith, John C., 60
Smith, Oliver P. 26
Smoot, Roland N., 4, 50

Snook (SSN 592), 72
Sobero, Guillermo, 128
Socialist Republic of Vietnam, xi, 83, 84, 86, 115, 149, 152
Socotra Island, Yemen, 83
Solaiman, Abu, 141
Solomon Islands, 1, 3
Somalia, 79, 83, 125, 129
Soo, Mary, 75
So San (North Korean), 134
South China Force (Seventh Fleet), 13
South China Sea, operations in,101, 122, 130, 135, 159; PRC, 99, 133, 157, 165; and Chinese civil war, 20; during First Indochina War, 38; during Korean War, 35, 41; during Vietnam War, 53–54, 59, 68, 71, 85; Soviets in, 79, 83–86; U.S. Navy in, 111, 121, 124
South Pacific Forces and South Pacific Area, commander of. *See* Halsey, William F.
South Sea Fleet, PLAN, 160, 167
Southeast Asia Cooperation against Terrorism, 137
Southeast Asia Treaty Organization, ix, 44–45, 52, 80
Southwest Pacific, vi, 1, 10, 13
Soviet Far East, 75, 87, 89, 92, 96, 100
Soviet navy, 79, 84, 89, 91, 98, 118
Soviet Pacific Fleet, 74, 79, 80, 83–84, 87, 89, 98, 129
Sovremenny-class guided missile destroyer (Soviet), 89; *88*
Spanish-American War, 48
Sparrow air-to-air missile, 59–60, 105
Special Detachment 88, 142
special forces, 76, 115, 120, 127–29, 139–41. *See also* SEALs
special operations, 31, 108, 121, 134, 170
Special Purpose Marine Air-Ground Task Force, 100
Sprague, Clifton A., 7, 10
Spratly Islands, 113, 122, 159
Spruance-class destroyer, 95
Sri Lanka, 79, 131
Stalin, Joseph, viii, 11, 14, 22, 33, 37; *11*
Stalwart (Singapore), 137
Standard Missile 3, 154
Steele, George P., 66–67, 171; *66*
Sterett (CG 31), 62, 86, 89, 96
Stickell (DD 888), 20
Stillwell, Richard, 77–78
Strike Fighter Squadron 81, 105
Struble, Arthur D., 8, 25–26, 33–34, 171; *25, 26*
Stump, Felix, 38, 48, 78
SU-15 Flagon (Soviet fighter), 87
Subic Bay, Philippines, 14, 19, 22, 48
Suisun (AVP 53), 34
Superferry 14 (Philippines), 140
Supreme Commander Southeast Asia Command, 9
Supreme Headquarters, Allied Powers Europe, 102
Surface Action Force, 42
Suzuki, Zenko, 90
"swing strategy," 89
Sydney (Australian), 122

Taepo Dong missiles, xii–xiii, 121
"Taffy 3," 7
Tai Ho (Chinese Nationalist), 41
Taipei, Taiwan, 33–34, 113
Tai Ping (Chinese Nationalist), 41
Taiwan, viii, 46–49, 89, 99–100, 113, 126, 157, 160, 163–66; government on, ix, 20, 22, 100; in World War II, 14, during post–World War II, 17; ship visits to, 19; during Korean War, 23, 25, 33–36, 46; and Taiwan Strait crises, xii, 40–42, 48–53, 85, 114–18
Taiwan Defense Command, 50
Taiwan Patrol Force, x, 34, 42, 50, 52, 113
Taiwan Relations Act, 113
Taiwan Strait, ix, 33, 35, 40, 48, 50, 55, 115–16
Taiwan Strait Crisis of 1954–1955, 40–43
Taiwan Strait Crisis of 1958, 48–52
Taiwan Strait Crisis of 1995–1996, 113–18
Takeshima/Dok-do Island, 122
Taliban, xii, 127
Tanaka, Kakuei, 83
Tang Jiaxuan, 124
Task Forces (TFs). TF 7, commander of, 25–26; TF 72, viii, 13, 34, 50; TF 73, 3, 13, 135–36; commander of, *137*; TF 74, 13, 168; TF 76, 1, 68–69, 137; TF 77, x, 25, 28–29, 55, 57–62, 74; commander of, 58; TF 78, xi, 9, 13; TF 79, 9; TF 95, 29
Task Groups (TGs). TG 70.7, 19; TG 74, commander of, 81; TG 74.4, 16; TG 76.4, 66; TG 76.8, 66; TG 77.4, 7; TG 79.1, 68; TG 79.4, 66
Tatham, Roy M., 41
Tawi Tawi Island, Philippines, 141
Tennessee (BB 43), 4; *5*
territorial waters, 50, 96, 131, 163, 167
terrorism, 125–39, 143–44, 150, 162
Tet Offensive, x, 63, 71, 76
Thailand, 100, 115, 144, 146, 150; and SEATO, ix, 44; in 1962 crisis, ix, 53; in *Mayaguez* crisis, 70; in exercises, 121, 135, 137–38, 168; and terrorists, 130–31, 139, 142–43
Thailand, Gulf of, naval operations in, 137–38. *See also* Siam, Gulf of
Thanh Hoa, Vietnam, 60
Theodore Roosevelt (CVN 71), 105, 106, 108
Theseus (British), 24
Thieu, Nguyen Van, 68; *65, 90*
3d Marine Aircraft Wing, 48
III Marine Amphibious Corps, 13, 15–16, 18
3d Marine Division, 45, 48
13th Marine Expeditionary Unit, 138
38th parallel, Korea, 13, 22, 31, 120
31st Marine Expeditionary Unit, 66, 123
Thomaston (LSD 28), 66
thousand-ship navy, xiii, 147
Tiananmen Square, xi, 20, 113
Tianjin, China, 13–15
Tibet, 44, 156
Ticonderoga (CG 47), 57–58
Ticonderoga-class guided missile cruiser, 95, 105

Tingey (DD 539), 45
Tobin, Paul E., 109
Togo, Heihachiro, 151
Tokyo, Japan, 3, 20, 33, 38, 46–47, 83, 131, 154, 163
Tomahawk land attack missiles, 92, 93, 104, 170
Tongling (Chinese), 119
Tonkin, Gulf of, U.S. Navy operations in, 56–62, 64, 75. *See also* Yankee Station
Tonkin Gulf Resolution, ix, 58
Tonkin region, 16, 39
Top Gun school. *See* naval air stations, Miramar, California
Topeka (CL 67), 18
Torrens (Australian), 121
Tortuga (LSD 46), 142, 153
Treaty of Mutual Cooperation and Security, xi, 156
Tripoli (LPH 10), 81, 107–8
Triumph (British), viii, 24
Truman, Harry S., viii, 11, 14, 17–25, 32–34, 37; *11*
tsunami, xiii, 144–46
Tucker (DD 875), 21
Tucson (SSN 770), *169*
Turner Joy (DD 951), 57, 86
Tuscaloosa (LST 1187), 68
typhoons, xiv, 47, 110
Tyson, Nora W., 136–37; *137*

Udaloy-class guided missile destroyer (Soviet), 89
UH-2 Sea Sprite, 59
UH-60 Black Hawk, 84
Uighurs, 156
Ultra intelligence, 4
United Kingdom, xii, 45, 82, 135
United Nations, 23–24, 77, 102, 121, 122, 129, 131; coalitions of, xi, 24–25, 103–4, 108; Convention on the Law of the Sea, 131, 164; International Maritime Organization, 131; peacekeeping, 125; Security Council Resolutions, 103 (UNSCR 661); 103 (UNSCR 665); 108 (UNSCR 687); 122 (UNSCR 1264); 135 (UNSCR 1874)
U.S. Air Force, x, 59, 76, 85, 161; Fifth Air Force, 2; 13th Air Force, 100
U.S. Army, xi, 1, 4, 7, 10, 27, 77, 85, 96, 106–8; Army Air Forces, 2, 9; 2nd Infantry Division, 38; 6th Infantry Division, 9; 7th Infantry Division, 27, 96; 37th Infantry Division, 9; 40th Infantry Division, 9; 43rd Infantry Division, 9; VII Corps, 104, 108; X Army Corps, 27–28; XIV Army Corps, 9; XVIII Airborne Corps, 108; XXIV Army Corps, 13–14
U.S. Bicentennial (1976), 83
U.S. Central Command, 101–2, 104, 108, 167; theater map, *101*
U.S. Coast Guard, 35, 136, 159,160; *159*; anti-infiltration patrols, x, 63–64; in 21st century maritime strategy, xiii, 148; Gulf War embargo patrol, 103; terrorists and pirates, operations against,127, 134–35
U.S. Congress, 58, 87
U.S. Defense Attaché Office Saigon, 68
U.S. embassies: Bangkok, 128; Beijing, 119; Manila, 128; Saigon, 58
U.S. Fifth Fleet, 108
U.S. First Fleet, 38
U.S. Fleet, commander in chief of, 1. *See also* King, Ernest J.
U.S. House of Representatives, 114
U.S.-Japan Joint Declaration on Security Alliance for the 21st Century, 118
U.S.-Japan Mutual Security Treaty, 155, 161
U.S. Joint Task Force, Timor Sea Operations, 122
U.S. Marine Corps, xiii. *See also individual divisions and units*
U.S. Naval Academy, 7, 25, 101
U.S. Naval Advisory Group Philippines, 18
U.S. Naval Base Subic Bay, Philippines, xii, 48, 69, 71,109, 111–12; 121; *109*,*112*
U.S. Naval Forces Central Command, commander of, 101, 104, 108, 167. *See also* Mauz, Henry H., Jr.; Arthur, Stanley R.
U.S. Naval Forces Western Pacific, vii–viii, 17–19, 21; commander of, 101,172. *See also* Cooke, Charles M., Jr.
U.S. Naval Hospital Subic Bay, Philippines, 48, 110
U.S. Naval Support Facility, Diego Garcia, 82
U.S. Pacific Command, 54, 81, 100, 102, 139; commander in chief/commander of, 48, 57, 78, 109, 143–44. *See also* Blair, Dennis; Fargo, Thomas; Sharp, Ulysses S. Grant; Keating Timothy J.; Larson, Charles R.; Prueher, Joseph, W.
U.S. Pacific Fleet, vii, 1, 38, 86, 99, 124, 143–44, 157–60; commander in chief/commander of, 48,143–44, 157. *See also* Doran, Walter F.; Foley, Sylvester R.; Hayward, Thomas B.; Lyons, James A.; Moorer, Thomas H.; Nimitz, Chester W.; Roughead, Gary; Stump, Felix B.
U.S. Third Fleet, vii, 2, 6, 8, 98
U.S. West Coast, 45, 50, 83
U.S.-Philippines Treaty of Friendship, Peace, and Cooperation, 111
U.S.-Republic of China Mutual Defense Treaty, 41
Ussuri River, 84
Utapao, Thailand, 144–45

Valley Forge (CV 45), 20–23, 28, 33; *23*
Van Buskirk, Scott R., 171
Vancouver (LPD 2), 66
Vandegrift (FFG 48), 160
Vendetta (Australian), 62
Victor I-class attack submarine (Soviet), 129
Viet Cong, 56, 63, 85, 129
Viet Minh, viii, 37–40
Vietnam Navy, x, 56, 63–64, 69–70
Vietnam People's Navy, 137
Vietnam War, 6, 52, 66, 74, 85–86, 99, 149, 152; confrontations of, 53, 79–80, 89; fleet bases in, 71, 111, 151; operations in, 55, 59, 62
Vietnamese Communists, 37, 53, 56, 58
Vincennes (CG 49), 97–98
Viraat (Indian), 132, 134

visit, board, search, and seizure operations, 134–36; *135*
V-J Day, 13
Vladivostok, Russia, 33, 80, 87, 91, 96, 121, 150–51, 167; *88*

Wadell (DDG 24), 96
Walker (DD 517), 75
Waller (Australian), xiv
Wang Wei, 124
Warramunga (Australian), 24
Al Wasitti (Iraqi), 103
Wasp (CVA 18), 38, 41 93
Wasp-class amphibious assault ship, 93
Watkins, James B., 92, 93, 99
weapons of mass destruction, xiii, 120, 134, 163
Wedemeyer, Albert C., 15
Weinberger, Caspar, 98
Weiss, Kenneth, 84
Wengen Gu, 160
Wen Rulang, 167
West Pakistan, 80
West Virginia (BB 48), 4
Western Pacific Naval Symposium, 147
whaleboats, 31–32
Whidbey Island-class dock landing ship, 93
White Beach, Okinawa, 8, 48, 137; *166*
Whitmire, Donald, 68
Wilkinson, Theodore S., 9
Willard, Robert F., 150, 160, 172
William H. Standley (CG 32), 96
Winter, Donald C., 146
Wisconsin (BB 64), 30, 102, 107–8
Wisecup, James P., 161
Wolmi Do, South Korea, 27
Wonsan, North Korea, 24, 27–28, 31–32, 76; *24*
World Trade Center, attack on, xii, 127; *127*
Wu Shengli, *160*

Xiamen, China, 33, 35, 41
Xining (Chinese), 119

Yalu River, 28–29
Yamashiro (Japanese), 6
Yamashita, Tomoyuki, 10
Yamato (Japanese), 4
Yangtze Patrol Force, 3, 13
Yangtze River, 13
Yankee Station, 59–61, 85
Yantai, China, 16
Yellow Sea/West Sea, 26, 33–34, 77, 162
Yeongheung Island, South Korea, 27
Yijiangshan Island, China, ix, 41
YMS 49, 14
YMS 516 (South Korean), *28*
Yokosuka, Japan, 19, 39, 46–47, 55, 108, 111, 146, 150–51, 163; during Korean War, 33, 46; post-Vietnam, 78, 83; ships forward-based at, 85, 102, 104–6, 117, 127, 129, 154, 167; during Vietnam War, 72–73, 83; *46, 149, 167*

Yorktown (CVA 10), 41
Yoshihara, Toshi, 157
Yoshikawa, Eiji, 148
Yousef, Ramzi, 128
Yudhoyono, Susilo Bambang, 143, 148

Zamboanga, Philippines, 128, 136
Zanoobia (Iraqi), *103*
Zhang Aiping, 84
Zhanjiang, China, 160, 167
Zhao Guojun, 126, 160
Zheng He (Chinese), 99
Zhu De, 115
Zumwalt, Elmo R. Jr., 13, 81, 89; *13, 81*

Vice Admiral Scott R. Van Buskirk, who assumed command on 10 September 2010, stresses the importance of the U.S. Seventh Fleet to peace and stability in the sometimes volatile Western Pacific.

www.ingramcontent.com/pod-product-compliance
Lightning Source LLC
Chambersburg PA
CBHW082119230426

43671CB00015B/2744